Business Impacts of COVID-19

The coronavirus disease (COVID-19) pandemic has caused serious disruptions to the economy and business activities. The COVID-19 crisis has also exposed important weaknesses in business and supply chains. It pointed to specific sectors of the economy, primarily related to services, that suffered the most. On the other hand, it has highlighted the great flexibility of the activities of entrepreneurs in their attempts to fight the crisis.

The role of government has also been important in tackling this pandemic crisis to contain the epidemic and adopt activities to help entrepreneurs who were most affected by the crisis. Numerous national aid and recovery packages have been announced to support businesses and workers. At the same time, financial decisions were made at the international level, resulting in the mobilization of huge funds that were intended to support the functioning of enterprises.

This book shares observations and conclusions from contemporary research and analyses, as well as from personal experiences in creating and implementing anti-crisis solutions in economies and enterprises caused by the COVID-19 pandemic on the economy and its entities. It will be of interest to researchers, academics, policymakers, and students in the fields of international business, economics, crisis management, and entrepreneurship.

Tomasz Bernat is a Professor of Economics and a Senior Researcher and Lecturer at the University of Szczecin, Poland.

Joanna Duda is a Professor of Management and a Senior Researcher and Lecturer at AGH University of Science and Technology in Krakow, Poland.

Routledge Studies in International Business and the World Economy

Chinese Organizations in Sub-Saharan Africa
New Dynamics, New Synergies
Edited by Terence Jackson, Lynette Louw and D. K. (Roshan) Boojihawon

The Oil Business and the State
National Energy Companies and Government Ownership
Øystein Noreng

Cultural Spaces in International Business
Theories and Applications
Edited by Taran Patel and Ahmad M. Salih

Science, Business and Universities
Cooperation, Knowledge Transfer and Entrepreneurship
Edited by Joanna Duda and Tomasz Bernat

International Entrepreneurship in Emerging Markets
Contexts, Behaviours, and Successful Entry
Edited by Vahid Jafari-Sadeghi and Léo-Paul Dana

Management Research, International Business, and National Culture
Evaluating Hofstede and GLOBE
Sunil Venaik, Paul Brewer and David Midgley

Business Impacts of COVID-19
International Business, Crisis Management, and the Global Economy
Edited by Tomasz Bernat and Joanna Duda

For more information about this series, please visit: https://www.routledge.com/Routledge-Studies-in-International-Business-and-the-World-Economy/book-series/SE0358

Business Impacts of COVID-19

International Business, Crisis Management, and the Global Economy

Edited by
Tomasz Bernat and
Joanna Duda

Routledge
Taylor & Francis Group
NEW YORK AND LONDON

First published 2024
by Routledge
605 Third Avenue, New York, NY 10158

and by Routledge
4 Park Square, Milton Park, Abingdon, Oxon, OX14 4RN

Routledge is an imprint of the Taylor & Francis Group, an informa business

Library of Congress Cataloging-in-Publication Data
Names: Bernat, Tomasz, editor. | Duda, Joanna (Economist) editor.
Title: Business impacts of COVID-19 : international business, crisis management, and the global economy / edited by Tomasz Bernat and Joanna Duda.
Description: 1 Edition. | New York : Routledge, 2023. |
Series: Routledge studies in international business and the world economy | Includes bibliographical references and index.
Identifiers: LCCN 2023005254 | ISBN 9781032437446 (hardback) | ISBN 9781032437453 (paperback) | ISBN 9781003368687 (ebook)
Subjects: LCSH: International business enterprises—Management. | COVID-19 Pandemic, 2020—Influence. | Crisis management. | Entrepreneurship.
Classification: LCC HD2755.5 .B88677 2023 |
DDC 658/.049—dc23/eng/20230330
LC record available at https://lccn.loc.gov/2023005254

ISBN: 978-1-032-43744-6 (hbk)
ISBN: 978-1-032-43745-3 (pbk)
ISBN: 978-1-003-36868-7 (ebk)

DOI: 10.4324/9781003368687

Typeset in Bembo
by codeMantra

Contents

Tables

Figures

Contributors

Anna Barwińska-Małajowicz is an Associate Professor of Economics at the University of Rzeszów, Poland. She is also Head of the Department of Economics and International Economic Relations. Her works analyze international economic relations, entrepreneurship, and the labor market. Her research has been published in a wide range of peer-reviewed journals. The author of nearly 200 scientific publications, she is an expert principal researcher on a number of Polish and European projects (labor market).

Joanna Brzyska is an economist and Assistant Professor at the Institute of Economics and Finance at the University of Szczecin, Poland. Her research interests are international economic relations and international trade. She is the author or co-author of numerous publications.

Magdalena Czerwinska is an Assistant Professor at Lublin University of Technology and head of the Department of Economics and Economic Management. She is an active member of many scientific societies, including the Polish Economic Society, the Scientific Society of Economic Informatics, and the Scientific Society of Organization and Management). Magdalena is the author of more than 50 papers; she specializes in knowledge management, e-health, information technology acceptance models, and health information.

Joanna Duda, is a Professor of Management, Senior Researcher, and Lecturer at AGH University of Science and Technology's Faculty of Management in Krakow, Poland. Her research interests are related to the issues that are encountered by small and medium-sized enterprises. She conducts her empirical studies in Poland, Germany, and Finland on the development barriers and financing strategies of the innovation activities of small and medium-sized enterprises in the context of globalization processes. She is the author or co-author of more than 130 scientific publications, including several monographs.

Aleksandra Gąsior is an Associate Professor, Senior Researcher, and Lecturer at the University of Szczecin, Poland. Her scientific interests are focused on the following areas: microeconomics, financial analysis, and restructuring. Her research has been published in a wide range of peer-reviewed journals, and she has published more than 100 scientific publications. She has participated in many international research projects that have been financed by national (Polish) and international funds. Currently, she is participating in an international project that is covered by the Erasmus+ fund.

Zofia Gródek-Szostak is an Assistant Professor in the Department of Economics and Business of Krakow University of Economics. She is an accredited consultant of the Polish Agency for Enterprise Development (PARP) in the field of pro-innovative consulting services the National Innovation Network (KSI) and general consulting services for the National Service System (KSU). She is the author of papers on the public financing of investments and R&D works and on implementing innovative solutions in enterprises. Her professional interests revolve around the motivation for the technical collaboration of enterprises as well as the assessment of the technological potential of enterprises.

Kristina Grumadaitė is a Researcher and Lecturer at Kaunas University of Technology (Lithuania) and St. Ignatius of Loyola University of Applied Sciences. Her research focuses on the formation of self-organization-based industrial systems, enabling innovation ecosystems, and the smart development of social systems as well as their organizational processes.

Magdalena Homa is an Assistant Professor in the Institute of Economic Sciences at the University of Wroclaw, Poland. Her scientific interests are focused on a few areas; namely, mathematics and statistics insurance (actuarial methods), financial econometrics, and financial mathematics. Her research has been published in a wide range of peer-reviewed journals.

Simeon Karafolas is a Professor of Accounting and Finance Department at the University of Western Macedonia in Greece. Prof. S. Karafolas is the Director of a Master Program on Banking Insurance and Finance at the same university. He is the author of papers and books on banking, finance, cooperatives, immigration, and regional development. He received research grants from the European Union for projects on banking and the financing of SMEs. His scientific interests include banking, finance, cooperatives, immigration, and regional development (e-mail: skarafolas@uowm.gr).

Miroslava Knapková is an Associate Professor at the Faculty of Economics of Matej Bel University in Banská Bystrica, Slovakia. She is the head of the Department of Economics; her scientific and research orientation has an economic-legal dimension. She focuses on analyses of labor market legislation and traditional and new forms of work (especially dependent self-employment) as well as workaholism, heavy time investment, work engagement, well-being, and work-life balance.

Damian Kocot is an Assistant Professor in the Department of Economic Informatics at the College of Economics at the University of Economics in Katowice. About ten years of work as a teacher at universities, his scientific interests include management and quality, IT outsourcing, IT support for business processes, IT support for public administration, electronic economy and e-business, creative organization, and information society. Author of 28 publications.

Anna Kozłowska is a Ph.D. of Economic Sciences in the Discipline of Economics; since 2016, she has been an Associate Professor in the Department of Microeconomics at the Institute of Economics of the Poznań University of Economics and Business. Her areas of scientific interest include economic growth and development, innovation and technological progress, Schumpeterian economics, business cycles, and direct foreign investment.

Natalia Krawczyk is a Ph.D. student at the Faculty of Management of AGH University of Science and Technology in Krakow, Poland. In her work, she analyzes benchmarking and management methods in the healthcare sector. She has experience in managing Polish medical entities.

Rafał Kusa is an Assistant Professor at AGH University of Science and Technology's Faculty of Management in Krakow, Poland. He received his Ph.D. degree from Krakow University of Economics. His research interests include entrepreneurship, strategic management, non-profit management, social entrepreneurship, and tourism management. He is the author or co-author of more than 80 scientific publications.

Renata Lisowska is an Associate Professor at the Department of Entrepreneurship and Industrial Policy of the University of Lodz's Faculty of Management. Her research interests include economics and small business management, financing business development, the management of innovative and research projects, and business consulting for SMEs. She also has many years' experience as a head of research projects and is the author or co-author of 100 scientific publications.

Radosław Luft is a Ph.D. at Kazimierz Pulaski University of Technology and Humanities in Radom, Poland. He is a member of the Business and International Finance Department. His research centers around the innovation and competitiveness of small and medium-sized enterprises, and he has more than 40 research publications that have been published in Poland as well as abroad.

Magdalena Maciaszczyk is an Assistant Professor at Lublin University of Technology's Faculty of Management in the Department of Marketing. A researcher since 2013, her scientific interests include consumer behavior, the prosumption and ethnocentrism of consumers, e-business, creative organizations and information society, and market innovations. Her approximate number of publications is 45.

Vanda Maráková is a Professor and Head of the Department of Tourism in the Faculty of Economics at Matej Bel University in Banska Bystrica, Slovakia. She has 20 years of experience in research and education in the field of economy and management; her main research topics include tourism management, entrepreneurship in tourism, corporate social responsibility, sustainability and competitiveness, and innovations in tourism. She has authored or co-authored more than 170 research publications, including 7 monographs that were published in Slovakia and abroad.

Monika Mościbrodzka is an Assistant Professor at the Institute of Economic Sciences at the University of Wroclaw, Poland. She is the author of several dozen articles that are related to the application of quantitative methods in economic analyses, which mainly concern the evaluation of financial investments and capital market properties.

Andriy Pekhnyk is an Associate Professor in the Department of International Economic Relations of the Faculty of International Relations at Ivan Franko National University in Lviv. His research interests include international business, transnational corporations, international management, cross-cultural business, and negotiations. He has many years' experience of participating in international research projects and is the author or co-author of more than 50 scientific publications.

Agnieszka Rzepka is a Professor at Lublin University of Technology in the Faculty of Management of the Department of Economics and Economic Management. She specializes in inter-organizational management, intellectual capital, self-management, and SMEs. Her current research is focused on teal organizations. She is the author of 135 papers, including 7 proprietary and collective monographs such as Innovation in the Digital Economy: New Approaches to Management for Industry 5.0. (2022).

Natia Shengelia is an Associate Professor at Georgian Technical University who has a Ph.D. in Social Sciences in Economics. In 2014, she was awarded the *President's Grant for Young Scientists* in Georgia. She is the author and co-author of more than 75 articles and monographs in different languages. With an *ACCA* International Advanced Diploma (UK) in Accounting, she is a graduate of Oxford Brookes University.

Her work experience spans eight years as a senior financial auditor and a risk and quality-assurance manager.

Katarzyna Sieradzka is a Ph.D. at Kazimierz Pulaski University of Technology and Humanities in Radom, Poland. A researcher and teacher in the Department of Economics at the Faculty of Economics and Finance, she specializes in issues that are related to the development of the enterprise sector, including sources of financing, innovation, and competitiveness. She is the author of many articles and the author or co-author of several books.

Bogusław Ślusarczyk is an Associate Professor of Economics at Karpacka Państwowa Uczelnia in Krosno, Poland. He works in the Department of Economics and International Economic Relations. His scientific interests focus on international economic relations, entrepreneurship, and competitiveness. His research has been published in a wide range of scientific journals worldwide; he has been the author or co-author of nearly 300 scientific publications.

Hanna Soroka-Potrzebna is an Assistant Professor at the Faculty of Economics, Finance, and Management at the University of Szczecin in Poland. Her scientific areas of interest include project management, risk management in projects, human resource management, and heuristics methods and techniques. She holds several project management certifications, including the PRINCE2® Foundation and the MoR® Foundation. Her research has been presented at several international conferences, and she has authored or co-authored more than 40 scientific publications.

Marcin Suder has been an Assistant Professor at AGH University of Science and Technology's Faculty of Management in Krakow since 2008; he received his Ph.D. degree from the same university. His research interests focus on the application of quantitative methods in economic and managerial studies, and he is the author or co-author of 46 scientific publications.

Izabela Szamrej-Baran is an economist and Assistant Professor at the Institute of Economics and Finance of the University of Szczecin. She is the author or co-author of many research publications; her academic research and teaching encompass economic and social policy, sustainable development, and the impact of diverse phenomena (e.g., the COVID-19 pandemic or fuel poverty) on the economy.

Agnieszka Szczepkowska-Flis is a Ph.D. of Economic Sciences in the Discipline of Economics. During the period of 2005–2018, she was an Assistant Professor in the Department of Business Activity at the Poznań University of Economics and Business; since 2019, she has been an Assistant Professor at the Department of Economics of Kazimierz Wielki University. Her areas of scientific interest include economic growth and development, innovation and technological progress, Schumpeterian economics, business cycles, and direct foreign investment.

Anna Wolak-Tuzimek is an Associate Professor at Kazimierz Pulaski University of Technology and Humanities in Radom, Poland. She is the head of the Department of Economics in the Faculty of Economics and Finance. Her research centers around the conditions of enterprise development. She studies the impact of corporate social responsibility on enterprise competitiveness and has authored more than 120 research publications, including 8 monographs that were published in Poland and abroad.

Maciej Woźniak is an Assistant Professor at the Faculty of Management of AGH University of Science and Technology in Krakow, Poland. His research interests cover a wide range of areas that include small and medium-sized enterprises and public policy. He has published findings in books and academic journals and has been the author or co-author of more than 50 scientific publications.

Patrycja Żegleń is a Doctor of Economics at the College of Social Sciences of the Institute of Economics and Finance at the University of Rzeszów, Poland. She graduated from Warsaw School of Economics; her scientific interests focus on public-private partnerships, entrepreneurship, and the economics of tourism. She is the author of more than 100 scientific publications and has taken part in several European projects (both scientific and didactic).

Preface

Introduction to Business Impacts of COVID-19: International Business, Crisis Management, and Global Economy

The coronavirus disease (COVID-19) was first identified in Wuhan, China, in December 2019. Since then, it has had an unprecedented social and economic impact on the entire planet and its people. Today (November 2022), more than 630 million people have been infected worldwide, and more than 6.5 million have died from it (WHO, 2022). The world we know is almost frozen in anticipation of the events to come. The economic and social effects that are related to the functioning of enterprises, people's ways of life, and the organization of society have changed for longer periods, and nobody knows how this will ultimately change us (Honey-Roses et al., 2020; Nicola et al., 2020).

There has been a significant decline in consumer spending (Chetty et al., 2020). At the same time, companies reduced investments and employment in order to cope with the fall in demand due to the lockdown (Campello et al., 2020). In the case of the most sensitive sectors of the economy, a significant number of companies decided to shutter their activities (Bartik et al., 2020). In particular, small- and medium-sized enterprises have been forced to close or downsize. The main reason for this was that they had relatively low financial liquidity and were repeatedly unable to adapt to the economic realities that were caused by the pandemic crisis.

It should also be noted that COVID-19 had a much stronger impact on those industries that required direct contacts and actions; these was associated with many restrictions – especially the movement of people (Škare et al., 2021).

The measures that were taken by governments in order to tackle the pandemic and COVID-19 have had a devastating global economic impact on economies (Kobayashi et al., 2021). World markets have plunged precipitously, unemployment has risen, and the incomes of tens of millions of people have decreased significantly (Ashraf, 2020). Businesses have faced declines in orders, the containments of expenses, and cost pressures such as rent, wages, tax payments, overall increases in commodity prices, insufficient demand, and difficulties finding alternative suppliers (Liu et al., 2021). Learning, improvisation, and resilience were essential for survival (Mariano, 2021). Consumers also felt the effects of the pandemic in which the boundaries between work and personal lives blurred while working, studying, and relaxing at home. Uncertainty about the risk of getting sick and becoming unemployed, and limiting governments to possibilities, changed their purchasing behavior, which led to a conservative attitude and a reduction of unnecessary spending, resulting in a sharp drop in company revenues.

The World Bank (The World Bank Group, 2022) estimates that the effects of COVID-19 have pushed an additional 100 million people into extreme poverty, reversing hard-won gains in development. Today, twice as many people are facing food insecurity – especially in those countries that were already fragile or affected by conflict. Nearly 1.6 billion students did not attend school for a time. Women were (and still are) more likely to lose their jobs and, at the same time, have greater needs for care and greater risks of gender-based violence.

From a theoretical and practical point of view, this situation has been the subject of many studies and scientific publications. As Torres et al. (2022) showed, 4,347 scientific papers were published in journals that were indexed in WoS during the period up to 2022. Their research identified those scientific areas that were most often discussed in these works; they were divided into 12 broad topics – the first five of which account for nearly 70% of all studies. These areas were financial markets, tourism and consumer behavior, policy and its socioeconomic effects, environmental and public impacts, and labor and gender impacts.

This publication covers the above-mentioned areas. It is a valuable collection of experiences and research on the effects of the pandemic. In this publication, the authors have shared their observations and conclusions from their research and analyses as well as from their experiences in creating and implementing anti-crisis solutions in economies and enterprises. This monograph deals with issues that are related to the impact of the crisis that was caused by the COVID-19 pandemic on the economy and its entities. First, it discusses general issues that are related to the impact of the pandemic on society and economy; e.g., the impact of the crisis on the economy in the context of the black swan theory, the actions that were taken by the governments of various countries in connection with the ongoing crisis that was caused by the SARS-CoV-2 pandemic (including relief measures that were important for reducing the tragic economic and social consequences), crisis management in the healthcare systems of selected European Union countries during the COVID-19 pandemic, supply and demand shocks that were triggered by the crisis (which can be catalysts for positive changes in the economic system), or the impact of the COVID-19 pandemic on learning and self-development, on interpersonal relationships in the areas of innovation and technology, and on the development of digital competencies.

The second part of the monograph focuses on those entities (mainly enterprises) that were most affected by the direct impact of the pandemic on their decisions and activities.

Topics such as changes in the factors of business competitiveness and the importance of inter-organizational cooperation during a crisis were discussed, and the dynamic capabilities of business entities that can enable them to respond quickly and effectively to changes in the environment, risk management in projects, consumer behavior during a pandemic, disruptions in supply chains, the impact of the COVID-19 crisis on financial markets, and the impact of the COVID-19 pandemic on international trade were also addressed.

Tomasz Bernat (University of Szczecin) and Joanna Duda (AGH University of Science and Technology)

References

Ashraf, B. N. (2020). Economic impact of government interventions during the COVID-19 pandemic: International evidence from financial markets. *Journal of Behavioral and Experimental Finance*, 27, 100371. https://doi.org/10.1016/j.jbef.2020.100371

Bartik, A. W., Bertrand, M., Cullen, Z. B., Glaeser, E. L., Luca, M., & Stanton, C. T. (2020). *How are small businesses adjusting to COVID-19? Early evidence from a survey* (Technical Report). National Bureau of Economic Research.

Campello, M., Kankanhalli, G., & Muthukrishnan, P. (2020). *Corporate hiring under COVID-19: Labor market concentration, downskilling, and income inequality* (Technical Report). National Bureau of Economic Research.

Chetty, R., Friedman, J. N., Hendren, N., & Stepner, M. (2020). *How did COVID-19 and stabilization policies affect spending and employment? A new real-time economic tracker based on private sector data* (Technical Report). National Bureau of Economic Research.

Honey-Roses, J., Anguelovski, I., Bohigas, J., Chireh, V., Daher, C., Konijnendijk, C., Litt, J. S., Mawani, V., McCall, M. K., Orellana, A., Oscilowicz, E., Sánchez, U., Nieuwenhuijsen, M. (2020). The impact of COVID-19 on public space: an early review of the emerging questions – design, perceptions and inequities. *Cities and Health*, 2021, VOL. 5, NO. S1, S263-S279 https://doi.org/10.1080/23748834.2020.1780074

Kobayashi, Y., Heinrich, T., & Bryant, K. A. (2021). Public support for development aid during the COVID-19 pandemic. *World Development*, 138, 105248. https://doi.org/10.1016/j.worlddev.2020.105248

Liu, N., Xu, Z., & Skare, M. (2021). The research on COVID-19 and economy from 2019 to 2020: Analysis from the perspective of bibliometrics. *Oeconomia Copernicana*, 12(2), 217–268. https://doi.org/10.24136/OC.2021.009

Mariano, S. (2021). Let me help you! Navigating through the COVID-19 crisis with prosocial expert knowledge behaviour. *Knowledge Management Research & Practice*, 19(4), 484–492. https://doi.org/10.1080/14778238.2020.1866445

Nicola, M., Alsafi, Z., Sohrabi, C., Kerwan, A., Al-Jabir, A., Iosifidis, C., Agha, M., & Agha, R. (2020). The socio-economic implications of the coronavirus pandemic (COVID-19): A review. *International Journal of Surgery*, 78, 185–193. https://doi.org/10.1016/j.ijsu.2020.04.018

Škare, M., Soriano, D. R., & Porada-Rochoń, M. (2021). Impact of COVID-19 on the travel and tourism industry. *Technological Forecasting and Social Change*, 163, 120469. https://doi.org/10.1016/j.techfore.2020.120469

The World Bank Group (2022). Responding to the COVID-19 Pandemic and Rebuilding Better, access on 10.11.2022: https://thedocs.worldbank.org/en/doc/bb1b191f6b1bd1f932d0ddc5492987ec-0090012021/original/WBG-Responding-to-the-COVID-19-Pandemic-and-Rebuilding-Better.pdf

Torres, D. A., Barrera Rodríguez A. M., & Echeverri Gutiérrez P. A. (2022). COVID-19 in business, management, and economics: Research perspectives and bibliometric analysis. *Brazilian Administration Review*, 19(3), e220016. https://doi.org/10.1590/1807-7692bar2022220016

WHO (2022). WHO Coronavirus (COVID-19) Dashboard, access on 10.11.2022: https://covid19.who.int

1 Socio-economic consequences of events at the beginning of the 21st century in view of the Black Swan theory

Anna Barwińska-Małajowicz, Bogusław Ślusarczyk, Patrycja Żegleń and Miroslava Knapková

Taleb's theory – literature review

"Black Swan. The Impact of the Highly Improbable," by N.N. Taleb (2014), presents an intriguing image of reality. The author addressed the problem of the *Black Swan* phenomenon, which are unpredictable events that occur suddenly and take a great toll on the life of an individual as well as on entire regions and countries. Whether it was the outbreak of the First World War, Hitler attaining power, the September 11, 2001, attacks in the United States, the 2008 financial crisis, or the coronavirus (COVID-19) pandemic, these events entirely changed the basis and the rhythm of life of entire societies. Their impact on the destiny of the world is enormous, whereas they are unpredictable and people try to rationalize them only once they have taken place (Bekiros et al., 2015; Lin, Tsai, 2019; Wang et al., 2019).

According to Taleb's concept, a *Black Swan* indicates an unpredictable event that has an immense impact on reality (Wells et al., 2017; Ponkin, 2019; Inayatullah, Black, 2020). At the same time, the author of this concept indicated the uselessness of historical data in attempts to predict *Black Swans*, which occur more frequently than commonly believed. Taleb gave the example of E.J. Smith, the captain of the Titanic who, in 1907 (five years before the disaster), said that "throughout his entire career, he had not dealt with an accident worth a mention; he had not even seen a shipwreck" (Piński, 2012).

The main threat does not lie solely in ignoring what we cannot predict but, primarily, in thinking that people have everything under control; this causes the risk to increase. Notably, *Black Swans* happen much more frequently than is commonly believed, and such events (and the knowledge that is acquired) should be used to predict and forecast the future, for example the economic future (Blasco, 2021). The problem with *Black Swans* is that we are not able to predict them; therefore, we ignore them completely. This contributes to the fact that we expose ourselves to

DOI: 10.4324/9781003368687-1

greater danger than in the hypothetical situation in which we consider their existence. According to Taleb, people are not able to react to such a phenomenon properly. They focus on the past and try to understand the error, and they create a behavior model for the future on the grounds of past events. This is not always effective.

Terrorist attacks of 2001 and their consequences

The terrorist attacks in the first decade of the 21st century that took place in the United States caused the losses of human life and material goods on a high scale as well as far-reaching consequences within various areas of life and the functioning of people (OECD, 2002). The effects of the terrorist attacks were extensive and affected practically every aspect of human life (social, economic, and political) (Sandler, Enders, 2008; Zakaria et al., 2019). This part of the article addresses the problem of the impact of the terrorist attacks of 2001 on entire economies and market segments as well as the enterprises and consumers that operated within them.

The passenger planes that were crashed into the World Trade Center, the Pentagon, and the Pennsylvania countryside resulted in serious consequences; this significantly destabilized the functioning of one of the global economic powers. The terrorist attacks accelerated and aggravated the economic recession in the United States, which was impending in 2001 and followed the crude oil price increase (from $10 to $37 a barrel) during the period of 1999–2000. According to the IMF and OECD, the terrorist attacks contributed to the decline of the American GDP. The speed of the economic growth in the United States declined from an estimated 1.4 to 0.9% during the third quarter of 2001 and down to 0.8% by the end of 2001. Furthermore, the terrorist attacks contributed to changes in the revenue and expenditure structure of the United States (a budget surplus of $128 billion was still recorded in 2001; however, a deficit of $158 billion emerged a year later and reached $347 billion by 2005) (Mazurek, 2012).

The losses that were recorded as a result of the attacks covered some markets, including the following:

1 goods and services;
2 raw materials and production;
3 financial.

The most important effects for **the goods and services market** covered the following:

- enormous drop in consumer trust (not only within the United States but also in Europe);
- fear of further attacks translated to a lower frequency of purchases and visits to public places (such as restaurants, cinemas, etc.) as well as to

losses within the tourist and transport market services (Belau, 2003) – in particular, those provided by airlines (Blake, Sinclair, 2003);
- decrease in turnover at enterprises operating in other sectors related to the hospitality and aviation services (requirement to introduce intensified checks resulted in the rise of service costs within the passenger as well as goods transport sector), including enormous losses for the hotel catering, entertainment, and tourist sectors ($6.4 billion) and for carriers ($7 billion);
- decrease in interest in fortunes of developing countries; rich countries would lock down more and did not invest nor prompt commerce within developing countries – this affected increases in developmental differences between rich and poor countries, intensified tensions of ethnic and religious backgrounds, and increased migration (Rodzinka, Hady, 2009).

The attack on the World Trade Center mainly affected the crude oil market (the price of a crude oil barrel before the attack was $25 – a month later, it was below $20, and at the end of 2001, it was below $18). The drop in crude oil prices was caused by the increasing recession, while the slower pace of economic growth caused lower demand for oil (which resulted in a price drop). In the second quarter of 2002, however, crude oil prices surged (which was caused by the risk of an outbreak of war between the United States and Iraq); the price per barrel reached almost $30.

Unfortunately, the gold market (a raw material that is often considered to be the safest investment) did not respond extensively to the terrorist attacks – the price of an ounce of gold before the attacks was just above $274, while it increased to about $290 shortly after the tragic events (a return to the pre-attack level was recorded by the end of October 2001).

Expenditures within the arms industry that were directed at protection against terrorism were of significance to production in the United States as well as in many European countries. During the period after the year 2001, expenditures on armaments increased regularly and were shaped as follows: in 2012, these constituted $711 billion in the US budget (4.7% of its GDP); in Great Britain – $63 billion (2.6% of its GDP); in France – $62 billion (2.3% of its GDP), in India – $49 billion (2.6% of its GDP); and in Japan – $59 billion (1% of its GDP).

The financial losses in the United States were estimated to be $83 billion. The cost of rebuilding the destroyed buildings and infrastructure was estimated to be $22 billion; removing the debris – more than $1 billion; and the losses of insurance companies – about $35–50 billion.

The most important effects on the financial markets were as follows:

- Immediately after the disaster, the International Forex Market suffered a standstill (the number of transactions shrank by about 80%).

- The American stock exchange market stopped for six days; the day of its reopening (September 17, 2001) saw share price reductions and a serious slump in the indices.
- The decrease in the European stock market indices (the value of the US dollar [USD] dropped, the Swiss franc [CHF] reached its highest level against the dollar in the past year and a half [CHF/USD 1.5670], and the rise of the price of American Treasury bonds, which were perceived to be the safest in the world and purchased during crisis situations).
- Indices drop on the Asian markets (including the Tokyo stock exchange).
- Soaring sales by stock investors in stock markets in other countries (such as Poland).
- The dramatic fall of the stocks of airlines and insurance companies (losses at a level of $13 billion).
- Interest rate reductions by ECB as well as CB in Switzerland, Taiwan, and Hong Kong.

In conclusion, the tragic events in the United States triggered a crisis in three powerful sectors: tourism, insurance, and aviation. In the wake of the attack, the numbers of airline travelers decreased significantly, which resulted in a turnover decline at many enterprises. The most adverse effects were suffered by the stocks of the airlines and insurance companies. A rise in insurance costs was recorded (including aircraft, ship, and building insurance). As compared to 2000, a significant decline in passenger traffic was recorded by airports, which had been among the biggest airports in the world (regarding passenger traffic) until then. The airports in Seoul (SEL), St. Louis (STL), and Boston (BOS) disappeared from the list, whereas the airport in San Francisco (SFO) went down in ranking the most – by 13 positions (Dziedzic, Olchowik, 2006, p. 12).

In the wake of the September attacks, the entire stock market infrastructure suffered seriously. During the session of September 17, 2001, the Dow Jones Industrial index value's loss was −7.1%, Nasdaq's was −6.9%, and the S&P 500's was −5% as compared to the closing levels before the attacks.

Furthermore, the events of 2001 resulted in increases in resources for security, the creation of anti-terrorist policies, and (in extreme instances) even restrictions of civil liberties in numerous countries (Dragu, 2011).

Socio-economic effects of crisis of 2007–2009

The crisis of 2007–2009 constitutes additional proof that there is no capitalism without the cyclicality of the macroeconomic reproduction process and that it is an inherent feature of the market economy (Benita, 2019; Chau et al., 2020; Beltran et al., 2021). This has been addressed by many prominent authors, including names such as K. Marx and J.M. Keynes, who emphasized the immanent crisis-inducing nature of capitalism in their considerations. However, they formulated utterly different conclusions; K. Marx predicted the inevitability of the fall of capitalism and its replacement with socialism free from conflict and free from crisis (Marks, Engels, 1956, pp. 55–56). Some authors provided unique immersions in their different approaches to the political economy and to the crisis with the understanding of Marx's crisis theory (Yagi et al., 2013; Meegan et al., 2018; Chau et al., 2020). One should also underline that the events of the 20th century and the initial years of the 21st century also provided a negative verification of the vision of K. Marks. On the other hand, Keynes (1936) believed that capitalism was an economic system that generated occurrences and processes that constituted the seedbed of crises that required that measures be undertaken to protect it against auto-destruction. He created the theory that underlay the economic policy, which aimed to prevent economic crises. In his work "The General Theory of Employment, Interest, and Money" (1936), he presented the concept of a so-called state-regulated economy (interventionism). He developed a demand-based production and employment model that he applied to explain the causes of high unemployment levels and low production levels, which were predominant in most industrialized countries during the 1930s. The main thesis that J.M. Keynes assumed was a statement that the size of production and employment were determined by global demand, whereas monetarists (headed by M. Friedman) presented arguments that the Keynesian analysis was useful in explaining the causes of the crises but was of little use in interpreting the inflation phenomenon. The postwar generation of economists became divided into those who:

- shared the views of J. M. Keynes that a state should become involved and increase demand in order to prevent the deepening of a recession;
- followed M. Friedman, who believed that the direct cause of the crisis of the 1930s was not a fall in demand but rather the depletion of bank deposits and reserves (which were the result of a bank panic).

Such a panic resulted in depositors withdrawing their savings, which led to many banks going bankrupt (Adelopo et al., 2018; Chen et al., 2018). According to monetarists, the fall in the money supply caused an overall demand fall, which effectively had an impact on the drop in outgoings, revenues, prices, and (eventually) employment levels. Hence, the fall of the monetary supply in the 1930s contributed to the aggravation of the credit crisis in the view of monetarists, and the Federal Reserve System's (Fed in short) operations only worsened the situation.

In order to avoid a repeat of the Great Depression, many economists conducted a technically sound description of the conditions and causes, mechanism and course, and in consequence, the course of the current economic crisis (Kobrak, Wilkins, 2013). In the conclusions of their studies, they established that periodical crises were the norm in capitalism; however, the lingering question was whether they were foreseeable and, if so, to what extent their effects could be limited.

This issue provides an area to present views, stances, or opinions regarding crises, including the 2007–2009 crises. The initial signs of the crisis in the real estate and high-risk mortgage (subprime mortgage) market that emerged in 2007 caused disbelief and fact denial. B. Bernanke, the Chair of the Fed, stated in Congress that "everything indicates that recently the impact of the bad credit problems on the rest of the economy and the financial markets has been significantly limited" (Bernanke, 2007). On the other hand, H. Paulson (the Secretary of the Treasury) underestimated the hazard of the crunch that was caused by such credits: "I do not believe they should pose any danger to the economy" (Carmichael et al., 2007). The facts were neglected even after the crisis outbreak and following the collapse of the Bear Stearns bank. H. Paulson stated this with his typical optimism: "I am expecting the future financial markets to be less dependent on the present confusion, but on the economic circumstances, especially from a recovery on the real estate market" (Paulson, 2008).

Furthermore, many commentators showed grand optimism (Beck, Garris III, 2019; Garcia, 2019), including D. Luskin – a stock market guru and financial market pundit who, despite the collapse of two giants on the mortgage market (Fannie Mae and Freddie Mac), anticipated that, in the nearest future, the United States would see economic recovery. He wrote:

> naturally, the economy has witnessed the emergence of dangerous phenomena, with the explicitly evident example of the take-over of mortgage market giants Fannie Mae and Freddie Mac or the tensions concerning the Lehman Brothers bank. Also, the unemployment rates went up slightly.

In his opinion, however,

> none of those phenomena entitle us to talk about a crisis or to exaggerate the comparisons to the great recession of the 30's. [...] Everyone who claims that we are in a recession phase, or that we are heading towards it, and especially those who talk about the worst recession since the 30's, use their private definition of recession (Luskin, 2008).

Meanwhile, as it emerged the following day (September 15, 2008), Lehman Brothers announced its bankruptcy, the real estate and mortgage market crashed, a global scale panic swept most countries in the world, and the crisis became a fact.

Many economists who have analyzed the causes of the 2007–2009 crisis outbreak claim that it was predictable because all previous crises introduced chaos and followed fixed patterns (Rapoport, Gerts, 2010). In an analysis of the conditions and the course of the global economic crisis, J.E. Stiglitz wrote: "The only surprise when it comes the crisis of 2008 was that it was a surprise for so many" (Stiglitz, 2010, p. 1). However, many referred to the *Black Swan* theory that was formulated by N.N. Taleb (2007), claiming that the financial crisis was a type of anomaly with far-reaching unpredictable effects. Therefore, we may need to agree with J.E. Stiglitz that the scope (areas) of the crisis was unpredictable: that it would be of a global reach and would cause such enormous effects that surprised so many (as depicted by J. E. Stiglitz).

According to the IMF, the pace of global trade growth dropped from a level of 9.4% in 2006 to a level of about 2.1% in 2009 due to the global financial crisis. The direct causes of the export revenue reduction in developing countries were decreasing raw material prices, a reduction in the demand of economically developed countries for goods that were exported by those countries, and the fall in the revenue that was generated by tourism.

According to data perceived from the World Bank, low interest rates affected a vast boost in granted mortgages and the relaxation of requirements regarding the assessment of the credit ratings of prospective clients, which increased the participation of the high-risk credit (subprime credit). "Bad" (uncollectable) debts increased, and information emerged about falls in asset values at increasing numbers of financial institutions. Bankruptcies (or losses of the liquidity of credit institutions) would cause a drastic fall in the trust in such institutions. In turn, the loss of trust generated a freeze of interbank market deposits. The burst housing bubble impacted the slump of demand for bonds. Furthermore, the value of the unpaid capital on American credit cards grew to $950M (more than 7% of the GDP in the United States), and the insolvency rate on the national scale rose to 7.3% of the GDP.

Such a high insolvency rate had undoubtedly originated from the high unemployment that was generated, which reached its peak level over the past 14 years (about 6.7%). The average unemployment level (also in the European Union) oscillated at a high level, i.e., 9.1%.

The financial crisis of 2007–2009 disrupted static (allocative) and dynamic efficiency in the global economy, caused a decline in economic growth (economic recession), depreciated customer satisfaction, the production structure of national savings, exacerbated income disparities, and triggered an increase in unemployment, poverty, and social inequalities. In the book "Crisis Economics" (2011, p. 35), N. Roubini and S. Mihm presented the anatomy of the crisis of 2007–2009 along with its causes, mechanisms, and effects. They established that "the last round of dramatic events did not belong among extremely rare and atypical phenomena. Its emergence was rather likely." The authors of this chapter do not entirely agree with the quoted statements; in our opinion, the mechanism of crisis generation does lie in the systemic assumptions of capitalism. It is difficult to predict the results of a crisis, its scope, and the depth of the inevitable social and economic consequences.

Scenarios related to economic situations of the selected countries affected by the coronavirus pandemic (economic crisis of 2020–2021)

As a set of methods and techniques that have the goal of generating strategies and insight for decision- and policy-makers (Batrouni et al., 2018), the scenarios and forecasts that were related to the global social and economic situation as a consequence of the COVID-19 pandemic were based on diagnoses of events that affected what would happen in the future (Heinonen et al., 2017; Perera et al., 2018). An important role is that of the simulations of events we try to predict on the grounds of our acquired experience and expertise (Moon, 2020; Rogers, 2020; Sohrabi et al., 2020). It has been observed that a broad debate is ongoing on whether the COVID-19 pandemic can be defined as a *Black Swan* or not (Dhara, 2020; Antipova, 2021; Selmi et al., 2021; Stavrova et al., 2020). However, what were unpredictable were the socio-economic consequences that were related to the global economic situation with the causes lying in the so-called lockdowns that were brought about by the COVID-19 pandemic.

According to the most optimistic scenario considered by the IMF (imf.org), the global economy has experienced losses that total $9 billion. This is more than the GDPs of Japan and Germany put together. Global economic growth is strongly negative, and a "partial recovery" is taking place in 2021. The situation was worsened by potential new cases of the illness, which resulted in the year 2021 being economically poorer than the previous year.

The effects of the pandemic on the European economy were seen in the decline in international import and export, i.e., escalation of the so-called *economic egoism* phenomena, which is being manifested through the countries that are becoming discouraged to cooperate and deepening the divisions within Europe. The next economic effect for Europe is the drop in company stocks within the sectors that have faced the biggest risk, such as the tourism sector. Effectively, the economies of the European Union member states are slowing down, and the financial debt is rising. Globally, the economic impact of the pandemic is clear across sectors and business forms, just as it is across countries. International trade exchange has declined due to restrictions on the international flow of production factors. In other words, the socio-economic consequences of the COVID-19 pandemic are tangible, and there is a lot to do to overcome the crisis (Jaderan Yazdani, 2020; Langley, 2021).

Global debt as an aftermath of events related to the coronavirus pandemic

The coronavirus outbreak started in the central Hubei Province of China. The spread of the disease across China and the entire world was a multilayered issue that affected all of the spheres of our lives (Brown, Wang, 2020, p. 247). The COVID-19 pandemic and its economic fallout have been devastating to public balance sheets. Countries are faced with additional spending needs to finance their health responses, provide support to households and companies, and invest in the recovery once the pandemic is under control (Hausmann, 2020; Leung et al., 2020; Verma, Gustafsson, 2020). At the same time, revenues are collapsing (Buheji et al., 2020; Ramesh, 2020), and global debts are projected to jump by 13% of GDP (from 83 to 96%). The IMF expects fiscal balances to turn sharply negative in developing countries (to -9.1 and -5.7% of GDP in middle-income and low-income countries, respectively) (Spiegel et al., 2020).

The debt of the emerging markets (i.e., 21 economies in the world such as Brazil, Chile, Pakistan, and China) has reached an amount of about $69 billion (that is, almost 200% of GDP). The countries with the highest debt are the United States, China, Japan, France, Great Britain, etc. One of the reasons for the government, local government, and enterprise sector to go into debt is the low level of interest rates, which is conducive to the incurrence of debt. Notably, the debt level was higher in 2020 than it was before the 2008 crisis. Global debt contributes to unemployment rises, declines in people's incomes, and (consequently) the global impoverishment of societies. The poorer the education levels of individuals, the worse fates they will face in the coming years (Ptak-Iglewska, 2020). Should the past pandemics be some guidelines, the toll for the poorest and most vulnerable social groups will be several times greater (Furceri et al., 2020). They refer to the recent study (http://www.igmchicago.org/surveys/inequality-and-the-covid-19-crisis/) of economists[1] who analyzed five of the most recent pandemics (SARS [2003], H1N1 [2009], MERS [2012], Ebola [2014], and Zika [2016]), and they verified the effects within five years following each event. They established that the Gini coefficient (i.e., the social dispersion measure) increased in those countries by 1.5% over the five years. According to the economists, this is a considerable rise, and it is really concerning that it increased despite governments' efforts to redistribute income to mitigate the effects of the pandemic. The factors that contributed most to such negative effects of the pandemic were loss of work, higher unemployment levels, and lower money transfers. Furthermore, economists observed that the extent that people will be hit by an economic crisis after a pandemic depends on their education levels. In accordance with the study by the IMF (https://www.imf.org/en/Publications/GFSR/Issues/2020/04/14/global-financial-stability-report-april-2020), these pandemics affected people of different levels of education in different ways. The difference was distinct – the pandemics did not have significant impacts on the employment of university-educated people, whereas there was a more than 5% slump in the employment of people with primary education in the following five years. Hence, it appears that the job losses that are related to a pandemic harm employees with primary education in a disproportionate manner. According to K. Georgieva (the managing director at the IMF), particular attention should be paid to preventing the long-term losses suffered by the sources of income of the least privileged. The IMF recommends that, in the case of inevitable future shocks (such as climatic changes), policy-makers should implement fundamental changes in order for their societies to initiate mechanisms of split risk and public assistance, which protect the most vulnerable much better than we do now.

The World Bank data on the real GDP rate in 2019 as well as in 2020 and 2021 indicate an economic recession on a global scale; according to World Bank forecasts, the economies of undeveloped countries will not note negative GDPs in 2021 (in contrast to highly developed and developing economies).

The World Bank has appealed to governments for quick firm policies in order to save jobs and support the poor. The institution announced that they have already commenced emergency response operations in 100 countries in response to the crisis that was triggered by the COVID-19 pandemic. To sum up, critical reflection on the coronavirus pandemic has to be combined with a review of how economists have defended economic growth as sustainable and inclusive regardless of systemic limits and multiple crises (Spash, 2020).

Conclusions

Addressing the negative examples of *Black Swans* and their socio-economic consequences, we should mention the so-called positive *Black Swans* (for example, Google or Facebook). These are examples of positive unpredictable events because nobody expected their global success on such a scale. Naturally, we could search for negative aspects of these undertakings; however, the benefits arising from them are evidence of their success and popularity.

Recapitulating, in light of the *Black Swan* theory regarding the 21st century's unpredictable events analyzed herein, we should establish that the consequences that were generated by such events and their circumstances were hardly predictable, considering their scope of impact and volume of dysfunctional events in numerous sectors of the world's economies. The diagnosis of such occurrences constitutes a basis to create forecasts and scenarios regarding the socio-economic consequences that were triggered by the COVID-19 pandemic. We may only estimate and assume the effects of the existing situation for a further global economic future with regard to individual consumers as well as businesses.

The results of the research and analysis presented in this chapter on the *Black Swan* theory (identified as an unpredictable event that has serious and universal consequences) in retrospect can be perceived as getting in the way of something (so-called hindsight bias) and may have important implications for financial markets and stock market investors. And in this area, comparisons are very often made to wildlife (bull market, bear market). The strategies of the activities of these organizations should be built in such a way as to be impervious to these types of events. They cease to be something unexpected then.

The research results also suggest to all business entities that elasticity in running a business plays a significant role; thanks to this, entrepreneurships can adjust to changes that are caused by unpredictable events, whereby one should emphasize that it would be easier for those companies whose digitization processes are highly advanced.

Note

1 The panel of scientists were from a range of universities including Harvard University, MIT University, Stanford, Yale, Princeton, and Berkeley. Among the economists who participated in the study were R. Hall, O. Hart, J. Stock, R. Thaler, K. Braicker, and M. Bertrand et al.

References

Adelopo, I., Lloydking, R., Tauringana, V. (2018) Determinants of bank profitability before, during, and after the financial crisis, *International Journal of Managerial Finance*, Vol. 14, Issue 4, pp. 378–398, ISSN: 1743-9132.

Antipova, T. (2021) *Coronavirus pandemic as black swan event.* [in:] Antipova, T. (eds.) *Integrated Science in Digital Age 2020. ICIS 2020. Lecture Notes in Networks and Systems*, Vol. 136, Springer International Publishing, Springer, Cham, https://doi.org/10.1007/978-3-030-49264-9_32, pp. 356–357.

Batrouni, M., Bertaux, A., Nicolle, C. (2018) Scenario analysis, from Big Data to black swan, *Computer Science Review*, Vol. 28, pp. 131–139, ISSN 1574-0137, https://doi.org/10.1016/j.cosrev.2018.02.001.

Beck, J.J., Garris III, R.O. (2019) Managing personal finance literacy in the United States: a case study, *Education Sciences*, Vol. 9, pp. 129, https://doi.org/10.3390/educsci9020129.

Bekiros, S., Boubaker, S., Nguyen, D.K., Uddin, G.S. (2015) Black Swan events and safe havens: the role of gold in globally integrated emerging markets, *MPRA Paper*, Vol. 73, pp. 317–334.

Belau, D. (2003) *The Impact of the 2001–2002 Crisis on the Hotel and Tourism Industry*. International Labor Organization (ILO), Geneva, Essay Paper.

Beltran, D.O., Bolotnyy, V., Klee, E. (2021) The federal funds network and monetary policy transmission: evidence from the 2007–2009 financial crisis, *Journal of Monetary Economics*, Vol. 117, pp. 187–202, ISSN 0304-3932, https://doi.org/10.1016/j.jmoneco.2019.12.006.

Benita, F. (2019) Trade openness, economic growth and the global financial crisis of 2007–2009 in Latin America, *Journal of International Development*, Vol. 31, Issue 5, pp. 411–431, https://doi.org/10.1002/jid.3411.

Bernanke, B.S. (2007) *The Economic Outlook*, zeznanie przed połączoną Komisją Gospodarczą w Kongresie, available at: https://www.federalreserve.gov/newsevents/testimony/bernanke20070328a.htm.

Blake, A., Sinclair, M.T. (2003) Tourism Crisis Management. Responding to September 11. *Annals of Tourism Research*, Vol. 30, Issue 4, pp. 813–832, https://doi.org/10.1016/S0160-7383(03)00056-2.

Blasco, G. (2021) The coronavirus: black swan and endowment shock, *Revista Galega De Economía*, Vol. 30, Issue 1, pp. 1–14, https://doi.org/10.15304/rge.30.1.7259.

Brown, K., Wang, R.C. (2020) Politics and science: the case of China and coronavirus, *Asian Affairs*, Vol. 51, Issue 2, pp. 247–264, https://doi.org/10.1080/03068374.2020.1752567.

Buheji, M., da Costa Cunha, K., Beka, G., Mavric, B., de Souza, Y.L., da Costa Silva, S.S., Hanafi, M., Yein, T.C. (2020) The extent of COVID-19 pandemic socio-economic impact on global poverty. A global integrative multidisciplinary review, *American Journal of Economics*, Vol. 10, Issue 4, pp. 213–224.

Carmichael, K., Cook, P. (2007) *Paulson Says Subpri Rout Doesn't Affect Economy*, Bloomberg.com, available at: http://www.bloomberg.com/apps/news?pid=20601087&zsid=aBblvvm.ISfo&refer=home.

Chau, M., Lin, C.Y., Lin, T.C. (2020) Wisdom of crowds before the 2007–2009 global financial crisis, *Journal of Financial Stability*, Vol. 48, pp. 100741, ISSN 1572-3089, https://doi.org/10.1016/j.jfs.2020.100741.

Chen, H.K., Liao, Y.C., Lin, C.Y., Yen, J.F. (2018) The effect of the political connections of government bank CEOs on bank performance during the financial crisis, *Journal of Financial Stability*, Vol. 36, pp. 130–143, ISSN 1572-3089, https://doi.org/10.1016/j.jfs.2018.02.010.

Dhara, S. (2020) *Coronavirus Outbreak: Is the COVID-19 Pandemic a Black Swan or A Gray Rhino Event? Part 1*, Firstpost, available at: https://www.firstpost.com/health/coronavirus-outbreak-is-the-covid-19-pandemic-a-black-swan-or-a-gray-rhino-event-part-1-8292051.html.

Dragu, T. (2011) Is there a trade-off between security and liberty? Executive bias, privacy protections, and terrorism prevention, *The American Political Science Review*, Vol. 105, Issue 1, pp. 64–78, http://www.jstor.org/stable/41480827.

Dziedzic, T., Olchowik L. (eds.) (2006) *Rynek lotniczy 2006*. Raport Wiadomości Turystycznych, Institute of Tourism, Warsaw.

Furceri, D., Loungani, P., Ostry, J. (2020) *How Pandemics Leave the Poor Even Further Behind*, available at: https://blogs.imf.org/2020/05/11/how-pandemics-leave-the-poor-even-farther-behind/.

Garcia, I. (2019) Historically illustrating the shift to neoliberalism in the U.S. home mortgage market, *Societies*, Vol. 9, pp. 6, https://doi.org/10.3390/soc9010006.

Georgieva, K. (2020) *The Global Economic Reset – Promoting a More Inclusive Recovery*, available at: https://www.imf.org/external/index.htm.

Hausmann, R. (2020) *Flattening the COVID-19 Curve in Developing Countries*, World Economic Forum, available at: https://www.weforum.org/agenda/2020/03/flattening-the-covid-19-curve-in-developing-countries/.

Heinonen, S., Karjalainen, J., Ruotsalainen, J., Steinmuller, K. (2017) Surprise as the new normal–implications for energy security, *European Journal of Futures Research*, Vol. 5, Issue 1, p. 12, https://doi.org/10.1007/s40309-017-0117-5.

Inequality and the COVID-19 Crisis, available at: http://www.igmchicago.org/surveys/inequality-and-the-covid-19-crisis/.

Innayatullah, S., Black, P. (2020) Neither a Black Swan nor a zombie apocalypse: the futures of a world with the COVID-19 coronavirus, *Journal of Future Studies*, Vol. 2., Available online: https://jfsdigital.org/2020/03/18/neither-a-black-swan-nor-a-zombie-apocalypse-the-futures-of-a-world-with-the-covid-19-coronavirus/.

International Monetary Fund (2020) *Global Financial Stability Report: Markets in the Time of COVID-19*, available at: https://www.imf.org/en/Publications/GFSR/Issues/2020/04/14/global-financial-stability-report-april-2020.

Jaderan, F., Yazdani, H.R. (2020) Identifying the components of macro-social capital to deal with outcomes of the corona virus, *Iranian Journal of Management Sciences*, Vol. 15, Issue 59, pp. 63–94.

Keynes, J.M. (1936) *The General Theory Of Employment Interest And Money*. Kessinger Publishing, Whitefish, MT.

Kobrak, C., Wilkins, M. (eds.) (2013) *History and Financial Crisis. Lessons from the 20th Century*. Routledge, London.

Langley, P. (2021) Economy and society in COVID Times, *Economy and Society*, Vol. 50, Issue 2, pp. 149–157, https://doi.org/10.1080/03085147.2021.1900653.

Leung, K., Wu, J.T., Liu, D., Leung, G.M. (2020) First-wave COVID-19 transmissibility and severity in China outside Hubei after control measures, and second-wave scenario planning: a modelling impact assessment, *The Lancet*, Vol. 395, Issue 10233, pp. 1382–1393.

Lin, W.Y., Tsai, I.C. (2019) Black swan events in China's stock markets: intraday price behaviors on days of volatility, *International Review of Economics & Finance*, Vol. 59, pp. 395–411, ISSN 1059-0560, https://doi.org/10.1016/j.iref.2018.10.005.

Luskin, D. (2008) Quit doling out that bad-economy line, *Washington Post*.

Marks, K., Engels, F. (1956) *Manifest komunistyczny*. Książka i Wiedza, Warsaw.

Mazurek, J. *Terroryzm a ekonomia*, available at: http://biznes.onet.pl.

Meegan, A., Corbet, S., Larkin, C. (2018) Financial market spillovers during the quantitative easing programmes of the global financial crisis (2007–2009) and the European debt crisis, *Journal of International Financial Markets, Institutions and Money*, Vol. 56, pp. 128–148, ISSN 1042-4431, https://doi.org/10.1016/j.intfin.2018.02.010.

Moon, M.J. (2020) Fighting COVID-19 with agility, transparency, and participation: wicked policy problems and new governance challenges, *Public Administration Review*, Vol. 80, Issue 4, pp. 651–656, https://doi.org/10.1111/puar.13214.

OECD (2002) OECD Economic Outlook No. 71 (Edition 2002/1), *OECD Economic Outlook: Statistics and Projections* (database), available at: https://doi.org/10.1787/data-00095-en.

Paulson Jr., H.M. (2008) *Washington Post*, 200 Lunch, Washington DC, available at: http://www.ustreas.gov/press/releases/hp981.htm.

Perera, T., Higgins, D., Wong, W.W. (2018) The evaluation of the Australian office market forecast accuracy, *Journal of Property Investment and Finance*, Emerald Group Publishing, School of Property Construction and Project Management, RMIT University, Melbourne, Vol. 36, Issue 3, pp. 259–272.

Piński, A. (2012) *Sekret czarnego łabędzia*, Obserwator Finansowy, (ed.) G. Jeż, Narodowy Bank Polski, ISSN 2956-3259, Warsaw, available at: https://www.

obserwatorfinansowy.pl/tematyka/makroekonomia/trendy-gospodarcze/sekret-czarnego-labedzia/.

Ponkin, I.V. (2019) Black Swan event as manifestation of uncertainties in public administration, *Mediterranean Journal of Social Sciences*, Vol. 10, Issue 2, pp. 9–15, ISSN 2039-2117,https://doi.org/10.2478/mjss-2019-0018.

Ptak-Iglewska, A. (2020) *Pandemia pogłębi nierówności społeczne*, available at: https://www.rp.pl/Gospodarka/200529504-MFW-Pandemia-poglebi-nierownosci-spoleczne.html.

Ramesh, S. (2020) *The Four Stages of Covid-19 Transmission and Why India Maintains It Is Not Yet in Stage 3, The Print*, available at: https://theprint.in/health/the-four-stages-of-covid-19-transmission-why-india-maintains-it-is-not-yet-in-stage-3/395349/.

Rapoport, A., Gerts, A. (2010) The global economic crisis of 2008–2009. Sources and causes, *Problem of Economic Transition*, Vol. 53, Issue 6, pp. 45–62.

Rodzinka, J., Hady, J. (2009) *Konsekwencje katastrof i aktów terroru dla gospodarek i przedsiębiorstw z branży lotniczej*, available at: http://e-finanse.com/archives/?page=wpabstracts&tab=attachments&task=download&type=attachment&id=630.

Rogers, A. (2020) *The Asian Countries that Beat Covid-19 Have to Do It Again*, WIRED, available at: https://www.wired.com/story/the-asian-countries-that-beat-covid-19-have-to-do-it-again.

Roubini, N., Mihm, S. (2011) *Ekonomia kryzysu*. Wolters Kluwer, Warsaw.

Sandler, T., Enders, W. (2008) *Economic consequences of terrorism in developed and developing countries: an overview.* [in:] *Terrorism, Economic Development, and Political Openness*, pp. 17–47, Cambridge University Press, New York, NY.

Selmi, R., Bouoiyour, J., Hammoudeh, S. (2021) *Negative oil: coronavirus, a black swan' event for the industry?.* [in:] Antipova, T. (ed.) *Integrated Science in Digital Age 2020, Lecture No*, Springer, Cham, https://doi.org/10.1007/978-3-030-49264-9_32, pp. 1–9.

Sohrabi, C., Alsafi, Z., O'Neill, N., Khan, M., Kerwan, A., Al-Jabir, A., Iosifidis, C., Agha, R. (2020) World Health Organization declares global emergency: a review of the 2019 novel coronavirus (COVID-19), *International Journal of Surgery*, Vol. 76, pp. 71–76, https://doi.org/10.1016/j.ijsu.2020.02.034.

Spash, C.L. (2020) The economy as if people mattered: revisiting critiques of economic growth in a time of crisis, *Globalization*, Routledge Francis & Taylor Group, London, https://doi.org/10.1080/14747731.2020.1761612.

Spiegel, S., Schwank, O., Obaidy, M. (2020) *UN/DESA Policy Brief #72: COVID-19 and Sovereign Debt*, available at: https://www.un.org/development/desa/dpad/publication/un-desa-policy-brief-72-covid-19-and-sovereign-debt/.

Stavrova, E., Paskaleva, M., Stoykova, A. (2020) Empirical analysis of black swan effect: evidence of China, *Economic Science, Education and the Real Economy: Development and Interactions in the Digital Age*, Issue 1, pp. 129–146.

Stiglitz, J.E. (2010) *Freefall: America, Free Markets, and the Sinking of the World Economy*. W. W. Norton & Company, New York.

Taleb, N.N. (2007) *The Black Swan: The Impact of the Highly Improbable*. Random House, New York.

Taleb, N.N. (2014) *Czarny Łabędź. O skutkach nieprzewidywalnych zdarzeń*. Kurhaus, Warsaw.

Verma, S., Gustafsson, A. (2020) Investigating the emerging COVID-19 research trends in the field of business and management: a bibliometric analysis approach, *Journal of Business Research*, Elsevier, Vol. 118 July, pp. 253–261.

Wang, Y., Cao, X., Sui, X., Zhao, W. (2019) How do black swan events go global? – Evidence from US reserves effects on TOCOM gold futures prices, *Finance Research Letters*, Vol. 31, ISSN 1544-6123, https://doi.org/10.1016/j.frl.2019.09.001, pp. 47–50.

Wells, C., Farhat, A., Richardson, C., Deering, T.R. (2017) A vine copula–GARCH approach to corporate exposure management, *Journal of Risk, Incisive Media*, Vol. 20, Issue 2, pp. 27–51.

Yagi, K., Yokokawa, N., Shinjiro, H., Dymski, G. (eds.) (2013) *Crises of Global Economy and the Future of Capitalism. An Insight into Marx's Crisis Theory.* Routledge, London.

Zakaria, M., Jun, W., Ahmed H. (2019) Effect of terrorism on economic growth in Pakistan: an empirical analysis, *Economic Research-Ekonomska Istraživanja*, Vol. 32, Issue 1, pp. 1794–1812.

2 Impact of COVID-19 on consumer behavior

Magdalena Maciaszczyk, Damian Kocot and Agnieszka Rzepka

Introduction

Fluctuations are an inevitable part of any economy. These usually occur cyclically, so they can be predicted (at least theoretically). There are, however, situations in which economic activity is interrupted by a completely random event. Such conditions redefine the current reality in unpredictable ways. The COVID-19 pandemic and the lockdown and social distancing mandates have become impulses that have had a significant impact on the economy and trade. The current situation has certainly changed the e-commerce markets all around the globe, as statistics show a significantly increased interest in online shopping.

Consumer behaviors are time-bound, place-bound, and habitual, as consumers develop habits concerning what, when, and where to buy. This is true when talking about consumption, shopping, market information searches, and even post-consumption habits of waste disposal (Sheth, Kellstadt, 2021). Additionally, these behaviors are highly contextual. The main contextual factors are the social situation of a consumer (like a family situation or work environment), the development of new solutions and technological changes that occur in society, and the regulations and rules (especially those that are related to public spaces).

Most of the above are more or less probable; however, there is also a highly unpredictable context that covers natural disasters. The 2020 COVID-19 pandemic has been such an unpredictable factor that has seriously disorganized consumption, production, and supply chains (Schmidt, Benke, Pané-Farré, 2021; Sheth, 2020).

The purpose of this chapter is to analyze the behavior of consumers during the coronavirus pandemic and examine the impact of the pandemic on buying habits as well as shopping. Different aspects of consumer behavior have been analyzed in a theoretical context and then compared with COVID-19 reality.

The main trends in consumer behavior have been presented with references to studies from different countries. The conclusions of the considerations that can be found in this chapter represent a proprietary model of consumer behavior, which is determined by external factors (such as

DOI: 10.4324/9781003368687-2

government-imposed measures) and internal factors (the need to protect one's health).

Consumer behavior in theoretical context

In economic theory, the term "consumer" is closely related to the theory of consumer choice and is understood as an entity that consumes and creates demand (Hands, 2010). The term is usually identified with a buyer who consumes purchased products and benefits from their utility value (Deber et al., 2005; Giese, Cote, 2000). In marketing theory, the consumer is seen as the starting point for marketing activities that are undertaken in the market for goods and services. These activities are aimed at aligning the marketing strategies of manufacturers and retailers with identifying consumer needs (Mothersbaugh et al., 2020; East et al., 2016; Bywalec, Rudnicki, 2002).

The current understanding of consumption remains in line with the postmodern paradigm (Eriksen, 2020) in which it is seen not only as a banal tool for satisfying needs but also as a way of finding exciting experiences and sensations (Jain, Aagja, Bagdare, 2017). It is essential that consumers can choose from a wide range of available goods and services. In addition to the possibility of satisfying needs, such choices enable the individual expression of one's personality, the development of one's passions, and the realization of one's dreams (Petruzzellis et al., 2021; Manthiou, Hickman, Klaus, 2020).

Consumers are therefore increasingly becoming informed market participants. They are becoming aware of the discomfort that is caused by limitations of the scopes of their activities and the fact that they have been reduced exclusively to the purchase aspect. They have therefore expressed their willingness to participate in other marketing activities. Being duly observed by manufacturers, this trend has led to the increased participation of buyers in the preparations of marketing offers (Gillis, Johansen, Vivek, 2018; Sharma, Conduit, Hill, 2017).

Much research throughout the world has proven that the COVID-19 pandemic has significantly changed consumer decisions and purchasing behaviors (Jo, Shin, Kim, 2021; Schleper, 2021; Silva et al., 2021a; Uthman, Aspitman, Karacsonyi, 2021; Ku et al., 2020).

Determinants of consumption during pandemic

The outbreak of the COVID-19 pandemic brought a new reality to consumers. New organizational problems in such areas as the purchasing process have emerged. These problems have been due to both external and internal factors. The external ones have included the measures that have been adopted by governments, while the internal ones have included consumers' awareness of the inevitability of change (even though they know that they have not been in a position to foresee the shape of the change). In addition, consumers have experienced an overwhelming sense of insecurity, which has led to stockpiling (especially during the early days of the pandemic). At the same time, they were afraid to leave their homes for fear of infection.

The increase in the number of COVID-19 cases has led to the introduction of so-called lockdowns. This happened in most countries that saw the spread of the coronavirus (Chaudhary, 2020; Guthrie, Fosso-Wamba, Arnaud, 2021). Companies that were of minor importance to the economy were temporarily closed, gatherings were banned, sporting and cultural events were canceled, travel restrictions were introduced, and the social distancing and isolation of the most vulnerable people occurred (Bonadio, Levchenko, Pandalai-Nayar, 2020; Chronopoulos, Lukas, Wilson, 2020). Some people gave up buying food in supermarkets in favor of small local shops. Home deliveries often replaced buying food and cooking at home (Coibion, Gorodnichenko, Weber, 2020; Esper, 2021). In such cases, however, direct contact with delivery people proved to be problematic.

With the appearance of the first cases, consumers began to take more interest in their health. They began to stockpile hygiene products and food (Sherman, Arthur, Thomas, 2021; Çelik, Köse, 2021; Dinić, Bodroža, 2020). As the number of cases increased, state institutions initiated nationwide emergency measures. During this period, we observed a particularly important change in the purchasing behavior of customers who refrained from traveling or commuting and who often preferred to shop online; thus, they visited stationary shops less frequently (Arora et al., 2020).

Stockpiling has become an omnipresent phenomenon, while panic-buying has led to the mass purchases of long-life products (Hall et al., 2020; Hobbs, 2020). In addition, stockpiling has often accelerated future purchases – especially of products such as toilet paper, medical supplies, or pasta. Between April and June 2020, the market experienced a medium-term decline in the sales of these products, as customers used up their supplies. However, the sales of fresh food, ready meals, chilled products, and beverages increased during this period, as their increased consumption was closely linked to the fact that customers stayed at home more often and stopped eating out (Brancaccio et al., 2021; Silva et al., 2021b; Horta, de Paula Matos, Mendes, 2021).

During the period of the COVID-19 pandemic, the value of the entire product basket has increased as compared to the same period in the previous year according to different sources. The sales of cosmetics and household cleaning products increased slightly more than those of food. The surveys also showed that sales of hand sanitizers increased by more than 2,000% as compared to the previous year depending on the country (Saienko, Palienko, Liulyova, 2020; Shetty et al., 2020; Berardi et al., 2020).

Changes in consumer behavior during COVID-19

The COVID-19 pandemic certainly has had an impact on consumer purchasing behavior. As already predicted, a major change in purchasing habits has been the wholesale purchase of food, hygiene products, and consumer goods. The reasons for this behavior are due to several factors; one of them is certainly the feeling of uncertainty (Altig et al., 2020; Andersen et al., 2020; Baldwin, di Mauro 2020; Bounie et al., 2020). It has encouraged people to follow COVID-19 news developments, as evidenced by increasing interest in news or government websites. This can also mean receiving conflicting news, which increases this uncertainty. The answer to this is the urge to stockpile supplies (Werner, 2020).

There is also the phenomenon of mob mentality, which illustrates how various factors lead individuals to imitate others. The belief that stockpiling is necessary is often reinforced when we see other people shopping and queuing in front of shops or we observe shortages of products in stores. One of the factors behind mob mentality includes a practical approach to shopping. If the number of people who can shop in a store at the same time is limited, the sight of people queuing up can often reinforce the decision to shop more.

The phenomenon of social isolation has led to many aspects of life being transferred to the virtual world. In February 2020, 27.9 million Poles used the Internet; in March, this number rose to 28.6 million, while the number of users fell to 28.2 million in April. Although a large part of society has access to the Internet, it is used for various purposes. According to research by the Central Statistical Office, the Internet was used to do the following in private matters (stat.gov.pl):

- search for information about products and services;
- use social networking sites;
- search for health-related information;
- use e-banking;
- post one's own content on the Internet;
- fill in official forms;
- obtain information from official websites;
- download official forms;
- use travel services;
- download game files;
- purchase goods and services;
- download software.

The above-mentioned reasons can easily be transferred to the coronavirus pandemic. Along with the COVID-19 outbreak, the most common purposes of Internet use included searching for information about goods and services, sending emails, and using social networking sites as entertainment. It is also likely that this trend will continue in the coming months. Users who want to offer information about their services or goods will want to work on the visibility of their sites on search engines. The ideal way to advertise in this case is via email or social media (Aziewicz, 2020). As people adapt to state regulations and restrictions, many of them have chosen and intensified digital activities and habits such as online streaming, online courses, or online fitness; however, they have also replaced some of the in-person aspects of their work and healthcare with solutions such as professional videoconferencing and telemedicine. What is more, videoconferencing and online chats have also replaced in-person meetings with friends (Arora et al., 2020). Regardless of age, more people have shifted to digital inclusion and new online communities called "third spaces" because of the deep anxiety that has been created by the COVID-19 pandemic (Shao, 2023).

An increasing number of consumers opt to shop online. A shift in their decision-making processes is observable. During times of pandemics, consumer behavior also changes as customers begin to explore the possibilities of e-commerce. An increasing interest in e-commerce can also be observed as a consequence of the limited offline shopping possibilities (Akhtar et al., 2020). Consumers are very interested in the possibility of having their parcels delivered to their homes; this minimizes the risk of coming into contact with other people, guarantees a comfortable and safe shopping experience, and ensures that products are obtainable quickly.

Secondary data sources from several countries/areas (including England, Germany, France, Canada, the United States, and Latin America) have shown that the main shopping trend during the COVID-19 pandemic has been pure online shopping. The retail-sales data in these countries have shown that retail sales in physical stores exceed 70% of total retail sales and retail e-commerce sales account for less than 30% (Sayyida et al., 2021).

In order to reach customers effectively, owners of online shops should be aware of the new shopping habits and the need to find suitable channels through which they can reach customers. According to Nielsen's predictions, the transfer to the online purchasing of food will probably remain at a much higher level than before the pandemic (Nielsen, 2020). It is highly probable that products and services that involve "high touch" or close proximity to others will be permanently impacted by the pandemic and will shift to online.

An important factor that determines consumer behavior during a pandemic is the inaccessibility or difficulty when accessing conventional offline sales channels. From March to May 2020, shopping centers and department stores limited their activities to the sales of food, personal care products, and medicine. During the next month, they worked in a sanitary regime. From the point of view of crisis management, going shopping has represented an unnecessary risk for consumers; each time, it is associated with the possibility of infection. This situation has forced certain adjustments on the supply side of the market (Kantar, 2020).

According to the International Monetary Fund (2020), the world economy shrank by 4.9% in 2020 due to the COVID-19 pandemic. Compared to 2019, the total retail value decreased by 20.5% (the period of January to February). The value of the online retail sales of physical goods increased by 3% (stat.gov.pl). Supermarkets (e.g., Carrefour) and smaller stores (e.g., Suning) adopted online ordering and pickup in stores (Ciesielski, 2020). As a result of these actions, supermarkets became the most frequently chosen sales channel for buyers during the pandemic (Kantar, 2020). The situation can be observed globally. Wallstreet Online (2020) named this trend and claimed that the COVID-19 pandemic and the fear that was connected to that initiated "a boom in online food retailing" (Alfonso et al., 2021; Gu, 2021; Dannenberg et al., 2020).

Determinants of consumer behavior in model approach

Restrictions on traditional ways of shopping and the need to comply with sanitary regimes have forced new consumer behavior and the need to adapt to current conditions. Introducing social distancing has also contributed to a decline in traditional forms of shopping. External factors (such as government-imposed measures) and internal ones (the shaping of consumer awareness and their conviction of the need for the protection of their own health) have resulted in a new model of consumer behavior; this includes a proactive interest in health, which results in customers purchasing sanitary products and food (often stockpiling them), being prepared for quarantines and functioning in the "new reality" that is characterized by restrictions, and the need to conform to the sanitary regime.

These considerations are presented in a proprietary model (Figure 2.1), which shows that the changes following the COVID-19 pandemic outbreak implied new consumer behavior. The pattern of consumer behavior in the new reality indicates the ability to cope with and adapt to different and changing situations.

It can be said that this proprietary model generates added value. Its contents may already be known to experts who deal with consumer behavior issues. Nevertheless, it may become an interesting proposition for members of management boards who have not dealt with this problem yet; this will allow them to repair the purchasing-management process, improve the functioning of their companies, and become acquainted with the literature on the subject concerning the problem of consumer behavior during a pandemic.

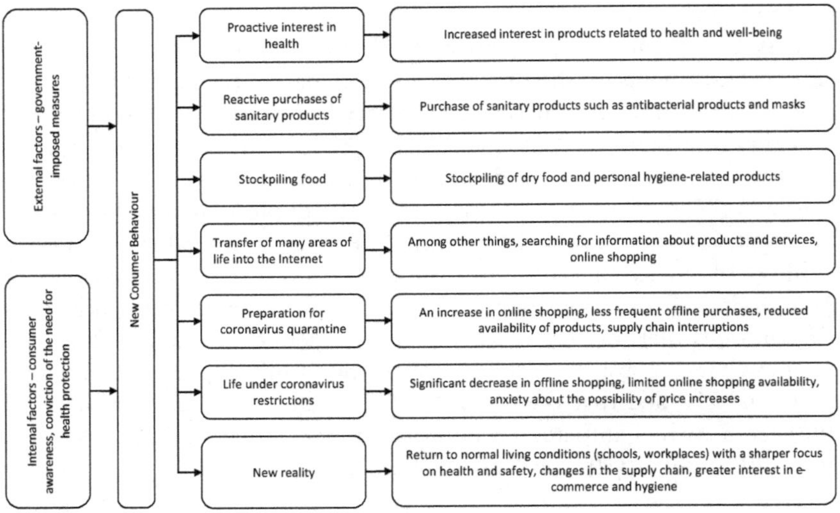

Figure 2.1 New model of consumer behavior during COVID-19.
Source: Authors' elaboration.

Recommendations for practical application by companies

The coronavirus pandemic has caused the collapse of many industries; however, some are experiencing rapid development. Among the latter is e-commerce, which is the result of the transfer of numerous aspects of life to the virtual world. It is therefore important to skillfully manage this area of the economy, the proper functioning of which depends on many factors. It is certainly a good idea to offer services through an online store. The digital market is constantly developing so that communication with customers is more efficient and faster and contributes directly or indirectly to conversion.

In addition, high competitiveness in the market means that the implementation of innovative solutions that attract customers has become necessary. Among other important issues are the development of complementary sales (e.g., sales promotions such as buying two items for a lower total price) and reaching out to new audiences through influencers who are aware of the brand they advertise. The development of online trading platforms such as Marketplace and the possibility of purchasing products from different categories in one place help attract consumers. During a pandemic, the customer wants comfort that allows him/her to order anything he/she might need in one place. Combining promotional offers from different shops on one website should become a reality.

As customers have been concerned about safety during the COVID-19 pandemic, companies should offer solutions that promote hygiene and pay attention to consumer health. Each stationary business should operate under a sanitary regime. Both traditional and online sellers should take great care to treat consumers as business partners. Consumers should be able to judge the level and quality of service. There should therefore be a continuous and uninterrupted transfer of knowledge between businesses and consumers; therefore, today's businesses are obliged to share knowledge with their consumers (Kocot, Wiench, Maciaszczyk, 2022).

Conclusions

The new economic reality has forced consumers to change their purchasing behaviors. Today, we can observe that a new model of consumer behavior has emerged and that it is conditioned by various factors. By far the most important of these is the issue of concern for one's own health and for compliance with the rules that are laid down by national authorities (Fielmua, Guba, Mwingyine, 2021; Untaru, Han, 2021).

The changes are reflected both in the structural approach to consumerism and in the growing importance of e-commerce. During times of social isolation, manufacturers communicate more actively with their customers via social media. This is especially true given that customers are afraid to shop in shopping centers because of health threats and, therefore, visit them less frequently (Moon, Choe, Song, 2021).

Therefore, the transfer of many areas of life into the virtual world has become a significant phenomenon. Customers are more willing to shop online (Saphores, Xu, 2021). At the same time, sellers are striving to meet the emerging needs of customers and comply with legal requirements. This way, they create innovative solutions for the sale and delivery of products. This trend is expected to continue in the foreseeable future (Maciaszczyk, 2016).

References

Akhtar, N., Nadeem Akhtar, M., Usman, M., Ali, M., and Iqbal Siddiqi, U. (2020) COVID-19 restrictions and consumers' psychological reactance toward offline shopping freedom restoration. *The Service Industries Journal*, *40*(13–14), 891–913.

Alfonso, V., Boar, C., Frost, J., Gambacorta, L., and Liu, J. (2021) E-commerce in the pandemic and beyond. *BIS Bulletin*, *36*, 1–6.

Altig, D. E., Barrero, J. M., Bloom, N., Davis, S. J., Meyer, B., Mihaylov, E., and Parker, N. B. (2020) American firms foresee a huge negative impact of the coronavirus, available at: https://www.frbatlanta.org/blogs/macroblog/2020/03/23/american-firms-foresee-a-huge-negative-impact-of-the-coronavirus.

Andersen, A. L., Hansen, E. T., Johannesen, N., and Sheridan, A. (2020) Pandemic, shutdown and consumer spending: Lessons from Scandinavian policy responses to COVID-19, available at: 2005.04630.pdf (arxiv.org).

Arora, N., Charm, T., Grimmelt, A., Ortega, M., Robinson, K., Sexauer, C., and Yamakawa, N. (2020) A global view of how consumer behavior is changing amid COVID-19, available at: https://wwwmckinsey.com/~/media/

McKinsey/Business%20Functions/Marketing%20and%20Sales/Our%20 Insights/A%20global%20view%20of% 20how%20consumer%20behavior%20 is%20changing%20amid%20COVID,20.

Aziewicz, A. (2020) Zachowania konsumentów w Chinach w warunkach epidemii COVID-19 (Consumer behavior in China under the COVID-19 outbreak). *Gdańskie Studia Azji Wschodniej, 17,* 174–177.

Baldwin R. B., di Mauro W., eds. (2020) *Mitigating the COVID Economic Crisis: Act Fast and Do Whatever It Takes.* London: CEPR Press.

Berardi, A., Perinelli, D. R., Merchant, H. A., Bisharat, L., Basheti, I. A., Bonacucina, G., and Palmieri, G. F. (2020) Hand sanitisers amid CoViD-19: A critical review of alcohol-based products on the market and formulation approaches to respond to increasing demand. *International Journal of Pharmaceutics, 584,* 119431.

Bonadio, B., Huo, Z., Levchenko, A. A., and Pandalai-Nayar, N. (2020) Global supply chains in the pandemic. National Bureau of Economic Research. (No. w27224), available at: vvzreddec pdfauthor=vic (nber.org).

Bounie, D., Camara, Y., and Galbraith, J. W. (2020) Consumers' mobility, expenditure and online– offline Substitution response to COVID-19: Evidence from French transaction data, available at: https://ssrn.com/abstract=3588373.

Brancaccio, M., Mennitti, C., Gentile, A., Correale, L., Buzzachera, C. F., Ferraris, C., Montomoli, C., Frisso, G., Borrelli, P., and Scudiero, O. (2021) Effects of the COVID-19 pandemic on job activity, dietary behaviours and physical activity habits of University Population of Naples, Federico II-Italy. *International Journal of Environmental Research and Public Health, 18*(4), 1502.

Bywalec, C., and Rudnicki L. (2002) *Konsumpcja.* Warszawa: Polskie Wydaw. Ekonomiczne.

Çelik, S., and Köse, G. G. (2021). Mediating effect of intolerance of uncertainty in the relationship between coping styles with stress during pandemic (COVID-19) process and compulsive buying behavior. *Progress in Neuro-Psychopharmacology and Biological Psychiatry, 110,* 110321.

Central Statistical Office, Statystyka związana z COVID-19 (Statistics connected with COVID-19) (2020), available at: https://stat.gov.pl/covid/.

Chaudhary, H. (2020). Analyzing the paradigm shift of consumer behavior towards E-Commerce during pandemic lockdown, available at: http: Analyzing the Paradigm Shift of Consumer Behavior Towards E-Commerce During Pandemic Lockdown by Himgiri Chaudhary: SSRN.

Chronopoulos, D., Lukas, M., and Wilson, J. (2020) Consumer spending responses to the COVID-19 pandemic: An assessment of great britain, available at SSRN: https://ssrn.com/abstract=3586723.

Ciesielski, M. (2020). *Gospodarka Bezkontaktowa – Świat Po Pandemii Się Zmieni | Obserwator Finansowy: Ekonomia, Debata, Polska, Świat,* available at: https://www.obserwatorfinansowy.pl/bez-kategorii/rotator/gospodarka-bezkontaktowa-swiat-po-pandemii-sie-zmieni.

Coibion, O., Gorodnichenko Y., and Weber M. (2020) *The Cost of The Covid-19 Crisis: Lockdowns, Macroeconomic Expectations, And Consumer Spending.* (No. w27141). New York: National Bureau of Economic Research.

Dannenberg, P., Fuchs, M., Riedler, T., and Wiedemann, C. (2020) Digital transition by COVID-19 pandemic? The German food online retail. *Tijdschrift voor economische en sociale geografie, 111*(3), 543–560.

Deber, R. B., Kraetschmer, N., Urowitz, S., and Sharpe, N. (2005) Patient, consumer, client, or customer: What do people want to be called?. *Health Expectations, 8*(4), 345–351.

Dinić, B., and Bodroža, B. (2020) "My precious... toilet paper": Stockpiling during the COVID-19 pandemic is related to selfishness, but not to fear. *Primenjena psihologija, 13*(4), 489–504.

East, R., Singh, J., Wright, M., and Vanhuele, M. (2016). *Consumer Behaviour: Applications in Marketing.* New York: Sage.

Eriksen, T. H. (2020) *Globalization: The Key Concepts.* London: Routledge.

Esper, T. L. (2021) Supply chain management amid the coronavirus pandemic. *Journal of Public Policy & Marketing, 40*(1), 101–102.

Fielmua, N., Guba, B. Y., and Mwingyine, D. T. (2021) Hand hygiene and safety behaviours at shopping centres in COVID-19: An observation in Wa township in Ghana. *Journal of Water, Sanitation and Hygiene for Development, 11*(3), 442–452.

Giese, J. L., and Cote, J. A. (2000) Defining consumer satisfaction. *Academy of Marketing Science Review, 1*(1), 1–22.

Gillis, W. T., Johansen, D., and Vivek, S. D. (2018) How customer engagement and customer participation translate across high-involvement purchases (like higher education), available at: https://digitalcommons.georgiasouthern.edu/amtp-proceedings_2018

Gu, S., Ślusarczyk, B., Hajizada, S., Kovalyova, I., and Sakhbieva, A. (2021) Impact of the COVID-19 pandemic on online consumer purchasing behavior. *Journal of Theoretical and Applied Electronic Commerce Research, 16*(6), 2263–2281.

Guthrie, C., Fosso-Wamba, S., and Arnaud, J. B. (2021) Online consumer resilience during a pandemic: An exploratory study of e-commerce behavior before, during and after a COVID-19 lockdown. *Journal of Retailing and Consumer Services, 61*, 102570.

Hall, M. C., Prayag, G., Fieger, P., and Dyason, D. (2020) Beyond panic buying: Consumption displacement and COVID-19. *Journal of Service Management, 32*(1), 113–128.

Hands, D. W. (2010) Economics, psychology and the history of consumer choice theory. *Cambridge Journal of Economics, 34*(4), 633–648.

Hobbs, J. (2020) Food supply chains during the COVID-19 pandemic. *Canadian Journal of Agricultural Economics/Revue canadienne d'agroeconomie, 68*(2), 1–6.

Horta, P. M., de Paula Matos, J., and Mendes, L. L. (2021) Digital food environment during the coronavirus disease 2019 (COVID-19) pandemic in Brazil: An analysis of food advertising in an online food delivery platform. *British Journal of Nutrition, 126*(5), 767–772.

International Monetary Fund (2020) World economic outlook report, available at: https://www.imf.org/en/Publications/WEO.

Jain, R., Aagja, J., and Bagdare, S. (2017) Customer experience–a review and research agenda. *Journal of Service Theory and Practice, 27*(3), 642–662.

Jo, H., Shin, E., and Kim, H. (2021) Changes in consumer behaviour in the post-COVID-19 era in Seoul, South Korea. *Sustainability, 13*(1), 136.

Kantar, (2020) Assessing the impact: a cross industry view on the impact of COVID in China, available at: Assessing the impact: A cross industry view on the impact of COVID in China – Understand people inspire growth – consulting (readkong.com).

Kocot, D., Wiench, P., and Maciaszczyk, M. (2022) *Inter-organization relationships on virtual level in terms of employee agility as determinant of Industry 4.0 era.* In: Rzepka, A., Olesiński, Z, Jędrych, E. (eds.) *Self-Management, Entrepreneurial Culture, and Economy 4.0. A Contemporary Approach to Organizational Theory Development.* London: Routlege, available at: https://www.routledge.com/Self-Management-Entrepreneurial-Culture-and-Economy-40-A-Contemporary/Rzepka-Olesinski-Jedrych/p/book/9781032081205

Ku, S., Cavusgil, S. T., Ozkan, K. S., Pinho, C. R. D. A., Pinho, M. L. C. D. A., Poliakova, E., … and Sharma, S. (2020) The great lockdown recession and international business. *Rutgers Business Review, 5*(1), 113–135.

Maciaszczyk, M. (2016) Konsument niepełnosprawny w dobie digitalizacji. Nasilenie postaw prosumenckich (Disabled consumers in the era of digitization. Increasing prosumer attitudes). *Nierówności społeczne a wzrost gospodarczy, 45*, 487–496.

Manthiou, A., Hickman, E., and Klaus, P. (2020) Beyond good and bad: Challenging the suggested role of emotions in customer experience (CX) research. *Journal of Retailing and Consumer Services, 57*, 102218.

Moon, J., Choe, Y., and Song, H. (2021) Determinants of consumers' online/offline shopping behaviours during the COVID-19 pandemic. *International Journal of Environmental Research and Public Health, 18*(4), 1593.

Mothersbaugh, D. L., Hawkins, D. I., Kleiser, S. B., Mothersbaugh, L. L., and Watson, C. F. (2020) *Consumer Behavior: Building Marketing Strategy.* New York: McGraw-Hill Education.

Nielsen. (2020). Key consumer behavior thresholds identified as the coronavirus outbreak evolves, available at: https://www.nielsen.com/us/en/insights/article/2020/key-consumer-behavior-thresholds-identified-as-the-coronavirus-outbreak-evolves/?utm_source=sfmc&utm_medium=email&utm_campaign=newswire&utm_content=3-18-2020

Petruzzellis, L., Colladon, A. F., Visentin, M., and Chebat, J. C. (2021) Tell me a story about yourself: The words of shopping experience and self-satisfaction. *Journal of Retailing and Consumer Services, 63*, 102703.

Saienko, M., Palienko, M., and Liulyova, L. (2020) Online sales: Impact of Covid-19. *Innovation, Social and Economic Chalenges*, 67–68.

Saphores, J. D., and Xu, L. (2021) E-shopping changes and the state of E-grocery shopping in the US-Evidence from national travel and time use surveys. *Research in Transportation Economics, 87*, 100864.

Sayyida, S., Hartini, S., Gunawan, S., and Husin, S. N. (2021) The impact of the covid-19 pandemic on retail consumer behavior. *Aptisi Transactions on Management (ATM), 5*(1), 79–88.

Schleper, M. C., Gold, S., Trautrims, A., and Baldock, D. (2021) Pandemic-induced knowledge gaps in operations and supply chain management: COVID-19's impacts on retailing. *International Journal of Operations & Production Management, 41*(3), 193–205.

Schmidt, S., Benke, C., and Pané-Farré, C. A. (2021) Purchasing under threat: Changes in shopping patterns during the COVID-19 pandemic. *PLoS One, 16*(6), e0253231, available at: Purchasing under threat: Changes in shopping patterns during the COVID-19 pandemic (plos.org).

Shao, Q. (2023). Pathway through which COVID-19 exacerbates energy poverty and proposed relief measures. *Energy for Sustainable Development: The Journal of the International Energy Initiative, 74*, 1–5.

Sharma, S., Conduit, J., and Hill, S. R. (2017). Hedonic and eudaimonic well-being outcomes from co-creation roles: A study of vulnerable customers. *Journal of Services Marketing, 31*(4/5), 397–411.

Sherman, C. E., Arthur, D., and Thomas, J. (2021) Panic buying or preparedness? The effect of information, anxiety and resilience on stockpiling by Muslim consumers during the COVID-19 pandemic. *Journal of Islamic Marketing, 12*(3), 479–497.

Sheth, J. (2020) Impact of Covid-19 on consumer behavior: Will the old habits return or die?. *Journal of business research, 117*, 280–283.

Sheth, J., and Kellstadt, C. H. (2021) Next frontiers of research in data driven marketing: Will techniques keep up with data tsunami?. *Journal of Business Research, 125*, 780–784.

Shetty, G., Nougarahiya, S., Mandloi, D., and Sarsodia, T. (2020) COVID-19 and global commerce: An analysis of FMCG, and retail industries of tomorrow. *International Journal of Current Research and Review, 12*(17), 23–31.

Silva, A. L. B. d, Limongi, R., Gomes, A. C., and Pimenta, D. (2021a) Chocolates and 'Legrias': Dilemma of the best sales channel. *Revista de Administração Contemporânea, 25*, e200235.

Silva, M. N., Gregório, M. J., Santos, R., Marques, A., Rodrigues, B., Godinho, C., Silva, C. S., Mendes, R., Graça, P., Arriaga, M., Freitas, G. (2021b). Towards an in-depth understanding of physical activity and eating behaviours during COVID-19 social confinement: A combined approach from a Portuguese national survey. *Nutrients, 13*(8), 2685.

Untaru, E. N., and Han, H. (2021) Protective measures against COVID-19 and the business strategies of the retail enterprises: Differences in gender, age, education, and income among shoppers. *Journal of Retailing and Consumer Services, 60*, 102446.

Uthman, D., Aspitman, A., and Karacsonyi, B. (2021) Changes in online shopping activities of generation Z students-A qualitative study on online purchase intent and impulsivity during Covid-19, available at: https://www.diva-portal.org/smash/get/diva2:1559844/FULLTEXT01.pdf

Wallstreet Online (2020), Corona-Angst Sorgt für Boom im Online-Lebensmittelhandel, available at: https://www.wallstreet-online.de/nachricht/12336847-virus-corona-angst-sorgt-boom-online-lebensmittelhandel

Werner, A. (2020) Konsument w czasach pandemii (Consumer in the times of pandemic). *Marketing i Sprzedaż*, (5), 1–3,available at: https://www.ican.pl/b/konsument-w-czasach-pandemii/Pi8VEmWEm

3 Effectiveness of fiscal stimuli during COVID-19

Comparative analysis of the USA, Germany, Greece, and Poland

Maciej Woźniak and Simeon Karafolas

Introduction

As crises are a permanent feature of the free market economy, many regulations and institutions have been developed in order to solve such problems. However, it was hard to be prepared for the crisis that was caused by the COVID-19 pandemic that started at the beginning of 2020. Therefore, it is labeled as a *Black Swan* event (Nicola, 2020). It has resulted in huge decreases in both aggregate demand and short-run aggregate supply. The former is connected with lower spending for intermediate products, consumer goods, and social consumption (such as restaurant visits, tourism, or trade fairs) (Bofinger et al., 2020). This is particularly dangerous, as the pandemic hit most of the countries in the world. Therefore, it is difficult for companies to offset lower demand in the domestic market by sending their products abroad. Furthermore, they must struggle with the short-run aggregate supply. This is connected with the fact that many firms rely on a just-in-time approach and have low inventories; therefore, production losses have spread rapidly worldwide because of a lack of inputs. In addition, many employees have been absent from work due to illness or quarantine. Moreover, there have been disruptions in transport infrastructure networks (Bofinger et al., 2020). In connection to this, it is likened to the economic scene of WWII (Nicola, 2020). As a response, many governments have implemented fiscal stimuli with enormously high values of funds. There are some studies about the measures that should be taken in response to the negative effects of this crisis (Gopinath, 2020; Gali, 2020; Gita, 2020; Shang-Jin, 2020; Huang et al., 2020; Bulin & Tenie, 2020; Djankov & Panizza, 2020; Odendahl & Springferd, 2020). It is difficult to assess whether these policies work. Although a final (or even mid-term) evaluation is still to come, there have already been preliminary results; however, there is a shortage of evaluation research about the effectiveness.

In connection with this, the authors decided to set the following aim for this chapter: an evaluation of the fiscal stimuli that were implemented in the

DOI: 10.4324/9781003368687-3

United States, Germany, Greece, and Poland during the COVID-19 pandemic. Therefore, the desk-research method was applied in unison with a comparative analysis. The findings could be important for both academics and practitioners who are responsible for implementing economic policy. This chapter extends the literature in the area of evaluation. Moreover, it contributes to the fiscal policy theory – particularly during an economic crisis.

The chapter is organized as follows. First, the theoretical approach is delivered, and the literature is reviewed. Then, the analysis of the data is discussed. The conclusions are drawn at the end of the chapter.

Theoretical background and literature review

The crisis that is connected with the COVID-19 pandemic has caused negative demand and supply shocks in the economy. According to macroeconomic theory, this results in a lower aggregate output in the short run and higher unemployment. Moreover, the negative demand shock brings a danger of deflation. There is a move down along the short-run Philips curve that explains the relationship between the rate of inflation and unemployment. On the contrary, the negative supply shock could cause higher inflation. Nevertheless, the economy is self-fulfilling in the long run and tends to achieve a macroeconomic equilibrium. There is a general agreement that governments should not wait to act. Otherwise, everybody will be dead then (as Keynes [1923] argued). Therefore, many economists advocate using fiscal or monetary policy to offset the demand shock. However, most of them argue that the first of these policies should be constrained to automatic stabilizers. A discretionary fiscal policy could only be implemented during a deep recession. Even then, one must take into consideration that there are many disadvantages of fiscal stimulus: crowding out, Ricardian equivalence, and time lags. Higher budget expenditures could crowd out private spending and investments. There is a general consensus that this may occur only when the economy is at full employment. The Ricardian equivalence suggests that consumers could decrease their spending in order to offset the expected growth of taxes in the future. As Krugman and Wells (2015) stated, there is no evidence of such behavior. The reason is that governments can borrow money at lower rates than private borrowers can. Moreover, any reductions in tax rates will increase output and income (Begg et al., 2014). The third disadvantage regards time lags in the formulation and implementation of the fiscal stimulus that could make the economy less stable. According to the OECD report (2020), however, the procedures were shortening significantly in many countries during the recession that was caused by the coronavirus, and the policy responses have been rapid. One must keep in mind, however, that it is much more difficult to propose and implement the appropriate fiscal stimulus that could mitigate the negative effects of a supply shock.

Nevertheless, the expansionary fiscal policy is inevitably connected with the growth of budget expenditures. This is particularly dangerous during a recession when there are lower revenues from taxes. This results in a deficit that increases the public debt and could lower long-run growth. In the worst-case scenario, there is also the risk of the insolvency of the government. The attempts to alleviate the negative effects of the last economic crisis significantly increased the public debt of some countries – particularly from the southern part of Europe. This caused serious problems for public finance, as the spread of interest rates rose dramatically. In connection with this, expansionary monetary policy is recommended as the main measure of stabilization (according to the Great Moderation consensus) (Sparsam & Pahl, 2021). However, if interest rates are already low, the economy falls into a liquidity trap (Krugman, Wells, 2015). Then, extraordinary incentives are required. Therefore, many governments decided to use fiscal stimuli during the previous crisis. The length and impact of this crisis have been the subjects of many studies, as have been the implemented measures (Stiglitz, 2010; Krugman, 2012, Woźniak, 2016; Karafolas & Woźniak, 2020). Therefore, a similar approach in economic policy could be observed in 2020 during the coronavirus crisis. However, the cause of the recession was novel in modern history (Ozili & Arun, 2020).

Therefore, the authors of this study have focused on the tools of discretionary fiscal policy, which could be realized in two ways: transfers from the budget or taxation. This is particularly important as their effect on the economy could have a greater impact because of the multiplier. Moreover, the details of the implemented schemes are of importance (Ginter, 2015; Guerkan, 2021). Transfers from the budget such as grants or subsidies for enterprises should have a greater influence on the economy than taxation. Their impact on companies is still under consideration, as the results of the previous studies have been inconclusive (Woźniak & Lisowski, 2016; Pellegrini & Muccigrosso, 2017; Howell, 2017; Woźniak & Matejun, 2018). Nonetheless, most of the research has covered not only the recession but also other phases of the economic cycle.

There have already been some works that regard the crisis that was caused by the coronavirus. Ozili and Arun (2020) carried out a study on the spillovers of the COVID-19 pandemic into major sectors of the global economy between March and April 2020. Moreover, they evaluated the influence of some policy measures on economic activity (EC) – the PMI index was used as a proxy. They concluded that fiscal stimulus had a positive impact on the level of EC. Furthermore, it appeared to be more effective in alleviating the effect of the crisis that was caused by the COVID-19 pandemic than the monetary policy was. They explained that the monetary policy alone could help calm the financial markets; however, this did not stop the recession. The reasons for this are connected with the peculiar circumstances – governments imposed social distancing, which rendered economic agents unable to engage in their activities. Moreover, as Krugman stated (2020), conventional monetary policy at a zero rate would become impotent during bad times. He mentioned that the USA was in a liquidity trap for 8 of the past 12 years, and Europe is still there. Therefore, the case for fiscal stimulus is overwhelming.

Huang et al. (2020) made a study about the experiences of economic policy measures that were implemented in China in response to the coronavirus crisis. They found that there was one important issue that was connected to the economy: "do whatever it takes." This macroeconomic policy should be fundamental. Hafiz et al. (2020) tried to evaluate the economic and financial policy that was implemented in the USA in order to mitigate the COVID-19 crisis. They found three priorities that were interrelated but potentially conflicting: providing social insurance and a safety net to people in need, managing systemic economic and financial risk, and encouraging critical spatial behaviors. Sarkodie and Owusu (2020) also found a trilemma but of an environmental, health, and economic nexus. They stated that environmental pollution declined and health systems improved, but there was economic deterioration throughout the coronavirus crisis.

As Layanza and Pennings (2020) suggested, the short-term aim of economic policy should be to avoid mass layoffs and bankruptcies rather than stimulating the economy. Their reason was that the latter is ineffective during supply-restricting enterprises. Therefore, Odendahl and Springferd (2020) argued that it was important to manage any future monetary and fiscal stimulus that should only be implemented in the medium run. Nevertheless, international coordination is essential since the COVID-19 pandemic is a global crisis (Layanza and Pennings 2020). Moreover, Bofinger et al. (2020) suggested the following principles for fiscal stimulus: timely, targeted, and temporary.

Therefore, several suggestions were made regarding where policies were needed (Gopinath, 2020; Gali, 2020; Shang-Jin, 2020; Huang et al., 2020; Bulin & Tenie, 2020):

- ensure funding for sick employees to stay at home and not be afraid of losing their jobs;
- provide liquidity to banks and other financial institutions – particularly to those lending money to SMEs;
- offer funds and suspensions of tax and interest payments to affected firms in order to help them meet their payrolls and cover any unavoidable expenses.

Some economists have suggested that SMEs may be less prepared for sharp disruptions (Gopinath, 2020; Shang-Jin, 2020) and cannot withstand liquidity or solvency risk (OECD, 2020). Therefore, there should be special schemes that are intended only for these companies.

Djankov and Panizza (2020) explained that deep recessions are examples of when large deficits should be run. However, Gali (2020) mentioned that even the massive purchase of issued debts by central banks through quantitative easing vehicles would not prevent the increase in the debt ratios of governments. This could result in putting public finances on an unsustainable path. Therefore, he suggested unrepayable funding by central banks – the purchase of government debt, followed by writing it off. Gali added, however, that the solution should be implemented only in emergency situations (such as the COVID-19 crisis) when other tools are ineffective.

As there has been a quite short time span since the outbreak of the COVID-19 pandemic, there have been only a few studies about any implemented fiscal stimuli. These studies, however, have focused on policy measures and giving suggestions regarding which of them should be used. The research of Ozlili and Arun regarded the global economy as a whole and being based on aggregate indicators. There is a need to make a study on the use of more macroeconomic gauges that should go into more detail. Therefore, the authors of this chapter decided to choose three countries that were the biggest economies in the world (the USA), the European Union (Germany), the Balkans (Greece), and Eastern Europe (Poland). The US federal government decided to stabilize household consumption by sending checks to its citizens. However, the Polish and German governments preferred to protect jobs and future tax bases by subsiding enterprises (Li & Maskin, 2021). Therefore, the following research questions were set:

Q1: What were the differences in the economic situations of the chosen countries before and throughout the crisis that was caused by the COVID-19 pandemic?

Q2: What kinds of fiscal stimuli were implemented in the chosen countries and were they effective?

Methodology and collecting data

The authors decided to conduct desk research and comparative analysis. The first of these methods included collecting data from existing resources; therefore, it is also called secondary research. The collected data are summarized and collated to increase the effectiveness of the study; it includes materials that are published in reports and similar documents. The authors used the official databases of the chosen countries' statistical offices. In the cases of Poland and Germany, this was Eurostat, and for Greece – the Hellenic Statistical Authority. In the case of the United States, we tapped two sources: the US Bureau of Labor Statistics and the

US Bureau of Economic Statistics. As this chapter was prepared at the beginning of July 2020, the data for the previous year were collected; this concerned the following indicators for each country:

a The growth rate of the gross domestic product (GDP) in constant prices. The data were seasonally adjusted and based on chain-linked volumes.
b The rate of employment. This was calculated as the number of people that were unemployed as a percentage of the labor force. However, there were small differences in the definitions between the European Union (EU) and the USA. In the former case, unemployed people aged 15 to 74 who are without work and are available to start work within the next two weeks. Moreover, they have actively sought employment at some time during the previous four weeks. In the USA, people are classified as unemployed if they are over 16 years old, do not have a job, have actively looked for work in the prior four weeks, and are currently available for work.
c The rate of inflation. As there are at least three different gauges, the authors chose the indicator for customer prices. Eurostat calculates the Harmonized Indices of Consumer Prices (HICP), which measure changes over time in the prices of consumer goods and services that are acquired by households. The US Bureau of Economic Statistics calculates the Personal Consumption Expenditures Price Index (PCE) which measures the prices that the people living in the United States (or those buying on their behalf) pay for goods and services.

In the next phase, a comparative analysis of the collected data was conducted. Moreover, the correlation coefficient for the relationship between the rate of inflation and the unemployment level was calculated. According to the theory, this relationship should be linear; therefore, the Pearson coefficient was chosen. The macroeconomic indicators were compared with the fiscal stimuli that were implemented during the COVID-19 pandemic. The data for the stimuli were gathered from the documents and websites of the government institutions; they included the following areas:

- transfers from budget to enterprises: grants, subsidies, loans, guarantees, etc.;
- fiscal incentives: tax breaks, national insurance allowances, etc.

Effectiveness is the ability to be successful and produce intended results. In connection with the aim of the chapter, the authors defined it as the degree to which any implemented fiscal stimulus alleviated the negative effects of the shocks in the economy – drop in the GDP, rise in unemployment, and deflation – that were caused by the COVID-19 pandemic.

This is usually intended for small- and medium-sized enterprises (SMEs); however, there were some differences in the definitions of these entities between the EU and the USA. In the former, SMEs are enterprises that meet the definition of staff headcount (no more than 250) and either turnover (no more than €50 million) or balance sheet (no more than €43 million). In the latter, the Small Business Administration (SBA) sets criteria based on the industry, ownership structure, revenue, and the number of employees (this may be as high as 1,500 employees, although the cap is usually 500). However, both the USA and the EU generally use the same threshold of fewer than ten employees for small offices. In the USA, small- and medium-sized manufacturers are referred to as SMMs. The US Department of Energy classifies them as having gross annual sales below $100 million, fewer than 500 employees at a plant site, and annual energy bills between $100,000 and $2.5 million.

US case

According to the US Bureau of Economic Statistics, the growth of the GDP in the United States in the second, third, and fourth quarters of 2019 was rather similar (about +2.0%). The rate of inflation during the second half of 2019 was also quite stable, as shown in Figure 3.1. The same was for the unemployment rate, which only changed a little. However, there was a very dramatic decrease in the GDP in the first quarter of 2020 (−5.0%). The forecast for the next quarter was even worse, as it was projected to be worse than −16%. There was only a small increase in inflation at the beginning of 2020; then, it started to decrease (from +1.8 to 0%). However, the rate of unemployment rose slowly in March

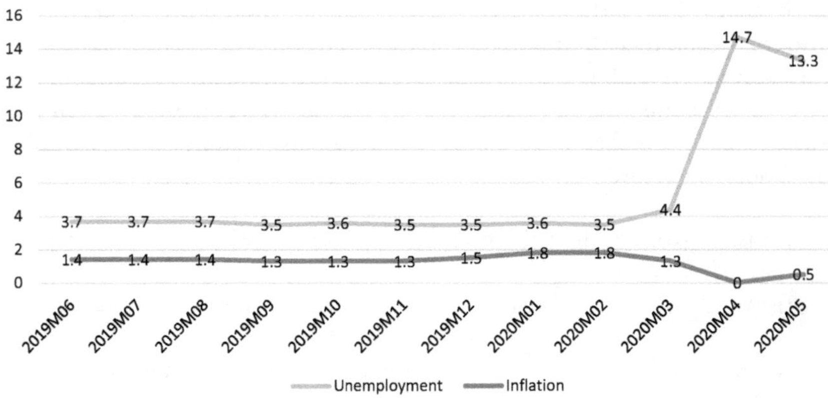

Figure 3.1 The rate of unemployment and inflation in the USA: 06.2019–05.2020.
Source: own elaboration based on US Bureau of Labour Statistics and US Bureau of Economic Statistics data.

but increased significantly (over +14%) in April. The relationship that was connected with the short-run Philips curve was very strong during the analyzed period. The Pearson correlation coefficient was −0.8503 (p value < 0.05).

The value of the fiscal stimulus for enterprises in the USA during the COVID-19 pandemic was as much as $500 billion for all sectors that were in danger because of the pandemic. Moreover, $350 billion in loans was intended as support for SMEs. An additional $250 billion was allocated to increase the benefits for unemployment. There were also schemes that were only for small enterprises; they were allowed to obtain loans under the Paycheck Protection Program. The $349 billion scheme was funded under the SBA. A small enterprise could get loans in order to guarantee eight weeks of payroll and other costs to help remain viable and allow its employees to pay their bills. If such a company already had a loan from SBA, the installments could be written off for six months. Moreover, small enterprises could apply for disaster loans from the Small Business Administration; these were the primary assistance for the repair and rebuilding of the private sector's disaster losses.

The outbreak of the COVID-19 pandemic at the beginning of 2020 induced the US government to offer additional loans for enterprises. Some of them were supposed to help companies meet their payrolls. There were also schemes for SMEs and even for small enterprises; this is rather consistent with the propositions from the literature review. It seems that all of these schemes together with the expansive monetary policy of the FED helped alleviate the drop in the inflation rate during the first half of 2020; however, they were not enough to stop the significant rise in unemployment and the decrease in the GDP.

German case

According to Eurostat, the growth rate of the GDP in Germany was already very low in 2019. There was even a little decrease during the second (−0.2%) and last (−0.1%) quarters. The rate of inflation was going down slightly in the second half of 2019, as shown in Figure 3.2. There were even two months of deflation (November 2019 and January 2020). However, the unemployment rate was quite stable; it only started to slowly increase from October 2019 through March 2020. Unfortunately, the GDP went down (−2.2% during the first quarter of 2020), and the forecast for the second quarter suggested that it could even reach −10% (or worse). Although there was the outbreak of the COVID-19 pandemic, the rate of inflation was quite low (and only in May 2020 did it decrease to 0%). The unemployment rate was stable; however, it rose during the second quarter of 2020 (from 3.5 to 3.9%). The relationship that was connected with the short-run Philips curve in Germany was very weak. The Pearson correlation coefficient was only −0.1008 (p value < 0.05).

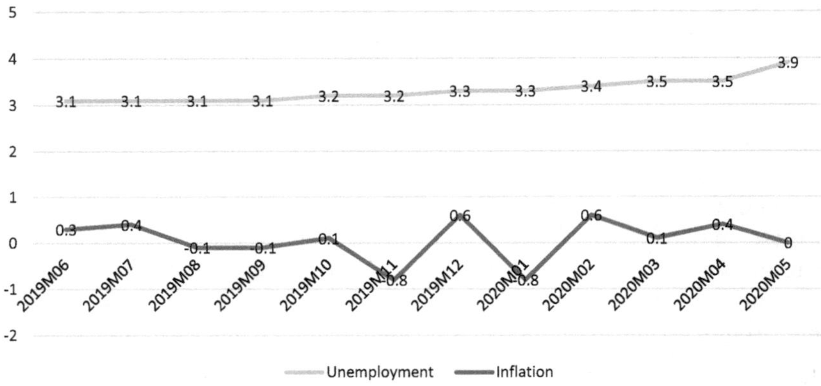

Figure 3.2 The rate of unemployment and inflation in Germany: 06.2019–05.2020.
Source: own elaboration based on Eurostat data.

Since the beginning of the COVID-19 outbreak, an additional €50 billion for small enterprises and self-employed has been allocated. Moreover, about €33.5 billion was intended to cover the decrease in fiscal revenues, as some corporate tax payables were suspended. An additional €7.5 billion was allocated to offset the suspended national insurance payments. Furthermore, €100 billion was intended as loans for enterprises that were facing financial difficulties. The German government also decided to set up a stabilization fund. Under the €400-billion fund, it was reserved for guarantees that could cover even 100% of loans. Each enterprise with fewer than five employees (and all self-employed people) was allowed to obtain up to €9,000 for three months. If a company had a staff of six to ten people, it could receive up to €15,000 (also for three months).

The German government decided to support enterprises during the crisis that was caused by the COVID-19 pandemic with loans, guarantees, grants, and suspended tax payables. There were schemes that were only for small companies as well; this is coherent with the proposals from the literature review. It seems that these measures were enough to alleviate the growth of unemployment and the fall of the inflation rate. This was also connected with the quantitative easing of the European Central Bank. Even though there was a drop in the GDP at the beginning of 2020, it was not very significant. Nevertheless, the forecast for the second quarter was much worse.

Greece case

The Greek economy had to face COVID-19 consequences shortly after a decade of economic recession (Karafolas, 2019; Karafolas & Woźniak, 2020). During the second and third quarters of 2019, substantial growth of the GDP was observed (2.6 and 3.7%, respectively); however, this did not continue into the fourth quarter of 2019. In 2020, the GDP fell sharply: −2.1% during the first quarter, −17.7% during the second, −10.8% during the third, and −7.6% during the last quarter of 2020 (Hellenic Statistical Authority, 2022). The inflation remained at a very low level, and deflation even appeared in several months. The high unemployment rate remained as a consequence of the previous years of the economic recession (Karafolas, 2019); it was 16.5% on average during the period of June 2019 through May 2020 (presenting a slight decrease during the first months of 2020).

The Greek government decided to allocate several billion euros to help the Greek economy. The state's financial help was supported by the EU Recovery Plan; starting in July 2021, Greece could use EU recovery and resilience funds to help its economy recover from the COVID-19 fallout (European Council, 2022). The Greek government through the umbrella of the Partnership Agreement for the Development Framework (2014–2020) financed several sectors of the economy that suffered from the COVID-19 pandemic. The government budgeted an allocation of €1.2 billion for interest subsidies (which reached 100%) on existing loans to small- and medium-sized enterprises that were affected by the COVID-19 pandemic measures; this was followed by a second round of €200 million. Around €2 billion was budgeted as guarantees (up to 80%) of new working capital loans for small- and medium-sized enterprises. Another €2 billion was considered for allocation to the working capital of SMEs that were under the suspension of work (or the restriction of operation) due to the COVID-19 pandemic; 40% of this amount was provided through the Partnership Agreement for the Development Framework, and 60% came from banks that cooperated in the *Entrepreneurship Fund II* program. Important allocations were focused on specific targets and sectors. A specific compensation of €500 million was considered for business support due to the appearance and spread of COVID-19; it focused on small enterprises and the self-employed with offers of €800 grants for a limited time period. Another amount of €680 million was considered for allocation as working capital subsidies to the sectors of services and tourism that were affected by the COVID-19 pandemic. Around €60 million was considered for start-up companies.

During the crisis that was caused by the COVID-19 pandemic, Greek enterprises and the self-employed were offered loans, subsidies, and suspended tax payables. The Greek government used special schemes with the support of EU funds through the umbrella of the Partnership Agreement for the Development Framework. The schemes that were used by the Greek government offered substantial help to small enterprises and the self-employed. Unemployment did not increase during this period; on the contrary, there was a slight decrease at the beginning of 2020. During this period, the phenomenon of increasing deposits appeared; their growth was 3.8% during the first half of 2020, 9.9% during the second half of 2020, and 4% during the first half of 2021 (Bank of Greece, 2022, author's calculations). This phenomenon was due to the fall in consumption and appeared in other countries as well.

Poland case

According to Eurostat, the growth rate of GDP in Poland was quite good during the second (+0.7%) and third (+1.2%) quarters of 2019. However, there was a slowdown (+0.2%) at the end of 2019. The rate of inflation in Poland was increasing during the second part of 2019 in opposition to the unemployment rate (which was going down, as shown in Table 3.1). The country's GDP decreased only a little at the beginning of 2020 (-0.4%). The forecast for the second quarter was, however, worse (a drop of about -4%). However, inflation started to decrease significantly at the beginning of 2020 and achieved 0% in April 2020. Then, it rose sharply in the next month. The unemployment rate remained almost the same. The relationship that was connected with the short-run Philips curve for Poland was quite weak. The Pearson correlation coefficient was -0.271121 (p value < 0.05).

The Polish government decided to allocate 100 billion PLN (around €24 billion) for enterprises: 25 billion PLN for microenterprises, 50 billion PLN for SMEs, and 25 billion PLN for large companies. The amounts of the subsidies depended on the scale of the revenue decrease. A company could obtain from 50 to 90% of subsidies for the salaries of its employees (the maximum was 2,600 PLN – around €620) if it sustained employment. Moreover, microenterprises could apply for a special loan of up to 5,000 PLN. The loan would be canceled if there were no layoffs in the company over the next few months. Furthermore, small enterprises could apply for a 50% decrease in national insurance payments. There were also some changes in corporate tax allowances, which could lower the fiscal payables.

Polish enterprises were offered loans, subsidies, and suspended tax payables during the crisis that was caused by COVID-19. There were special schemes that were only intended for SMEs; this is also coherent with the suggestions from the literature review. It seems that these schemes worked quite well. Inflation decreased only a little, which was connected with the lower interest rates that Poland Central Bank proposed. There was a very small increase in the unemployment rate; moreover, the GDP went down slightly at the beginning of 2020 (although the forecast for the second quarter was worse).

Conclusions

The crisis that was caused by the COVID-19 pandemic hit the global economy in an unpredictable way. Governments tried to alleviate the

Table 3.1 Rate of Unemployment and Inflation in Poland: June 2019 through May 2020

Rate/Time	*2019 M06*	*2019 M07*	*2019 M08*	*2019 M09*	*2019 M10*	*2019 M11*	*2019 M12*	*2020 M01*	*2020 M02*	*2020 M03*	*2020 M04*	*2020 M05*
Unemployment	3.3	3.2	3.1	3.1	3.0	2.9	2.9	3.0	3.0	2.9	2.9	3.0
Inflation	0.2	0.0	-0.1	0.1	0.3	0.1	0.6	0.7	0.6	0.2	0.0	0.8

Source: own elaboration based on Eurostat data

negative effects through appropriate economic policies (even though it was not an easy task). Therefore, the authors of this chapter posed two research questions and then made attempts to answer them.

Q1: What was the difference in the economic situation in the chosen countries before and throughout the crisis that was caused by the COVID-19 pandemic?

The economy in the chosen countries before the coronavirus crisis was in a quite good shape. There was growth in the GDPs of the USA, Greece, and Poland. The unemployment rate was rather low (except for Greece), and inflation was kept under control in all of the analyzed countries. Although the outbreak of the COVID-19 pandemic had a negative impact on all four economies, it seemed to be particularly dangerous for the USA; there was significant growth in the country's unemployment rate. In the three other countries, only a small number of employees lost their jobs. However, there was a sharp decrease in the GDP in Germany (even though it was not as high as it was in the USA and Greece). The gross domestic product of Poland seemed to be hit much less, as the drop was quite moderate. Nevertheless, the inflation rate in all four countries dropped, and deflation was avoided. Moreover, the relationship that was connected with the short-run Philips curve (measured by the Pearson correlation coefficient) was very strong in the USA, rather weak in Poland, and very weak in Germany and Greece.

Q2: What kinds of fiscal stimuli were implemented in the chosen countries, and were they effective?

There were some differences in the fiscal stimuli that were implemented in the analyzed countries. The USA decided to offer loans for enterprises, whereas Poland, Greece, and Germany provided grants, subsidies, guarantees, and suspended tax payables. Nevertheless, the governments of all four countries designed special fiscal stimuli for microenterprises with fewer than ten employees, small companies, or all SMEs. However, one must keep in mind that there were differences in the definitions of SMEs between the USA and the EU. Moreover, some of the schemes were intended to help enterprises meet their payrolls. These policy measures were rather consistent with proposals that were derived from the literature and were effective in Germany and Poland. In the case of the USA, however, the effectiveness seemed to be quite low when taking the dramatic increase in unemployment and drop in the GDP into consideration. This finding was explained by Joseph Stiglitz, who stated that the US policy was badly designed and costly (Stiglitz, 2021).

The answers to the research questions enabled us to realize the goal of this chapter, which was to evaluate the fiscal stimuli for enterprises that were implemented in the chosen countries during the COVID-19 pandemic. Therefore, one can state that the schemes seemed to have been effective in Germany, Greece, and (particularly) Poland. Taking the analyzed data into consideration, however, this did not alleviate the negative effects of the coronavirus crisis in the USA. It is possible that these fiscal stimuli will have a positive impact in the second half of 2020.

The study has some constraints as well. First of all, it has been only half a year since the outbreak of the COVID-19 pandemic, so the results are preliminary. Moreover, the set of analyzed indicators is rather small: GDP, unemployment, and inflation. Therefore, there is a need to make further research, which would cover a longer period of time. This research could then be based on some statistical analysis. The results of such an evaluation would be more reliable and could encompass more indicators than showing mere socio-economic changes.

References

Begg D., Vernasca G., Fischer S., Dornbusch R. (2014) *Economics*. McGraw-Hill, London.

Bofinger P., Dullien S., Felbermayr G., Fuerst C., Huether M., Sudekum J., Di Nauro B. W. (2020) Economic implications of the COVID-19 crisis for Germany and economic policy measures, in: R. Baldwin, B. W. di Mauro, *Mitigating the COVID economic crisis: Act fast and do whatever it takes*, CEPR Press, London: 167–178.

Bulin D., Tenie I. P. (2020) Preliminary assessment of the COVID-19 pandemic impact on the tourism industry. *Global Economic Observer*, *8*(1), 41–46.

Council of the European Union, (2022) *COVID-19: the EU's response to the economic fallout*. https://www.consilium.europa.eu/en/policies/coronavirus/covid-19-economy/.

Djankov, S., & Panizza, U. (2020). *COVID-19 in developing economies*. Centre for Economic Policy Research: 385.

Gali J. (2020) Helicopter money: The time is now, in: R. Baldwin, B. W. di Mauro, *Mitigating the COVID economic crisis: Act fast and do whatever it takes*, CEPR Press, London: 57–62.

Ginter M. (2015) Pomoc publiczna jako źródło finansowania MŚP na przykładzie Wielkopolski. *Acta Universitatis Nicolai Copernici. Zarządzanie*, *42*(2), 151–163.

Gopinath, G. (2020). Limiting the economic fallout of the coronavirus with large targeted policies. *Mitigating the COVID economic crisis: Act fast and do whatever it takes*, vol 1 41–48.

Gita G. (2020) Limiting the economic fallout of the coronavirus with large targeted policies, in: R. Baldwin, B. W. di Mauro, *Mitigating the COVID economic crisis: Act fast and do whatever it takes*, CEPR Press, London: 41–48.

Guerkan C. (2021) The constitution of neoliberal governmentality from early neoclassical economics to public choice theory, in: J. Maesse, S. Puehrinhger, T. Rossier, P. Benz, *Power and influence of economists. Contibutions to the social studies of economics*, Routledge, London: 73–89

Hafiz H., Oei S. Y., Ring D. M., Shnitser N. (2020) Regulating in pandemic: Evaluating economic and financial policy responses to the coronavirus crisis. *Boston College Law School Legal Studies Research Chapter*, (527).
Hellenic Statistical Authority, (2023) Quarterly Gross Domestic Product, seasonally adjusted, current prices, https://www.statistics.gr/en/statistics/-/publication/SEL84/-, (received on January 2023)
Howell A. (2017) Picking 'winners' in China: Do subsidies matter for indigenous innovation and firm productivity? *China Economic Review*, *44*, 154–165.
Huang Y., Lin C., Wang P., Xu Z. (2020). Saving China from the coronavirus and economic meltdown: Experiences and lessons. Available at SSRN 3570696.
Karafolas S. (2019), Crisis consequences on the structure of the Greek banking system. *Financial Studies*, *23*(4), 1–20.
Karafolas S., Woźniak M. (2020) The development of small enterprises during and after economic crisis: Comparative analysis of Greece and Poland, *12th International Conference, Economies of the Balkan and Eastern European Countries EBEEC 2020*, May 29–31, Opatija, Croatia.
Keynes J. M. (1923) *A tract on monetary reform*. Macmillan, London.
Krugman P. (2012) *End this depression now!*. W. W. Norton & Company, New York, NY.
Krugman P. (2020) The case for permanent stimulus, in: R. Baldwin, B. W. di Mauro, *Mitigating the COVID economic crisis: Act fast and do whatever it takes*, CEPR Press, London: 213–219.
Krugman P., Wells R. (2015) *Macroeconomics*. Worth Publishers, New York, NY.
Li D. D., Maskin E. (2021) Government and economics. An emerging field of study. *Journal of Government and Economics*, *1*, 100005.
Nicola M., Alsafi Z., Sohrabi C., Kerwan A., Al-Jabir A., Iosifidis C., … Agha R. (2020) The socio-economic implications of the coronavirus and COVID-19 pandemic: A review. *International Journal of Surgery*, *78*, 185–193.
Odendahl, C., & Springford, J. (2020). 16 Bold policies needed to counter the coronavirus recession1. *Mitigating the COVID Economic Crisis: Act Fast and Do Whatever*, *145*: 145–150.
Ozili P. K., Arun T. (2020). Spillover of COVID-19: Impact on the global economy. Available at SSRN 3562570.
Pellegrini G., Muccigrosso T. (2017) Do subsidized new firms survive longer? Evidence from a counterfactual approach. *Regional Studies*, *51*(10), 1483–1493.
Sarkodie S. A., Owusu P. A. (2021) Global assessment of environment, health and economic impact of the novel coronavirus (COVID-19). *Environment, Development and Sustainability*, *23*, 1–11.
Shang-Jin W. (2020) Ten keys to beating back COVID-19 and the associated economic pandemic, in: R. Baldwin, B. W. di Mauro, *Mitigating the COVID economic crisis: Act fast and do whatever it takes*, CEPR Press, London: 71–76.
Sparsam J., Pahl H. (2021) Macroeconomics and monetary policy as autonomous domains of knowledge and power. Rational expectations, monetarism and the Federal Reserve, in: J. Maesse, S. Puehrinhger, T. Rossier, P. Benz, *Power and influence of economists. Contibutions to the social studies of economics*, Routledge, London.
Stiglitz J. E. (2010) *Interpreting the causes of the Great Recession of 2008. Financial system and macroeconomic resilience: Revisited*. Bank for International Settlements, Basel.

Stiglitz J. E. (2021) The proper role of government in the market economy: The case of the post-COVID recovery. *Journal of Government and Economics, 1*, 100004.

Woźniak M. (2016) Access of enterprises to bank credit in Poland before and after economic crises, in: J. Kaczmarek, K. Żmija, *Expectations and challenges of modern economy and enterprises: Problems – concepts – activities*, Foundation of Cracow University of Economics, Kraków: 117–124.

Woźniak M., Lisowski R. (2016) Relationship between fiscal instruments and investments of industrial SMEs and LEs in Poland. *Managerial Economics, 17*(2), 261–276.

Woźniak M., Matejun M. (2018) Cost-effectiveness analysis of financial support instruments for small and medium-sized enterprises in the European Union. *Acta Universitatis Lodziensis. Folia Oeconomica, 339*(6), 41–56.

Websites

Eurostat, https://ec.europa.eu/eurostat
US Bureau of Labour Statistics, https://www.bls.gov
US Bureau of Economic Statistics, https://www.bea.gov
US Small Business Administration, https://www.sba.gov/
https://www.fintiba.com/corona/
https://www.express.co.uk
https://www.spiegel.de
https://www.pism.pl
https://wgospodarce.pl
https://www.coronavirus.gov/smallbusiness
https://www.bankofgreece.gr/en/statistics/monetary-and-banking-statistics/deposits
https://www.consilium.europa.eu/en/policies/coronavirus/covid-19-economy/
https://www.espa.gr/el/Pages/espa_covid.aspx
https://www.statistics.gr/en/statistics/-/publication/

4 Innovation and digital competencies as important factors of economic development in Industry 4.0 and during COVID-19

Agnieszka Rzepka, Magdalena Czerwinska and Natia Shengelia

Introduction

Industry 4.0 (Roblek, Meško, & Krapež, 2016), an approach that changes the way that companies operate, was initiated in Germany at the Hannover Messe in 2011. The primary goal of Industry 4.0 is to achieve accuracy and precision as well as a higher degree of automation (Thames, & Schaefer, 2016). Very often, Industry 4.0 is associated with the Fourth Industrial Revolution. The concept of the Fourth Industrial Revolution (Hermann, Pentek, & Otto, 2016) means a simultaneous compilation of three independent elements: the real world of production machines, the virtual world, and information technology. This revolution is characterized by the development of so-called superautomation and artificial intelligence. Rapid technical and technological changes such as the development of hyperautomation and, above all, IT are leading to new solutions such as the 5G system or the development of the Internet of Things (IoT) (Moeuf, Pellerin, Lamouri, Tamayo-Giraldo, & Barbaray, 2018) and creating convenient opportunities to improve the functioning of enterprises.

A key aspect of the Fourth Industrial Revolution is the increase in the efficiency, flexibility, and automation of internal business processes, the integration of value chains, and the advancement of innovation in service design using the wide availability of data that has been enabled by various technologies. Therefore, companies seek to understand how Industry 4.0 technologies can be implemented in order to increase their current productivity and provide more competitive offers to new and existing customers (Czerwinska, 2020).

Unlike the previous industrial revolutions (the First Industrial Revolution of coal and steel from the early 18th century, the Second at the turn of the 19th and 20th centuries [the revolution of chemistry, the automotive industry, and electricity], and the Third of the 1960s [the revolution

DOI: 10.4324/9781003368687-4

of automation]) (Rzepka, & Olesinski, 2020), the current transformation is progressing at a much faster pace. This is due to the fact that each new technology gives rise to a newer, even more efficient one, and the current one is a concept that is closely related to the development of the IoT as well as the digitization, progressive robotization, and automation of production processes (Rodak, & Gracel, 2017). The changes are clearly recognized by all types of enterprises (Smit, Kreutzer, Moeller, & Carlberg, 2016), which pay attention to the main key to success – digital competence and innovation in the era of Industry 4.0. The Fourth Industrial Revolution, which connects the physical world with the digital one, opens up great opportunities for companies (King, 2018). Industry 4.0 should therefore be considered as part of the larger megatrend of digital transformation, covering many industries – in particular, the financial and logistics sectors (Miskiewicz, 2019).

The adoption of new technologies to enhance, change, or even disrupt business models from an operations and strategic perspective to gain a competitive advantage is well established in the literature (Makkonen, Johnston, & Javalgi, 2016; Kim, So, & Je, 2019; Saebi, Foss, & Linder, 2019).

The introduction of new digital solutions and new production methods is much faster now. This is possible thanks to the use of technologies and innovations that have become the driving force of this revolution.

Digital competence

The crisis that was caused by the COVID-19 pandemic accelerated digital transformation around the world and opened up new opportunities offered by Industry 4.0 for economic development and the improvement of life. The coronavirus pandemic has accelerated the pace of digitization and automation.

The new socio-economic situation requires a new employee profile – a 4.0 engineer with specific competencies and skills that work well in the new reality.

One of the categories of these skills (which has gained a lot of importance under the current pandemic conditions) is digital skills.

Digital competence involves the confident, critical, responsible use of, and engagement with digital technologies for learning, working, and participating in society. It includes information and data literacy, communication and collaboration, media literacy, digital content creation (including programming), safety (including digital well-being and competencies related to cybersecurity), questions related to intellectual property, problem-solving, and critical thinking (The Council Recommendations, 2018).

They apply to all participants of the digital world (i.e., consumers, average Internet users) but also to Information and Communication

Technology (ICT) specialists and employees who support modern technologies and are required to have special digital skills that exceed the basic level.

Digital competencies include technical competencies, the ability to significantly use digital technologies at work, study, and everyday life, the ability to critically evaluate digital technologies, and the motivation to participate and engage in a digital culture (Ilomäki, Paavola, Lakkala, & Kantosalo, 2016).

It should be remembered that digital competencies do not equal the actual/frequent use of digital technologies (Janssen, Stoyanov, Ferrari, Punie, Pannekeet, & Sloep, 2013).

Due to the pandemic situation, the issues of digital competencies have once again become of interest to European Union (EU) bodies. Among other issues, this problem has been undertaken by the European Commission in a document dated July 1, 2020 (Proposal for a Council Recommendation, 2020). According to the Commission, more than 90% of jobs already require digital skills.

In an earlier EU document (The Council Recommendation of May 22, 2018, on key competencies for lifelong learning [The Council Recommendation, 2018]), there was a call on member states to support the development of basic digital skills and increase the level of digital competence in their entire populations. In contrast, the Commission's communication on the Digital Education Action Plan (Communication from the Commission, 2018) set out 11 actions to help member states make better use of digital technology in education and develop digital competencies and skills. For the implementation of these activities, a three-year perspective (2018–2020) was adopted. In addition, the Council's recommendation of December 19, 2016, on Upskilling Pathways: New Opportunities for Adults (The Council Recommendation, 2016) provided provisions for offering people with low levels of skill, knowledge, and competence the opportunity to acquire minimum skill levels.

Over the past four years, the level of digital skills in the EU has steadily increased, reaching 58% of people with at least basic digital skills, 33% with above basic digital skills, and 61% with at least basic programming skills (data from 2019) (Eurostat, 2020). Socio-demographic aspects have had a great impact on skill indicators. For example, 82% of young people (16–24 years), 85% of people with high formal educations, 68% of employed or self-employed people, and 87% of students have at least basic digital skills. However, only 35% of people aged 55–74 years and 30% of pensioners and inactive people have basic skills (European Commission, 2020).

The European Commission quickly responded to the new challenges that arose from the onset of the COVID-19 pandemic by introducing a number of measures in the areas of digitization.

Among others, The Digital Skills and Jobs Coalition brings together member states, companies, social partners, nonprofit organizations, and education providers who take action to tackle the lack of digital skills in Europe. These activities can increase the competitiveness of EU member states. The European Commission's Digital Decade Communication aims to achieve a target of 20 million ICT professionals in the EU by 2030.

The National Coalitions for Digital Skills and Jobs are partnerships between entities whose business is to improve digital skills at the national, regional, or local levels in EU member states. In Poland, such an entity is the Broad Alliance for Digital Skills. In other member states, there are also similar entities (e.g., the French National Coalition, DigiKoalice in the Czech Republic, and INCoDe.2030 in Portugal). Apart from the European Union, there are also activities that are aimed at developing digital skills. An example is ASEE – the American Society for Engineering Education. ASEE is a nonprofit organization of individuals and institutions that are committed to furthering education in engineering and engineering technology.

The COVID-19 pandemic also made economic entities aware of the need to care for the development of digital competencies (Zamfir & Aldea, 2020; Winarsih, Indriastuti, & Fuad, 2021).

Innovation

An enterprise that strives to achieve market success (Nagji, & Tuff, 2012) should strive to introduce innovations and, thus, be called an innovative organization.

The terms "innovation" and "innovativeness" are often equated (Cho, & Pucik, 2005). In management sciences, innovativeness is considered to be an important attribute of an enterprise, manifesting itself in its ability to innovate. Therefore, innovativeness can be called the ability to create something new or to introduce significant changes (Hilami, Ramayah, Mustapha, & Pawanchik, 2010).

Innovation is one of the factors that affect the achievement of competitive advantage by enterprises. Its importance is growing along with the progressing globalization processes in the social, economic, and environmental dimensions (Rzepka, 2019). In the Polish economy, the level of innovation remains low, scoring the fourth-worst rating in the European Union Member State Ranking – European Innovation Scoreboard 2019 (Hollanders, Es-Sadki, & Merkelbach, 2019). According to the authors of the Smart Industry Poland report (Piatek, 2018), Polish entrepreneurs treat innovation as being too expensive, time-consuming, and risky; this is why they usually do not associate their long-term development strategies with it. As indicated by the Central Statistical Office Report, the share of innovative enterprises in Poland during the period of 2015–2017 was only 18.5% in industry and 10.4% in services; during the period of 2016–2018, these increased to 24% and 20%, respectively (GUS, 2018). In EU countries, on the other hand, the share of innovative companies exceeds 50% on average (European Commission, Eurostat, 2020). The above data show that the Polish economy faces the serious challenge of achieving at least the average level of the other EU countries.

The use of advanced ICT technologies makes it possible to tailor production more precisely to different customer expectations while maintaining low costs, high quality, and efficiency. New business models (including artificial intelligence and incremental manufacturing) are accelerating the transformation processes in the industry and changing current business practices and market structures (Grabowska & Saniuk, 2022). They also require the introduction of new management models.

In Poland, small- and medium-sized enterprises constitute more than 99% of all economic entities (of which 96% of enterprises are micro-enterprises) (Report of Polish Agency for Enterprise Development, 2018); their share in the national GDP exceeds 50% and constitute a workplace for 69% of all employees.

Compared to large businesses in the world (USA, UK), Small Medium Enterprises (SMEs) have been the hardest hit by the COVID-19 pandemic, as sectors like retail, food services, hospitality, entertainment services, and construction activities are overrepresented by SMEs (Albaz, Mansour, Rida, & Schubert, 2020). Whether it be running a small business in the hospitality sector or operating a small accounting firm, introducing the right processes or technology is a big financial imposition. Coupled with reduced consumer demand, it is no surprise that many SMEs are currently experiencing challenging times (Mizen, 2020).

Due to the permanent increase in consumer requirements, their skillful building of competitive advantage through digital competence and innovation is increasingly important. As indicated by the report of the Ministry of Entrepreneurship and Technology and Siemens, the most commonly used technologies in the surveyed enterprises were the automation of production lines, data analytics and production optimization, and the use of software that reduces the cost of prototyping. Among the least popular technologies that are associated with Industry 4.0 and implemented by companies were artificial intelligence, Big Data, and cloud computing (*Smart Industry Poland Report*, 2018).

The outbreak of COVID-19, which caught the world unaware and unprepared, has significantly ruined business activities, with serious adverse effects on small businesses (Humphries, Neilson, & Ulyssea, 2020). Many businesses of all sizes have since implemented technologies such as virtual teams, Zoom virtual meetings, synchronous remote learning, and other technologies (Ting, Carin, Dzau, & Wong, 2020; Webster, 2020). Furthermore, many small businesses have also been able to utilize new techniques to adapt and improvise their business models (Puddister & Small, 2020; Vaccaro, Getz, Cohen, Cole, & Donnally, 2020).

The use of technology during this pandemic has also enabled and fostered community and civic spirit. In the UK and the USA, small- and medium-scale firms (Akpan, 2020), universities, and 3D-printing enthusiasts used their printers to create personal protective equipment to help alleviate the shortage of such materials during the early stages of the pandemic (Iddawela, 2020).

Innovation and digital competencies in empirical research

In June 2020, the authors conducted a study whose purpose was to find out the degree of the impact that the COVID-19 pandemic had on studying and self-development as well as interpersonal relationships.

The authors mainly wanted to know the attitudes and opinions of students regarding the impact of the COVID-19 pandemic (Kraus, Clauss, Breier, Gast, Zardini, & Tiberius, 2020) on the area of innovation and technology as well as on digital competencies in the aspect of Industry 4.0 development.

The study was conducted on a group of students from the Lublin University of Technology, from full-time and part-time first-cycle studies as well as from post-graduate MBA studies. The study was dominated by MBA students – they constituted 74.2% of the respondents. The research was of a pilot nature. The research tool used was a structured questionnaire that contained closed questions (six main questionnaire questions and three metric questions). The research was carried out by using the CAWI (computer-assisted web interview) method.

The socio-demographic characteristics of the respondents are presented in Table 4.1. The dominant group in the study was men (57.1%). The largest group of respondents (77.1%) was people who were more than 25 years old.

Table 4.1 Socio-Demographic Characteristics of Respondents

Variable	%
Age	
18–22	5.8
23–24	17.1
Over 25 years	77.1
Sex	
Women	42.9
Men	57.1
Status	
Student	22.9
A working student	2.9
MBA student	74.2

Source: Own study on the basis of conducted research.

Impact of COVID-19 on the perception of development factors of enterprises

Innovation in research

In terms of the number of people affected, the geographical coverage of the COVID-19 pandemic and its duration were much more extensive than the other epidemics that had attacked humanity after World War II. The economic impact of the current pandemic will also be greater due to the growing number and intensity of international links in Industry 4.0.

The COVID-19 pandemic surprised entrepreneurs and forced rapid adaptations to changing conditions. Many enterprises, in almost all sectors, had to adapt to the so-called new reality, as research shows.

In April 2021, the Livespace team conducted an online survey regarding the condition of sales during the pandemic. The study was conducted by using an online questionnaire. The survey involved 80 respondents – mainly people from companies with business-to-business relationships (82.5%) and with Polish-majority capital (91.25%). As many as 50% of the respondents were the owners and managers of companies, and the other 50% were sales department managers.

The survey showed that 65% of the respondents noted decreases in sales that were caused by the COVID-19 pandemic. Only 7.5% of the respondents indicated that the pandemic situation had had a positive effect on their businesses. For 50% of the respondents, the greatest challenges were the need to change plans and strategies and find financial (17.5%) and other (10%) support, including panic among managers and decreases in purchasing decisions on the part of clients.

The data that are presented above were also reflected in the report entitled "The situation of Polish enterprises and the labor market after lockdown" (report of the Polish Economic Institute and the Polish Development Fund, 2020) from a survey that was conducted in April/May 2020 among business owners or decision-makers in enterprises about their situations and plans after the coronavirus epidemic coming to Poland. The study was conducted by means of computer-assisted telephone interviews (CATI) on a random-quota sample of 400 companies. The survey showed that 60% of the companies experienced decreases in revenues. Demand was also falling, with nearly half of them reporting decreases of 25%. In addition, every fourth enterprise had problems with settling liabilities and 30% with enforcing claims. In addition, 67% of the companies experienced a decrease in revenues at the turn of April and May 2020 as compared to the result from March – an increase of 10% when compared to the situation a month earlier. A total of 12% of enterprises had already reduced employment, and a further 12% declared further redundancies. Companies from the trade sector and large- and medium-sized enterprises sacked the most employees, with a 60% reduction in 1–25% of the crews.

In the service sector and micro-enterprises, on the other hand, the strategy for reducing the salaries of entire crews dominated. The report showed that the situation of Polish companies remained uncertain, but fewer and fewer intended to use "radical survival strategies." Managers were looking for solutions for survival and in the perspective of further development.

The above research shows that companies do not fully adapt to changing conditions. Today, each manager should look at the development of their company in perspective, adapt its products and services to changing conditions, and implement innovations.

As part of the research that was conducted among students of the Lublin University of Technology, the respondents were asked to comment on innovation in the context of the situation that was caused by the COVID-19 pandemic.

The respondents strongly agreed that the studied university emphasizes modern technologies. It is important that more than half of the respondents agreed with the statement that the university was prepared to use new solutions and adapt to changing conditions. The above data indicate that, nowadays, institutions such as universities cannot lag behind; they must be flexible and adapt their offers on an ongoing basis, taking advantage of emerging opportunities in the area of innovation.

Relationships are an important area that covers the implementation of modern solutions. The respondents agreed that the pursuit of a common goal was the basis for building relationships between them. All of the respondents confirmed that teamwork was the basis for building lasting relationships during such a difficult time. Today, each enterprise should focus on social capital and the relationships that exist in the organization. Implementing innovations and then applying them in a given team is the basis for shaping attitudes and implementing the subsequent competencies in a team.

Innovation is essential; almost 75% of companies say that innovation is one of the top three management priorities, and 35% put it first. This is not surprising; a winning innovation strategy combined with the right innovation system can make a huge difference. It should be noted, however, that innovation is difficult. Only about 30% of companies think they are good at it; so, this is a growing challenge (Long, Iñigo, & Blok, 2020). Digital technologies and data require even the strongest innovators to constantly master new possibilities and develop faster and more efficient research and development processes.

Digital competencies

The digital revolution and new technologies undoubtedly affect the desired professional profiles in an economy that is based on Industry 4.0. An additional determinant in the form of the COVID-19 pandemic has now emerged. We have felt its influence, and we feel it in all areas of our lives. The subject of the considerations in question is the impact of the pandemic situation on the sphere of digital competencies. How did the pandemic change our perception of digital competence? Did it reveal shortcomings in this area, or did new needs arise? Has the current situation meant that the role of digital competence in the modern world is increasing?

Digital technology is currently playing a major role in social and economic development. We have been observing for some time now the gradual spread and implementation of technologies that are related to the phenomenon of Industry 4.0. Industry 4.0 has had (and continues to have) a strong and heterogeneous impact on the labor market, causing a change in organizational activities and competencies. It initiates the emergence of new professions, qualifications, skills, and competencies; it also affects the growing digitization of the labor market and the need for employees to master the use of new technologies and additional skills. It seems that the pandemic has dramatically accelerated certain processes and phenomena that are associated with the digitization of our lives. It forced radical changes for which we were not fully prepared; we needed to reevaluate our priorities and modify our lifestyles and work.

In many areas, the development of Industry 4.0 and the pandemic work in a similar fashion and on a strengthening basis. First, both phenomena are similar because of their impacts on society. Second, the consequences of the pandemic have affected the technological revolution. Over the past few months, pillars of Industry 4.0 (such as the role of some new professions, the need for digital skills that are required of enterprises, or the fear of technology) have been redesigned (Melluso et al., 2020). We have had to change our approach to work and be more open to change. In the digital revolution, technology has often been seen as a potential cause of job destruction. In the current pandemic reality, it is a support for citizens because it alleviates the problems that are caused by forced distances in the workplace. The boundaries between working time and leisure time have changed (due to the conditions of work and distance learning), and the ability to deal with the stress that is caused by constantly being in a network environment is gaining importance. All of this leads to a change in mentality toward the acceptance of radical changes in one's way of working: in particular, greater openness to technology.

The concept of lifelong learning and human development has been promoted for a long time. The COVID-19 pandemic has demonstrated the importance of immunity and adaptability when facing new limitations. New realities at work lead to the consolidation of new skills and the emergence of new professional profiles. First of all, we already know that employees who possess digital skills are absolutely necessary. Digital skills in an enterprise are no longer an element of competitive advantage but a *sine qua non* of survival. Second, there is demand in the labor market for professions that are related to risk management, ensuring compliance with safety regulations and (in particular) the monitoring of biological hazards. A particular emphasis is placed on soft skills such as time management, creativity, and resilience.

Industry 4.0 sparked a debate about the impact of technology on the labor market. The current pandemic situation has given these discussions additional dynamics and has shown that the introduction of Industry 4.0 solutions is becoming a necessity for us.

The COVID-19 pandemic has shown how important digital resources have become for our economies and how networks and connectivity, data, artificial intelligence (AI), and basic and advanced digital skills are important for socio-economic development, making everyday life and work possible under pandemic conditions.

Digital skills are the foundation of a digital society (Kwasek, Maciaszczyk, Kocot, & Depta, 2021). They allow one to use digital services and engage in basic online activities (the European Commission, 2020). This is especially important when mobility is limited, which occurred during the COVID-19 pandemic. Under these conditions, the appropriate digital skills allow citizens to access information, goods, and services. Recent months have revealed the need to strengthen basic and advanced digital skills (despite the improvements in this area). Last year saw an improvement in Internet users' basic and advanced digital skills (those of graduates and ICT specialists). In 2019, the percentage of people with at least basic digital skills reached 58% (an increase from 55% in 2015). However, a significant proportion of the EU population still do not have basic digital skills despite the fact that most jobs already require them. In 2018, around 9.1 million people worked as ICT specialists in the EU (employment in this industry increased by 1.6 million people over the last four years). However, there are still no ICT specialists in the labor market: 64% of large enterprises and 56% of SMEs that recruited ICT specialists in 2018 reported that they had problems finding employees. The biggest problems in this respect have occurred in Romania and the Czech Republic, where at least 80% of companies have reported difficulties finding ICT specialists. There is also a gender-imbalance issue, as only one in six ICT professionals are women. The best situations in terms of the supply of ICT specialists in the labor market are in Finland, Sweden, and Denmark, where the Digital Economy and Society Index (DESI) is at the highest level.

Despite the fact that as many as 85% of EU citizens used the Internet in 2019, only 58% of them possessed at least basic digital skills. Although the current crisis may have a positive impact on increasing the number of Internet users, it should be remembered that the development of digital skills does not occur automatically with increased use of the Internet. The leaders in this respect are Iceland (85%) and Norway (83%), while the worst situations are evident in Romania (31%) and Bulgaria (29%). The rate for Poland is 44%.

The current COVID-19 pandemic has shown just how important digital resources have become for our economies and how basic and advanced digital skills sustain our economies and societies. Although 85% of citizens were already using the Internet in 2019, only 58% had at least basic digital skills before the COVID-19 crisis. Therefore, having an Internet connection is not enough; it must be combined with the right skills. Digital skills include both basic usage skills (which allow for participation in the digital society and the consumption of digital goods and services) and advanced skills (which enable employees to operate in the digital economy).

In Europe, there is a clear mismatch in new technology skills between the academic offer and industry demand (European Commission, 2019). Most member states face shortages of ICT specialists and technicians, and the COVID-19 crisis has further widened this gap.

As part of the research that was conducted among students of the Lublin University of Technology, the respondents were asked to comment on digital skills in the context of the situation that was caused by the COVID-19 pandemic. The test results are presented in Figures 4.1 and 4.2.

More than half of the respondents (62.9%) noticed that the necessity of distance learning has forced them to develop their own digital competencies. Only every third respondent did not think so (of which only 5.7% of these respondents categorically said that they did not see the need to develop digital skills in order to fully benefit from remote education and work). Perhaps there are those who assess their digital competencies very highly and, therefore, do not see the need for changes in this area. This is very likely, because as many as 88.6% of the respondents admitted that they had sufficient skills to use remote teaching and work tools.

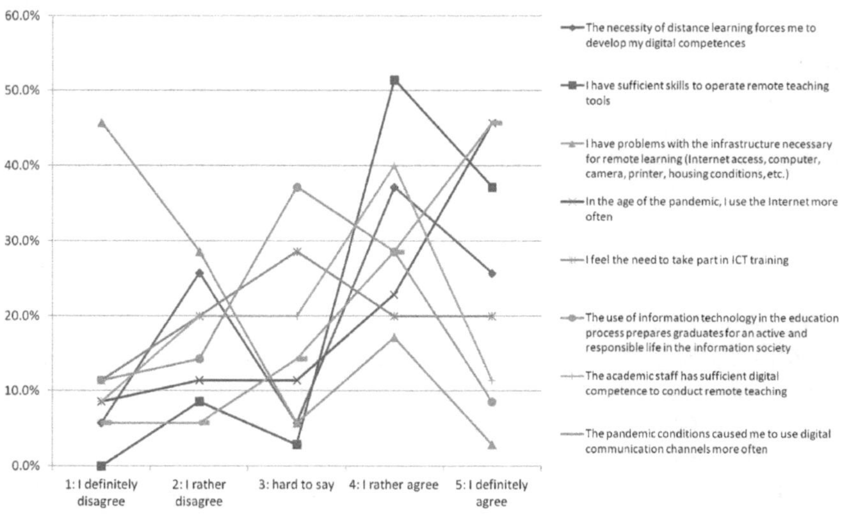

Figure 4.1 The use of innovation and technology in the aspect of the pandemic.

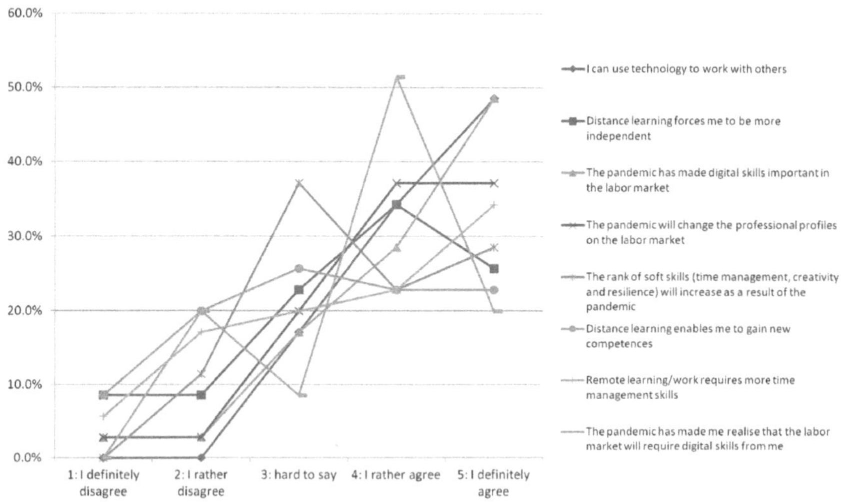

Figure 4.2 Impact of relationships on shaping attitudes in the face of a pandemic.

Of the respondents, 82.8% said that they could use technology to collaborate with others.

The situation looks good with the infrastructure that is necessary for learning and remote work (Internet access, computer, camera, printer, housing conditions, etc.). Only one in five respondents complained about deficiencies in this respect.

Around two-thirds of the respondents (68.6%) admitted that, during the pandemic, they have used the Internet more often (for private, professional, and educational purposes). Digital communication channels (such as email, social media, chats, Skype, Messenger, etc.) have also been more commonly used during the pandemic. Nearly three-fourths (74.3%) of the surveyed students admitted to this.

For 40% of the respondents, the pandemic situation and the need to function in a digital reality have generated the need to participate in training in the ICT area; this is dictated by the desire to better rediscover themselves in a changed reality.

More than one-third of the respondents (37.1%) believed that the use of information technology in the education process prepares graduates for an active and responsible life in the information society. Thanks to various forms of remote education, they are able to better find a place in a labor market that requires an increasingly broad range of digital competencies.

Despite the fact that the pandemic situation was a surprise and created the need to introduce remote teaching and work without prior preparation, actions in this area were positively evaluated by the respondents. Around half of them (51.4%) highly valued the preparation of academic staffs for conducting remote teaching. Only 8.5% of the respondents definitely negatively assessed the competencies of university employees for distance education.

At the same time, 60% of them noted that distance learning has forced them to become more independent and active in the process of learning about knowledge. They were also aware of the fact that remote learning and work require more time-management skills and the ability to separate work time and leisure time when free time, work, and study all occur in the same physical space, e.g., at home (57.1% of the respondents).

The respondents also referred to the impact of the pandemic on the labor market and the changing requirements for future employee competencies.

More than three-fourths of the respondents (77.1%) said that the pandemic had made digital skills more and more important in the labor market and that they would become an increasingly important element of employee competencies that determine finding good jobs. A similar-sized group (71.4% of the respondents) admitted that the pandemic had made them aware that the labor market would require, specifically, new or developed digital competencies from them. None of the given answers strongly denied such a statement.

The respondents predicted that the pandemic would change the professional profiles in the labor market (74.3% of the responses). According to 51.4% of the respondents, the ranks of soft skills (such as time management, creativity, and resilience) would increase.

Nearly half (45.7%) believed that e-learning would enable them to acquire new competencies that are desired in the labor market, every fourth respondent (25.7%) was not able to assess it unequivocally, and 28.6% spoke negatively about the possibility of gaining new competencies through remote education. Such a large diversity of answers was probably dictated by the fact that it was difficult to assess the effectiveness of distance learning in such a short time perspective.

Practical recommendations

The results of the conducted research and the ideas that are included in this chapter allow us to draw a number of recommendations for practical use:

1 Entrepreneurs are often considered to be those who, with their creative abilities, can fix problems or who will assist society in bouncing back or provide benefits to society; however, they can also be under pressure to overcome the challenges of delivering solutions. Entrepreneurship involves assessing opportunities and coming up with innovative ideas.
2 Today, each manager should look at the development of their company in perspective, adapt its products and services to changing conditions, and implement innovations.

3 During the age of Industry 4.0, digital innovation is forcing a paradigm shift in business and operating models. This is why it is such an important challenge for today's companies to support the ongoing processes of digital transformation, in terms of both production methods and the utilized business models and processes.
4 In addition to the intensive work of introducing innovations in the field of digital technology, a fundamental change in the approach to human resources management is also required. High-quality personnel are necessary to fully exploit the potential of new technologies.
5 Creating new solutions to raise awareness of the importance of innovative action is a good direction for change.

Conclusions

Today, the main advantages of an innovative organization/enterprise in the face of the pandemic can be found in its high flexibility and market expansiveness, efficient exchange of resources, quick responses to external opportunities, and partner support in difficult situations. These allow businesses to not only survive the crisis (or crises) and develop by achieving more and more ambitious goals but also to overcome the autonomous thinking of enterprises (or even the fear of cooperation that results from distrust).

There is a shift that is taking place in the world of entrepreneurship. Occasionally, a situation can be very difficult and may require different and varied solutions. It may be worthwhile to check whether a current business model is working properly, the style of a company's operation should be altered, new markets and distribution channels ought to be sought, organizational changes ought to be carried out, or innovative solutions should be implemented. A chance for companies that have suffered a pandemic could be a change in the model of their business or foreign expansion.

The research results showed that students at the Lublin University of Technology generally accepted the need for innovative activities and the development of digital competencies in response to both Industry 4.0 and the crisis that was caused by the COVID-19 pandemic. They also illustrated their equally positive approach to didactic technologies and distance learning. As many as 74.3% of the respondents stated that they "found themselves in a new reality."

Combined with the perceived increase in digital skills, such a positive perception also changed the students' perspectives regarding their future work. The pandemic has caused them to perceive their competencies differently. Digital competencies are becoming more and more important for them.

The coronavirus pandemic has only confirmed that the shaping of knowledge and entrepreneurial attitudes based on digital competencies is a determining factor for future professional success. Knowledge as well as entrepreneurial and employee competencies that are rooted in digital skills determines professional success during the era of Industry 4.0.

The COVID-19 pandemic has confirmed that, nowadays, not only are those skills a competitive advantage, but they are also a form of survival during economic lockdowns. The pandemic has also highlighted the fact that the future belongs to Industry 4.0. The ongoing automation of industrial practices and traditional manufacturing will lay the foundation of economic development, and it is a prerequisite for business entities, employees, and consumers to learn to function in this virtual environment.

References

Academic offer and demand for advanced profiles in the EU, European Commission, JRC, 2019.

Albaz A, Mansour T, Rida T, Schubert J. *Setting Up Small and Medium-size Enterprises for Restart and Recovery*. McKinsey & Company, 2020.

Akpan I. J. Sciento metric evaluation and visual analytics of the scientific literature production on entrepreneurship, small business ventures, and innovation. *Journal of Small Business & Entrepreneurship*, 33, 1–29, 2020, https://doi.org/10.1080/08276331.2020.1786229.

Cho H. J., Pucik J. Relationship between innovativeness, quality, growth, profitability, and market value. *Strategic Management Journal*, 26 (6), 555–575, 2005, https://doi.org/10.1002/smj.461.

Communication from the Commission on the "Digital Education Action Plan", COM/2018/022 final.

Czerwinska M. *Knowledge and perception of Industry 4.0 among the students of Computer Science*, Routledge, Taylor & Francis Group, London, 2020, in print.

Digital Economy and Society Index (DESI) 2020. *Thematic Chapters*. European Commission, Brussels, 2020.

Grabowska S., Saniuk S. Development of business models in the fourth industrial revolution: Conditions in the context of empirical research on worldwide scope companies located in Poland. *Journal of Open Innovation: Technology, Market, and Complexity*, 2022, 8 (2): 86.

Hermann M., Pentek T., Otto B. Design principles for industrie 4.0 scenarios. *System Sciences (HICSS), 49th Hawaii International Conference, IEEE*, 3928–3937, 2016, https://doi.org/10.1109/HICSS.2016.488.

Hilami M. F., Ramayah T., Mustapha Y., Pawanchik S. Product and process innovativeness: Evidence from Malaysian SMEs. *European Journal of Social Science*, 16 (4), 552–557, 2010.

Hollanders H., Es-Sadki N., Merkelbach I. *Innovation Union Scoreboard 2019*. European Commission, Maastricht Economic and Social Research Institute on Innovation and Technology (MERIT), Luxemburg, 2019.

Humphries J.E., Neilson, C., Ulyssea G. The evolving impacts of COVID-19 on small businesses since the CARES Act. 2020.

Iddawela Y. Social distancing app developed by students and alumni goes live. *The London School of Economics and Political Science 2020*, Accessed 15 July

2020, http://www.lse.ac.uk/News/Latest-news-from-LSE/2020/d-April-20/Social-distancing-app-developed-by-students-and-alumni-goes-live.

Ilomäki L., Paavola S., Lakkala M., Kantosalo A. Digital competence–an emergent boundary concept for policy and educational research. *Education and Information Technologies*, 21 (3), 655–679, 2016, https://doi.org/10.1007/s10639-014-9346-4.

Individuals' Level of Digital Skills, Eurostat, 2020, http://ec.europa.eu/eurostat/web/products-datasets/-/isoc_sk_dskl_i.

Innovative Activity of Enterprises in Poland in 2015–2017, Statistical analysis, Central Statistical Office (GUS), Warsaw, 2018.

Innovative activity of enterprises in Poland in 2016–2018, Signal information, Central Statistical Office (GUS), Warsaw, 2018.

Innovative enterprises as % of total enterprises – by size class and type of innovation, European Commission, Eurostat, 2020.

Janssen J., Stoyanov S., Ferrari A., Punie Y., Pannekeet K., Sloep P. Experts' views on digital competence: Commonalities and differences. *Computers & Education*, 68, 473–481, 2013, https://doi.org/10.1016/j.compedu.2013.06.008.

Kim H. K., So W. H., Je S. M. A big data framework for network security of small and medium enterprises for future computing. *The Journal of Supercomputing*, 75 (6), 3334–3367, 2019.

King A. Industry 4.0 and SMEs. *RMIT University*, 2018, 46.

Kraus S., Clauss T., Breier M., Gast J., Zardini A., Tiberius V. The economics of COVID-19: Initial empirical evidence on how family firms in five European countries cope with the corona crisis, 2020. *International Journal of Entrepreneurial Bahavior & Research*, 26 (5), pp. 1067–1092, 2020.

Kwasek A., Maciaszczyk M., Kocot M., Depta A. Sustainable remote work market–diagnosis of digital IT, information and functional competences in the aspect of equal opportunities. *European Research Studies Journal*, 24 (2B), 213–226, 2021.

Long T. B., Iñigo E., Blok V. Responsible management of innovation in business. [in:] Laasch O., Jamali D., Freeman R. E., Suddaby R. *Research Handbook of Responsible Management*. Cheltenham: Edward Elgar, 2020, chapter 40.

Makkonen H., Johnston W. J., Javalgi R. R. G. A behavioral approach to organizational innovation adoption. *Journal of Business Research*, 69 (7), 2480–2489, 2016.

Melluso N., Fareri S., Fantoni G., Bonaccorsi A., Chiarello F., Coli E., Manafi S. *Lights and shadows of COVID-19, Technology and Industry 4.0*, 2020, arXiv preprint arXiv:2004.13457.

Miskiewicz R. Challenges facing management practice in the light of Industry 4.0: The example of Poland. *Virtual Economics*, 2 (2), 37–46, 2019, https://doi.org/10.34021/ve.2019.02.02(2).

Mizen, R. SMEs hit hardest by COVID-19 job losses, 2020. Retrieved from: https://www.afr.com/policy/economy/smes-hit-hardest-by-COVID-19-job-losses-20200910-p55u7l

Moeuf A., Pellerin R., Lamouri S., Tamayo-Giraldo S., Barbaray R. The industrial management of SMEs in the era of Industry 4.0. *International Journal of Production Research*, 56 (3), 1118–1136, 2018, https://doi.org/10.1080/00207543.2017.1372647.

Nagji B., Tuff G. How to manage an innovation portfolio. *Harvard Business Review Poland*, 115, 25–28, 2012.

Piatek Z. *Smart Industry Poland 2018*, Industry 4.0 Modern Industry Portal, 2018, http://przemysl-40.pl/index.php/2018/05/10/jakajest-innowacyjnosc-polskich-msp-raport-smart-industry-polska-2018/.

Proposal for a Council recommendation on A Bridge to Jobs - Reinforcing the Youth Guarantee and replacing Council Recommendation of 22 April 2013 on establishing a Youth Guarantee, COM/2020/277 final, CELEX number: 52020DC0277.

Puddister, K., Small, T. A., Trial by Zoom? The Response to COVID-19 by Canada's Courts. *Canadian Journal of Political Science/Revue Canadienne de Science Politique*, 5, 2020, https://doi.org/10.1017/S0008423920000505.

Report on the state of the SME sector in Poland, Report of Polish Agency for Enterprise Development, Warsaw, 2018.

Roblek V., Meško M., Krapež A. A complex view of Industry 4.0. *Sage Open*, 6 (2), 1–11, 2016, https://doi.org/10.1177/2158244016653987.

Rodak A., Gracel J. Transformation to industry 4.0 [in:] *How to do IT. Technologies for Business – Special Edition*, Poland, Harvard Business Review, 2017.Retrieved from: https://www.hbrp.pl/b/transformacja-do-przemyslu-40/PiYIsMRNo

Rzepka A. Innovation, inter-organizational relation, and co-operation between enterprises in Podkarpacie region in Poland. *Procedia Manufacturing*, 30, 642–649, 2019, https://doi.org/10.1016/j.promfg.2019.02.091.

Rzepka A., Borowiecki R., Olesiński Z. Towards economy 4.0: Evolution of management. [in:] *Industry 4.0 in Poland – On Time or too Late?*. New York, Routledge, Taylor & Francis Group, 2020, in print.

Saebi, T., Foss N. J., Linder S. Social entrepreneurship research: Past achievements and future promises. *Journal of Management*, 45 (1), 70–95, 2019.

Smart Industry Poland 2018. Innovation in the sector of micro- and small and medium-sized production enterprises in Poland, Research report, Ministry of Entrepreneurship and Technology/Siemens, Warsaw, 2018.

Smit J., Kreutzer S., Moeller C., Carlberg M. *Industry 4.0*, Study for the ITRE Committee, Policy Department A: Economic and Scientific Policy, European Parliament, Retrieved from: http://www.europarl.europa.eu/RegData/etudes/STUD/2016/570007/IPOL_STU(2016)570007_EN.pdf (access April 2, 2019).

Ting, D. S. W., Carin L., Dzau V., Wong T. Y. Digital technology and COVID-19. *Nature Medicine*, 26 (4), 459–461, 2020.

Thames L., Schaefer D. Software-defined cloud manufacturing for Industry 4.0. CARV in Bath, United Kingdom, Paper presented in *The 6th International Conference on Changeable, Agile, Reconfigurable and Virtual Production*, 52, 12–17, 2016, https://doi.org/10.1016/j.procir.2016.07.041.

The Council Recommendation of 19 December 2016 on upskilling pathways: New opportunities for adults (2016/C 484/01).

The Council Recommendation of 22 May 2018 on key competencies for lifelong learning (2018/C 189/01).

The situation of Polish enterprises and the labor market after lockdown, Report of the Polish Economic Institute and the Polish Development Fund, 2020, http://pie.net.pl/.

Ulyssea. The evolving impacts of COVID-19 on small businesses since the CARES Act (April 26, 2020). Cowles Foundation Discussion Paper No. 2230, 2020, Available at SSRN: https://doi.org/10.2139/ssrn.3584745.

Vaccaro, A. R., Getz, C. L., Cohen B., Cole B., Donnally, I. Practice management during the COVID-19 pandemic. *The Journal of the American Academy of Orthopaedic Surgeons*, 28 (11), 464–470, 2020.

Winarsih, Indriastuti M., Fuad K. Impact of Covid-19 on digital transformation and sustainability in Small and Medium Enterprises (SMEs): A conceptual framework. [in:] Barolli L., Poniszewska-Maranda A., Enokido T. (eds) *Complex, Intelligent and Software Intensive Systems. CISIS 2020. Advances in Intelligent Systems and Computing*, vol. 1194. Cham, Springer, 2021, https://doi.org/10.1007/978-3-030-50454-0_48.

Webster, P. Virtual health care in the era of COVID-19. *The Lancet*, 395 (10231), 1180–1181, 2020.

Zamfir A. M., Aldea A. B. Digital skills and labour market resilience. *Postmodern Openings*, 11 (1Supl2), 188–195, 2020, https://doi.org/10.18662/po/11.1sup2/151.

5 Crisis management in selected countries of the European Union during the COVID-19 Pandemic

Natalia Krawczyk

Introduction

Over the course of 2019 and 2020, SARS-CoV-2 virus rapidly spread in China and eventually reached many other countries. As a result, the World Health Organization's (WHO's) Emergency Committee announced a global health threat on January 30, 2020 based on the increasing number of recorded cases around the world. The first clinical symptom of COVID-19, a disease that is caused by SARS-CoV-2, is pneumonia. Gastrointestinal symptoms may also occur. Clinical symptoms in infected patients usually include fever, cough, nasal mucosa hyperemia, shortness of breath, fatigue, and other symptoms of upper respiratory tract infection. Current research shows that some infected people are asymptomatic (Velavan, Meyer, 2020). Since February 26, 2020, coronavirus has been detected in people living on all continents, except Antarctica (McAleer, 2020).

This virus became a great global threat for which the world was not prepared. According to the Global Health Security (GHS) Index, data from 2019 show that the average overall GHS score was 40.2 out of a possible 100, while high-income countries reported an average score of 51.9. The analyzed index showed that, collectively, international preparedness for epidemics and pandemics is at a very low level. In addition, the GHS Index identified major problems in the country's ability to prevent, detect, and respond to health crises. The existence of significant gaps in healthcare systems; vulnerability to environmental, political, and socio-economic threats; and failure to comply with international standards may interfere with the preparedness for and response to an epidemic (GHS Index, 2019).

In this regard, the WHO and the United States Center for Disease Control and Prevention issued guidelines for infection control, screening, and diagnosis in the general population; however, there are still limited acute treatments of critically ill patients with severe illness due to COVID-19 (Alhazzani et al., 2020).

Therefore, an attempt was made to analyze the six best European healthcare systems in the context of the COVID-19 pandemic and compare them with the Polish system. The main purpose of this chapter is

DOI: 10.4324/9781003368687-5

to analyze the crisis management of the selected European Union states during the COVID-19 pandemic. The study was based on literature research and desk research in the field of healthcare systems in the Netherlands, Denmark, Belgium, Finland, Luxembourg, Sweden, and Poland. This was followed by an analysis of management during the crisis that was caused by the coronavirus pandemic.

Euro Health Consumer Index

The Euro Health Consumer Index (EHCI) was published in 2018. The EHCI has been developing annual assessments of the performance of national healthcare systems in Europe since 2005. The results were based on 46 indicators that were grouped into six categories: patient rights and information, availability of medical care, treatment results, scope and extent of services, prevention, and use of pharmaceuticals (HCP, 2019). The EHCI compares 35 countries using indicators and focuses on creating health policies in different countries, choices that are made by beneficiaries, levels of service, and access to information (Nieszporska, 2018).

The obtained results of the EHCI ranking as a comparative index for national health systems confirmed that there is a group of EU member states that have good health systems from the point of view of the consumer (patient). Scoring was intentionally done in such a way that the probability of receiving the same results was maximally minimized. The results published in the report show that there were eight European countries that belonged to the "800 Club" – those that scored at or above 800 from a theoretical maximum of 1,000 (HCP, 2019).

In this research, only European Union states were analyzed; therefore, the following countries were purposely skipped: Switzerland (which achieved the best score – 893 points) and Norway (which also does not belong to the EU). The study covered 6 countries that were in the "800 Club" (which were in the top 10 of the 35 analyzed European countries) as well as the Polish healthcare system. Poland was chosen for this comparison because, despite its very low health index score (32nd place in the ranking), it achieved very good results (HCP, 2019) in the context of its low number of cases reported and low mortality rate as a result of COVID-19 (both on European Union and global scales) (WHO, 2020a).

Figure 5.1 shows the total scores for EHCI 2018 for the analyzed countries in this study.

The Netherlands has been a state with an exemplary healthcare system since 2005. In the EHCI 2018 ranking, it came in second with 883 points (after Switzerland, which is not analyzed in this research) (HCP, 2019). The country's healthcare system combines competing healthcare insurance options, a single-payer system for long-term care, and local tax-financed social care. The Dutch government regulates and manages three programs

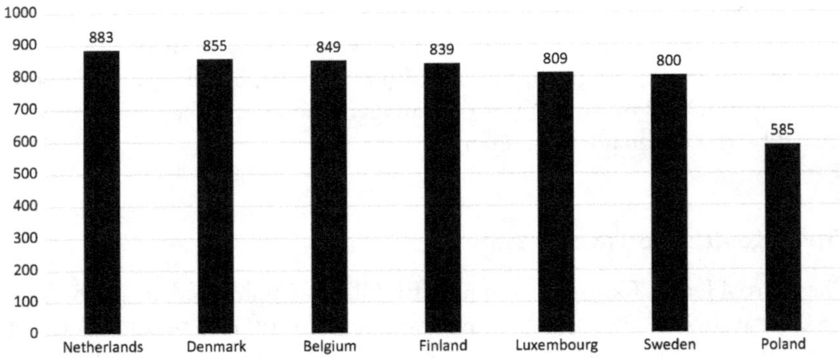

Figure 5.1 Total EHCI 2018 scores for Finland, Denmark, Netherlands, Belgium, Luxembourg, Sweden, and Poland (HCP, 2019). EHCI, Euro Health Consumer Index.

that provide universal insurance coverage. The relatively large financial outlays into the healthcare sector in the Netherlands have had a significant impact on this success (OECD, 2019). In practice, coordination problems often occur in every functioning healthcare system, while Dutch experts try to regularly monitor and solve them (Toebes, San Giorgi, 2014).

The next country is Denmark, which scored 855 points in the EHCI (HCP, 2019). This is a country where health expenditure is steadily increasing; currently, this is 25% higher than the EU average. The public fund covers 84% of all health expenditures, while other fees are paid by patients (mainly for dental and pharmaceutical services). The Danish system is decentralized in regard to the provision of health services; however, it is centralized in terms of general planning and regulation at a national level. National health authorities set standards and assess the quality of the care (OECD, 2019a).

Belgium is also distinguished by a system in which their total health expenditure is higher than the EU average. It scored 849 points in the analyzed European ranking (HCP, 2019). Most of the services in this country are covered by public money, while some are funded by voluntary health and household insurance. Federal authorities are responsible for regulations that are related to health insurance and the health care budget. In order to improve cooperation between the federal authorities, regions, and communities, inter-ministerial conferences are organized in Belgium (OECD, 2019b).

In the case of Finland (which scored slightly lower than Belgium – 839 points), the healthcare system works just as well (HCP, 2019). The government finances the healthcare sector at 75%, while the other expenses are covered by patients. The Finnish healthcare system is regulated at the local level; local authorities play an important role in the purchase and provision of health services. There is the National Social Insurance Institution, which runs the statutory National Health Insurance system by financing medicine, travel costs that are related to care and illness, maternity benefits, and co-financing healthcare in the workplace (OECD, 2019c). The healthcare system in Finland has a centralized structure; it aims to reduce costs and increase patient decision-making capacities (Keskimäki et al., 2019).

Similar to the countries that were described above, Luxembourg (809 points in the EHCI ranking) also spends well above the EU average on healthcare (HCP, 2019). As much as 84% of its health expenditure is financed public expenditure, while the remainder is covered by patients or by voluntary health insurance. Luxembourg has a compulsory social insurance system with a single payer – the Caisse Nationale de Santé national health insurance. Caisse Nationale de Santé includes a system of healthcare, sick leave, and long-term care insurance. The responsibility of managing the healthcare system is very centralized (OECD, 2019d).

Sweden was the last country that was classified as an "800 Club" member thanks to a score of 800 points in the EHCI (HCP, 2019). It has the third largest health expenditure in the EU, and most of it is publicly funded (84% – like in Luxembourg). The Swedish government is responsible for regulation and supervision, whereas the country is divided into 21 counties that are responsible for financing, purchasing, and providing health services. Health expenditure is covered mainly from local taxes as well as government contributions. There is ongoing work to reduce the waiting times for scheduled operations and improve the functioning of the healthcare sector (OECD, 2019e).

In comparison, Poland scored only 585 points, which resulted in it placing fourth from the bottom of the 35 analyzed European countries (HCP, 2019). Poland finances almost 70% of its expenditures with public money (which constitutes a smaller share than the EU average), while the remaining part comes from patients. The distance that separates Poland from the other countries that were examined in the study seems to be very large in this respect. The healthcare system in Poland is based on social insurance. The Ministry of Health oversees the system, while the National Health Fund is the buyer and payer of health services under reimbursed services. This diverse structure is a major impediment to effective system coordination. In 2017, Poland introduced the "hospital network" initiative to support the integration of outpatient and hospital care (OECD, 2019f).

Management of health system with regard to COVID-19

The health models of the countries presented above were analyzed in terms of the management of the healthcare system during the COVID-19 pandemic. This part of the chapter describes the necessary plans, responses to the pandemic, and methods of system management to ensure their continued functioning. This study includes data that were published by the Worldometer portal and the World Health Organization, including mechanisms for responding to crisis situations and how to provide information. Table 5.1 summarizes the results that were obtained under the EHCI 2018 ranking and the results regarding the pandemic in the analyzed countries that were published by Worldometer.

COVID-19 attacked 213 countries and territories around the world (Worldometer, 2020). Figure 5.1 shows the total number of COVID-19 cases per million in the selected European Union countries that were analyzed in the study. In contrast, Figure 3.2 shows the same number of fatal cases per million as a result of COVID-19.

Table 5.1 Planning Documents in Field of Crisis Management

Country	*EHCI 2018 total scores*	*Number of cases per million population (COVID-19)*	*Number of deaths per million population (COVID-19)*	*Planning document in the field of crisis management*
The Netherlands	883	2,961	358	National pandemic response plan
Denmark	855	2,227	105	Mathematical model (SEIRS) regarding behavior and infection rates
Belgium	849	5,360	843	Risk monitoring and management system
Finland	839	1,311	59	National Preparedness Plan for an Influenza Pandemic
Luxembourg	809	7,427	176	National protection concept
Sweden	800	7,312	227	Pandemic response plan
Poland	585	969	41	National Strategic Management Plan

EHCI, Euro Health Consumer Index.
Source: Worldometer (2020) and HCP (2019).

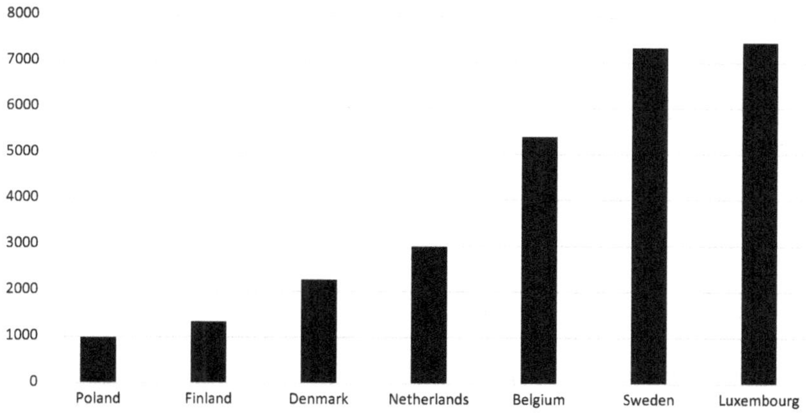

Figure 5.2 Total number of COVID-19 cases per million (Worldometer, 2020).

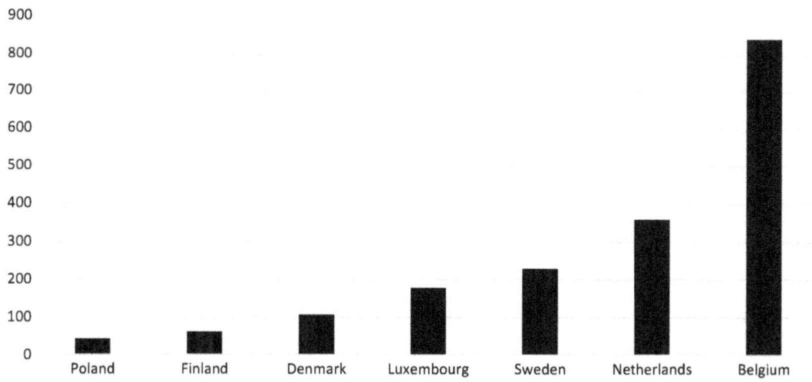

Figure 5.3 Total number of deaths from COVID-19 per million population (Worldometer, 2020).

It should be noted that these values are constantly changing. The data were analyzed during the crisis and not after it; therefore, the study is of a pilot nature and will also be repeated after the end of the pandemic (when the data stabilizes).

Nevertheless, the results that are shown in Figures 5.2 and 5.3 encourage one to undertake an analysis on this topic. The question arises as to what may be the reason that the best health systems in the European Union have had very poor results during the crisis. In the countries of the "800 Club" group, the number of cases of infections and mortality has been very high. In contrast, the number of patients and deaths in Poland (which obtained a very low result in the EHCI 2018 ranking and where the health care system was very poorly assessed in a pandemic situation) has been very small.

In comparison, the number of cases from March 4, 2020 to July 8, 2020 was 969 per million in Poland, while during the period of February 15, 2020 to July 8, 2020, there were 1,311 cases per million recorded in Finland; during the same period, Belgium experienced 5,360 cases, and Sweden counted 7,312. From February 27, 2020 to July 8, 2020, Denmark experienced 2,227 cases per million, and the Netherlands reported 2,961. During the period of February 29, 2020 to July 8, 2020, the highest number of cases per million of all of the analyzed countries was recorded in Luxembourg – 7,427.

In the case of deaths per million, these values were as follows during the same general period: Poland – 41; Finland – 59; Denmark – 105; Luxembourg – 176; Sweden – 227; the Netherlands – 358; and Belgium – up to 843 (Worldometer, 2020). Therefore, an attempt was made to analyze the crisis management systems in these countries.

Finland

The Finnish pandemic preparedness measures are primarily based on the national preparedness plan for a flu pandemic. Currently, the multi-sector readiness model was used where each sector is responsible for their readiness due to the situation regarding COVID-19. Several ministries are involved (WHOb, 2020b).

The COVID-19-ready model functions as the approach of the entire government and ministry, and their reporting is coordinated by the prime minister's office. According to the national pandemic contingency plan, management relationships during a pandemic are determined in accordance with the government's civil government model. Municipalities are responsible for maintaining social distancing. Hospital district infectious disease practitioners act as planning experts at the regional and local levels. Also, several universities participate in epidemic modeling and advise the government. In connection with the outbreak of COVID-19, a coronavirus coordination group (VN COVID-19) was created on February 13, 2020 to plan, manage, and coordinate healthcare and social welfare measures. Following the coronavirus outbreak, the government declared a state of emergency in the country on March 16, 2020. In accordance with Art. 86 of the extraordinary act, the Ministry of Social Affairs and Health decided that medical personnel should be quarantined for 14 days after returning from abroad (WHO, 2020b).

In Finland, an exit strategy plan was developed and published on May 5, 2020; on May 6, the government adopted a resolution on the hybrid plan strategy to manage the COVID-19 crisis. This meant moving away from extensive restrictive measures to more-targeted restrictions. The "hybrid strategy" was largely based on the "testing, tracking, isolation, and treatment" approach. The first restrictions in Finland concerned restrictions on major public events, school operations, restaurant operations, and travel restrictions, and the country provided protections for the elderly and other at-risk people. In addition, hygiene and social distancing practices were tightened. Starting on June 1, 2020, these restrictions were reduced (GCD, 2020).

Denmark

A mathematical model (SEIRS) was developed in Denmark (Statens Serum Institut, SSI) to support decision-making. The model is based on assumptions about behavior and infection rates and was supplemented with international data in the field of COVID-19. The report presents various scenarios based on various policy re-openings and directly supports policy-making. On May 29, the Danish government and its regions agreed on a national plan to restore patients' rights to health services. On June 30, the Danish Health Authority published a summary of revised guidelines on how to increase clinical activities while preventing the spread of COVID-19 (DHA, 2020).

A set of emergency provisions regarding the pandemic was adopted, which mandated the isolation and treatment of sick people, limited meetings and gatherings, curtailed transport and travel, and suspended rules regarding the right to choose a hospital and the right of quick access. The right to suspend other legal requirements in exceptional circumstances was also specified. The national security council (chaired by the Prime Minister) decided on crisis management; this group consisted of the Ministers of Justice, Foreign Affairs, Defense, and Finance, permanent secretaries, the Minister of Health, and Director of the National Health Authority, and the Director of the Statens Serum Institute. The Prime Minister assumed strong leadership. A task force was responsible for assessing and managing the resources that were needed during the pandemic. There was good coordination between the different levels of government, and they had no significant differences in the approaches of the five regions (WHO, 2020b).

The Netherlands

In the field of crisis management, the Netherlands introduced a national pre-pandemic response plan for COVID-19. The plan describes the overall action in the event of an infectious disease crisis and concerns public health services. It describes which measures should be taken at what phase of the crisis, who is responsible for determining the phase of the crisis, and how to modify it. In the Netherlands, no emergency legislation was issued regarding the healthcare system, except for certain requirements for medical personnel who were involved in the care of COVID-19 patients. The responsible institution for COVID-19 is the National Institute of Public Health and Environment (RIVM). An appointed epidemic management team advise the Prime Minister and his cabinet on necessary matters. Restrictions on maintaining specific distances between people and at public meetings were also introduced (WHO, 2020b).

In addition, public health organizations were responsible for tracking contacts. The government examined the idea of a COVID-19 application on mobile phones and developed an application that protected privacy (WHO, 2020b).

Belgium

In Belgium, crisis management is based on groups of essays that cooperate with ministries and the government (such as Group of Experts in charge of the Exit Strategy). The Interfederal Testing & Contact Tracing Committee was also appointed, which is responsible for staffing the call center and staff training and is in close contact with other experts and consulting groups, in particular with the Interministerial Conference on Public Health.

Belgium has a monitoring and risk management system based on the national focal point for International Health Regulations (WHO, 2020). The national focal point consists of a risk assessment group and a risk management group.

A scientific committee on COVID-19 was set up to provide better scientific knowledge on the virus's evolution and to help optimize Belgium's preparation. In March 2020, the National Security Council was formed, which included the Prime Minister and deputy prime ministers, and was expanded to include the ministers-presidents of the regions and communities. This collegiate body makes all decisions that are related to crisis management.

In addition, the federal government has been given special powers to act without going through ordinary legislative procedures in order to respond to emergency situations that are related to exceptional circumstances. Extraordinary legal measures were also taken to quickly address shortages in the field of protective equipment, medical supplies, and diagnostic tests. Units that operate in Belgium are responsible for ensuring the coordination of all authorities in the state for the purpose of communication and strategic management, the development of legal regulations, and risk management (WHO, 2020b).

Luxembourg

In June, the Luxembourg Parliament adopted two COVID-19 laws that set out the legal framework of the country's response, including on the subject of mandatory protective measures to be applied after the state of emergency expired. The first law focused on limiting mass gatherings, adopting protective measures such as masks, and testing and isolating infected people. The other concerned health restrictions that were related to business, sport, culture, and other generally available activities. The

Parliament adopted the extension of the initial ten-day state of emergency for a maximum period of three months.

In Luxembourg, crisis management is coordinated by the High Commission for National Protection. The High Commission for National Protection is responsible for planning and implementing the national concept of protection. The crisis unit is responsible for analyzing any situation in the country, establishing the overall strategy of the state's reaction, and initiating, coordinating, and providing implementations of all measures to deal with the crisis. The government set up an advisory committee with experts from various sectors to assess the impact of measures that were regularly taken in the fight against COVID-19 (WHO, 2020b).

Sweden

Sweden has contingency plans for influenza pandemics at the national, regional, and local levels. These plans also apply to other major outbreaks of infectious diseases, such as COVID-19. The parliament made legislative changes that would temporarily increase the powers of the government to be able to quickly take action. The Public Health Agency coordinates pandemic preparedness at the national level and supports planning at the regional and local levels (where the operational work is carried out). In each region, there are doctors who deal with infectious diseases and, in accordance with the pandemic plan, provide assistance in the region. The regions that are responsible for healthcare in Sweden are also responsible for the care of patients with suspected infections.

The individual regions of Sweden are responsible for the healthcare and treatment of COVID-19 patients. Municipalities also have plans for a pandemic and crisis, as do hospitals. In Sweden, the Government Office, Public Health Agency, National Council for Health, and Social Welfare and Social Security are all involved in the fight against COVID-19. Each of these institutions has a different scope of responsibility.

The government entrusted the Public Health Agency with the responsibility of coordinating work and increasing the number of COVID-19 samples that were tested in Sweden. The National Council for Health and Social Care was entrusted with the task of identifying the most vulnerable groups. The government agreed to release medical devices with information in languages other than Swedish. COVID-19 is subject to mandatory notification in accordance with the Infectious Diseases Act; therefore, doctors and laboratories constantly provide data that are analyzed by the Public Health Agency on a daily basis (WHO, 2020b).

Poland

In Poland, there are regulations regarding the control of infections and infectious diseases in humans that determine the status of a national epidemic. In connection with this legislation, national blocking and isolating measures could be legally introduced, and additional funding could be allocated to the healthcare system for the examination and treatment of infectious diseases. The COVID-19 epidemic was announced by the Chief Sanitary Inspectorate. The epidemic status was announced in March. In April 2020, restrictive measures were introduced in the form of social distancing. Decisions were made to shut down schools and universities, close non-essential stores and recreational facilities, and maintain social distancing.

On March 29, 2020, the government introduced specific legislation that contained targeted solutions for the prevention and mitigation of COVID-19. The Minister of Health has been responsible for managing the healthcare system during the COVID-19 pandemic. The Minister decided to appoint 19 entities as single-name hospitals. The Minister of Health coordinates research and health communication and is responsible for sending information.

The Chief Sanitary Inspectorate is responsible for detecting cases. People showing symptoms are obligated to report to local sanitary and epidemiological units. The Chief Sanitary Inspector or the voivodeship sanitary inspector is entitled to request information, take specific preventive or control measures, and make appropriate decisions in accordance with their jurisdictions regarding the distribution of medicine, medical devices, and personal protective equipment (WHO, 2020b).

Conclusions and recommendations

Conclusions

Despite the fact that the conditions for the emergence and spread of pandemic viruses are known in the world, their effects cannot be fully determined. Therefore, the preparation of crisis plans by healthcare units should become a basic undertaking that enables the proper functioning of medical facilities and the continuity of health services. In activities that can reduce the scope of a pandemic and minimize its effects, healthcare institutions should cooperate with other organizations such as government administrations, local or regional administrations, and universities and research units; they should also collaborate with experts. In all of the analyzed healthcare systems, such cooperation occurs, and various types of crisis plans are developed; these systems have achieved different results during the COVID-19 pandemic. It is worth noting that even those countries with the most-developed and well-financed health sectors did not cope well with the crisis.

In this research, the selected healthcare systems and the manner of crisis management during the COVID-19 pandemic from February 15, 2020 to July 09, 2020 have been analyzed. The presented studies indicate that there is no correlation between the result in the EHCI 2018 and the effectiveness of crisis management, whose results can be related to the number of cases and deaths that have been caused by COVID-19. Countries that achieved very good results and were in the EHCI "800 Club" during the COVID-19 pandemic showed a very high number of confirmed cases and deaths.

In addition, it can be concluded that crisis management in the context of central management is more effective than in the case of the decentralization of power in this respect. Countries whose healthcare systems were managed centrally showed lower incidences and deaths (Poland, the Netherlands, Denmark) than those countries where there was a division of responsibilities (for example, by regions).

Crisis management is a very complex issue; therefore, an analysis of this issue requires a multi-dimensional research approach. The presented preliminary studies are burdened with restrictions that resulted from the lack of the stabilization of the results and the small number of publications on this subject. Due to the very important nature of the issues in both the social and management contexts, further research in this direction will be conducted.

Recommendations

Specifically, the researcher recommends the following based on the analysis and interpretation of the results:

1 Considering the possibility of further spread of the COVID-19 virus, new emergency plans should be developed in detail, or existing plans should be adapted to current needs.
2 Healthcare establishments should use benchmarking methods and cooperate with other entities and organizations in order, inter alia, to exchange good practices, knowledge, and experiences.
3 Authorities who oversee national crisis management strategies should analyze and implement central governance models in the context of the COVID-19 pandemic.

References

Alhazzani, W., et al., 2020. Surviving Sepsis Campaign: Guidelines on the Management of Critically Ill Adults with Coronavirus Disease 2019 (COVID-19). *Intensive Care Medicine*, 46(5), pp. 854–887.

DHA, 2020. Coronavirus/COVID-19, https://www.sst.dk/en/English, (accessed on 9 July 2020)

GCD, 2020. Ministry of Social Affairs and Health, https://valtioneuvosto.fi/-/10616/valtioneuvoston-periaatepaatos-suunnitelmasta-koronakriisin-hallinnan-hybridistrategiaksi?languageId=en_US (accessed on 9 July 2020)

GHS Index, 2019. Available online: https://www.ghsindex.org/ (accessed on 29 June 2020)

HCP, 2019. Euro Health Consumer Index 2018, https://healthpowerhouse.com/media/EHCI-2018/EHCI-2018-report.pdf (accessed on 25 June 2020)

Keskimäki, I., et al., 2019. Finland: Health System Review. *Health Systems in Transition*, 21(2), pp. 1–166.

McAleer, M., 2020. Prevention Is Better Than the Cure: Risk Management of COVID-19. *Journal of Risk and Financial Management*, 13, 46.

Nieszporska, S., 2018. The Polish Healthcare System Towards the European Union Challenges. *On European Integration*, pp. 1084–1091.

OECD, 2019. State of Health in the EU, The Netherlands: Country Health Profile 2019, https://ec.europa.eu/health/sites/health/files/state/docs/2019_chp_nl_english.pdf (accessed on 25 June 2020)

OECD, 2019a. State of Health in the EU, Denmark: Country Health Profile 2019, https://ec.europa.eu/health/sites/health/files/state/docs/2019_chp_da_english.pdf (accessed on 25 June 2020)

OECD, 2019b. State of Health in the EU, Belgium: Country Health Profile 2019, https://ec.europa.eu/health/sites/health/files/state/docs/2019_chp_be_english.pdf (accessed on 25 June 2020)

OECD, 2019c. State of Health in the EU, Finland: Country Health Profile 2019, https://ec.europa.eu/health/sites/health/files/state/docs/2019_chp_fi_english.pdf (accessed on 25 June 2020)

OECD, 2019d. State of Health in the EU, Luxembourg: Country Health Profile 2019, https://ec.europa.eu/health/sites/health/files/state/docs/2019_chp_lu_english.pdf (accessed on 25 June 2020)

OECD, 2019e. State of Health in the EU, Sweden: Country Health Profile 2019, https://ec.europa.eu/health/sites/health/files/state/docs/2019_chp_sv_english.pdf (accessed on 25 June 2020)

OECD, 2019f. State of Health in the EU, Poland: Country Health Profile 2019, https://ec.europa.eu/health/sites/health/files/state/docs/2019_chp_poland_english.pdf (accessed on 25 June 2020)

Toebes, B., San Giorgi, M., 2014. Dutch Realities: Evaluating Health Care Reform in the Netherlands from a Human Rights Perspective. *In The Right to Health*, pp. 403–436.

Velavan, T. P., Meyer, C. G., 2020. The COVID-19 Epidemic. *Tropical Medicine & International Health*, 25(3), 278.

WHO, 2020a. WHO Coronavirus Disease (COVID-19) Dashboard, https://covid19.who.int/ (accessed on 9 July 2020)

WHO, 2020b. COVID-19 Health System Response Monitor, https://www.covid19healthsystem.org/mainpage.aspx (accessed on 11 July 2020)

Worldometer, 2020. Worldometer COVID-19 Data, https://www.worldometers.info/(accessed on 9 July 2020)

6 European alternative market behavior during the COVID-19 pandemic

Monika Mościbrodzka

Introduction

In Europe, the coronavirus epidemic started at the beginning of March 2020. The situation in European countries like Spain, Italy, Germany, France, and the United Kingdom worsened day after day, both in terms of the number of new cases and the death toll. However, Italy was the EU country that suffered the most; moments later, the frightening statistics were reported by other European countries as well.

The economic situation of individual countries was affected by the rising panic, on the one hand, and by all of the implemented restrictions and limitations, on the other hand. This referred to the national stock exchanges as well (Vasileiou, 2020). All of the stock exchanges around the world (essentially, stock investors) reacted in a similar manner to the information of the coronavirus pandemic (i.a., by selling their shares). According to experts, the smaller the market, the bigger the consequences of that sale; during moments of crisis, global investors tend to withdraw their investments from markets of lower sizes and liquidity (Gacki, 2020).

Studies on the impact of pandemics on stock market reactions have already appeared in the literature. Ambros et al. (2020) examined the impact of changes in COVID-19 news on eight different stock markets during the first two months of the coronavirus crisis in 2020. They did not find evidence that stock returns were sensitive to the changes in COVID-19 news, but there was strong evidence that changes in COVID-19 news increased stock market volatility in European markets. In the work of He et al. (2020b), the authors showed that COVID-19 had a negative but short-term impact on the data from stock markets in the People's Republic of China, Italy, South Korea, France, Spain, Germany, Japan, and the United States. However, there was no evidence that COVID-19 negatively affected these countries' stock markets more than the global average. Having said this, most analyses of this type that have been carried out have concerned only regulated markets.

This chapter focuses on the issue of how alternative markets reacted to the pandemic. Since alternative markets are less liquid than regulated markets, such markets are intended for small and medium enterprises that

DOI: 10.4324/9781003368687-6

have no possibility of raising capital through the introduction of shares into regulated markets. As reported by experts, small enterprises suffered the most during the pandemic. On the other hand, the biggest turnover in share trading was achieved by the innovative enterprises from biotechnological and gaming industries as well as by the companies that informed the public about their involvement in business that was focused on fighting coronavirus (which comprised the majority of the alternative markets at that time). Such conclusions are consistent with research on the impact of pandemics on market performance (He et al., 2020a).

Hence, the aim of this chapter is to provide an answer to the question of how (if at all) did the pandemic influence the behavior of European alternative markets. Since the market index is representative of the market condition, this value has been analyzed both in terms of the distribution of its rates of return and of the correlation with other stock indices that are typical of alternative trading systems (ATSs).

In the first section of this chapter, the behavior of the rates of return on particular indices was analyzed. It was also verified whether the pandemic had a significant impact on their distribution. Thereby, the aim of this section is to verify a hypothesis that the pandemic led to a decrease in the expected rates of return on stock indices, while the investment risk (measured by the standard deviation of the rates of return) increased. In the second part of this chapter, the short-term connections between the stock exchanges (expressed by the correlations between the rates of return on the main indices of individual stock exchanges) were analyzed. The purpose of this analysis was to verify a hypothesis that the "contagion effect," which occurred in several countries, was also observed on the markets of small and innovative companies; in other words, the effect of mutual "crisis contagion" that was related to the pandemic was also observed on alternative markets. The aim of the last part is to verify the hypothesis that the pandemic had a significant impact on the long-term relationships between stock exchanges.

The empirical research employs the daily continuously compounded rates of return on eight indices that represented the situation on alternative stock exchanges between May 9, 2018 and May 11, 2021. Despite the fact that these markets have been functioning in Europe for more than 20 years, they went under various transformations (including changes in their supervisory entities). Therefore, it was difficult to establish the common window function for the main indices that functioned at this moment on these markets. Certain exchanges did not have their main indices (for example, the Greek Alternative Market [ENA]), and other exchanges did not publish or defer the publications of their listings (for instance, the Cyprian Emerging Companies Market). In order to include the biggest number of ATSs into the analysis, the research period was narrowed down to a three-year period.

Alternative markets in Europe

Over the last decades, many changes have been observed on capital markets all around the world. Not only did financial instruments and investors evolve but also the institutions that provided the concentration of demand and supply through the organization of trading. Additionally, a noticeable increase in the propensity to risk-taking by investors could be observed during this period. These changes led to institutional innovations, followed by legislative changes; one such change was the ATS. Alternative financial markets, which offer the issuing and trading of securities for smaller entities, have been developing worldwide for more than 50 years. These markets are focused on providing access to capital for smaller and dynamically developing enterprises (which plan to undertake innovative and capital-intensive investments) as small- and medium-sized enterprises are sources of increases in innovation in all industries (Dibrell et al., 2008).

In various academic papers (e.g., Michelacci & Suarez, 2004), it is indicated that stock exchanges are significant factors that support quickly developing entrepreneurial companies and, despite certain limitations, possible benefits encourage entities to introduce their shares to public trading. Contrary to the American market, European exchanges never inclined to allow newly created companies to access the public market. However, the standards of the US financial system implied that the alternative platforms help businesses by facilitating their access to capital and by dealing with funding problems (Mendoza, 2008). According to the Federation of European Securities Exchanges, alternative markets or segments may be defined as markets that are organized according to different rules and regulations than in case of the main markets (FESE, 2008).

According to the concept of an alternative market, the promotion of entities with promising prospects of growth involves simplified formalities and lower entrance fees and costs that are related to the functioning on the market when compared to the primary stock market. The simpler and cheaper entrance procedures (which imply lower costs when raising capital) result in higher investment risk. However, this is compensated by the potentially high return that results from increasing stock prices (Hadro & Pauka, 2018).

Rates of return on stock index behavior

The time series that are related to financial data share certain features that distinguish them from other economic series. A precise description of these features may be found, i.a., in the works by Bollerslev (1994), Engle and Patton (2001), and Dempsey (2020). Starting from this point, we will focus on changes in the mutual behavior of time series on the financial market during the pandemic, namely, on the characteristic incidents that repeated on the market during the so-called crisis (stylized facts). The research sample was divided into two parts: the pre-pandemic period

(May 2018–December 2019) and the pandemic period (based on the time when the first cases of COVID-19 occurred in Europe).

The markets that are analyzed in this chapter are as follows (together with the country and the main index)[1]:

- Nasdaq First North (Sweden, Finland, Iceland, and Denmark; Index – First North All-Share);
- Mercado Alternativo Bursatil (Spain; Index – IBEX MAB All-Share);
- AIM Italia (Italy; Index – FTSE AIM Italia);
- AIM London (Great Britain; Index – FTSE AIM All-Share);
- Euronext Growth (Belgium, Portugal, and France; Index – Euronex Growth All-Share);
- Scale (Germany; Index – Scale All-Share Performance);
- NewConnect (Poland; Index – NCIndex);
- Axess (Norway; Index – Oslo Axess All-Share).

Although the number of European alternative markets is slightly greater, the analysis includes only those markets that had their own main indices.

The first stylized fact is an increase in the volatility of the rates of return during financial perturbations.

The values of the indices of individual alternative markets and their rates of return are presented in the diagrams in Figure 6.1. As it may be observed (and this refers to all of the analyzed stock indices), there was a decline in the index value at the beginning of 2020 (which lasted up to April 2020). On the other hand, one may notice a higher volatility of the rates of return during this period. However, it should be emphasized that this decline was recorded regardless of the previous tendencies of the indices. An interesting fact is that after April 2020, all of the indices recorded rapid increases in their prices, which may have indicated the short-term effect of the pandemic in the sector of small enterprises. Furthermore, increasing investor activity can be observed after the pandemic's outbreak on the exchanges from ATSs. According to Piotr Borowski (a member of the WSE Management Board), the most popular companies among investors on alternative markets are those that belong to the gaming, biotechnological, IT, and e-commerce sectors during times of pandemics.[2] Additionally, those companies that informed the market about their involvement in the fight against the coronavirus recorded more transactions on their shares during the pandemic. These were mainly small entities; therefore, their growing popularity among investors may have been immediately mirrored in the share prices on the markets from ATSs.

Another characteristic of the distribution of rates of return is the different market behaviors during "good" and "bad" times, which are related to the rise and decline in the rates of return. When considering the whole research period (Table 6.1), one may notice that the distribution of the

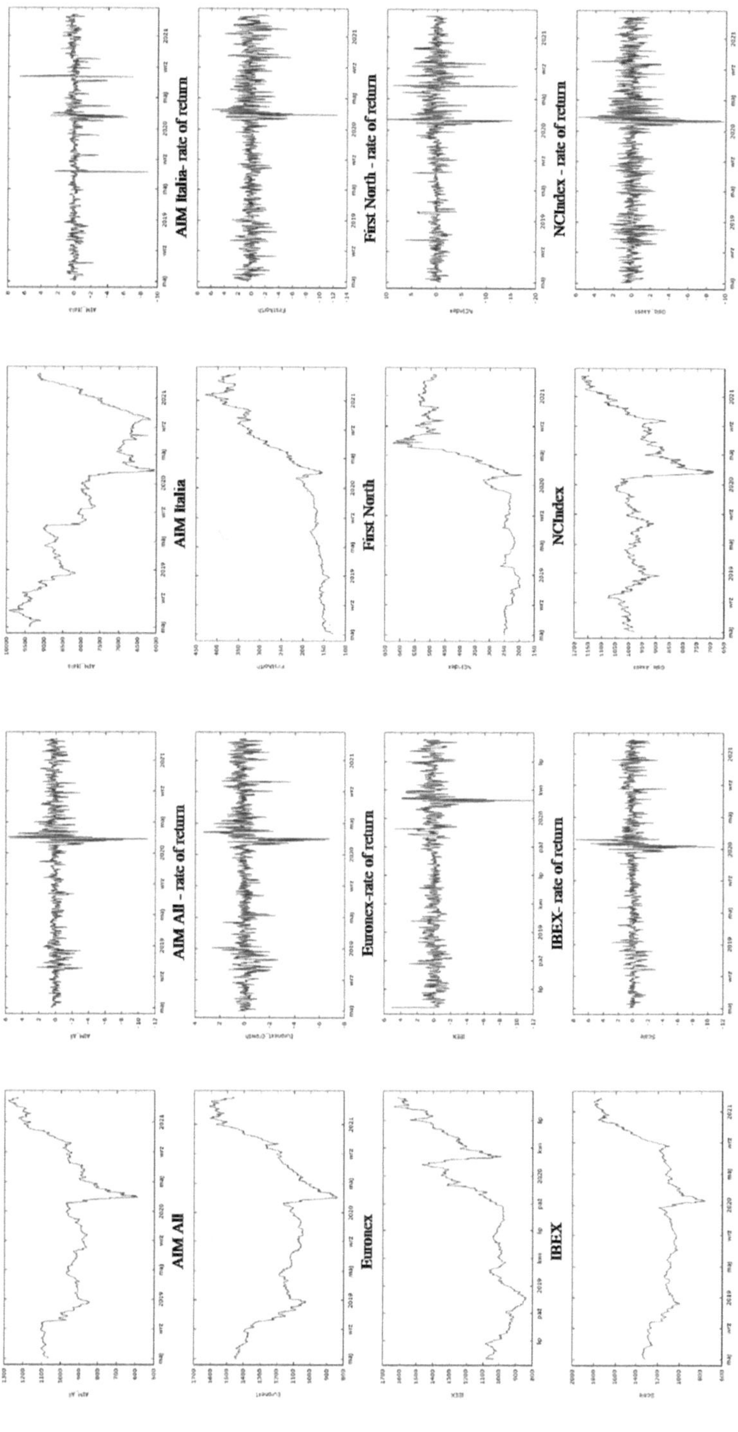

Figure 6.1 Stock indices and their rates of return between 09 May 2018 and 11 May 2021. ATS, alternative trading system.

Source: Own study based on the collected data available on the exchange websites of given ATS.

Table 6.1 Descriptive Statistics of Rates of Returns on Indices during Whole Research Period (Jointly Pre-Pandemic and Pandemic Period), Pre-Pandemic Period, and Pandemic Period

	Index	*Mean*	*Standard deviation*	*Median*	*Skewness*	*Kurtosis*	*Q1*	*Q3*	*IQR*	*Min*	*Max*
Total research period	IBEX	0.0736	1.1942	0.0513	−1.8620	20.6200	−0.4925	0.6468	1.1393	−11.9960	5.0686
	AIM_Italia	−0.0034	0.8747	0.0675	−2.9846	31.5260	−0.2433	0.3727	0.6160	−8.8867	6.7046
	AIM_All	0.0240	1.0950	0.1102	−2.3401	23.6320	−0.2513	0.4570	0.7083	−11.1000	5.7713
	FirstNorth	0.1451	1.4412	0.2230	−1.2404	9.3114	−0.5289	0.9306	1.4595	−12.5320	6.0532
	Euronext	0.0129	0.8271	0.0860	−1.9227	13.1300	−0.3289	0.4464	0.7753	−6.7828	3.3743
	Scale	0.0385	1.1525	0.0755	−1.5263	19.6230	−0.3629	0.5403	0.9033	−10.8850	7.7536
	NCIndex	0.0874	2.0180	0.0733	−1.5397	15.2290	−0.6501	0.8023	1.4524	−16.2520	9.9358
	Oslo Axess	0.0213	1.2653	0.0678	−1.4471	10.7020	−0.5146	0.6866	1.2011	−9.8320	5.8424
	Index	*Mean*	*Standard deviation*	*Median*	*Skewness*	*Kurtosis*	*Q1*	*Q3*	*IQR*	*Min*	*Max*
Pre-pandemic period	IBEX	0.0515	0.8842	−0.0351	1.0478	4.5825	−0.4753	0.4825	0.9577	−2.7711	5.0686
	AIM_Italia	−0.0375	0.6747	0.0090	−5.8036	71.4040	−0.2610	0.2705	0.5315	−8.8867	2.4847
	AIM_All	−0.0293	0.6565	0.0736	−1.1203	4.3453	−0.2769	0.3160	0.5929	−3.3865	2.3472
	FirstNorth	0.0812	1.0170	0.1532	−0.3976	1.1325	−0.4885	0.7268	1.2153	−3.7830	3.2358
	Euronext	−0.0722	0.6165	−0.0147	−0.5904	2.9898	−0.3785	0.2826	0.6611	−2.7268	2.6743
	Scale	−0.0375	0.6906	−0.0204	−0.3299	2.9319	−0.3602	0.3405	0.7006	−3.0472	2.9567
	NCIndex	−0.0058	1.1517	−0.0280	0.5307	4.4651	−0.5150	0.4836	0.9986	−4.1161	6.3269
	Oslo Axess	0.0153	0.9062	0.0644	−0.3703	1.0034	−0.4907	0.5679	1.0586	−3.6912	2.5282

	Index	*Mean*	*Standard deviation*	*Median*	*Skewness*	*Kurtosis*	*Q1*	*Q3*	*IQR*	*Min*	*Max*
Pandemic period	IBEX	0.1190	1.6604	0.2486	−2.5116	15.4600	−0.5250	0.9729	1.4979	−10.9960	3.9631
	AIM_Italia	0.0381	1.0684	0.1312	−1.9296	17.1420	−0.2228	0.4690	0.6918	−7.0195	6.7046
	AIM_All	0.0889	1.4595	0.1720	−2.1787	15.7580	−0.2228	0.6435	0.8663	−11.1000	5.7713
	FirstNorth	0.2229	1.8281	0.3478	−1.3557	7.3010	−0.5553	1.2335	1.7888	−12.5320	7.0532
	Euronext	0.1165	1.0181	0.2442	−2.3249	12.4540	−0.2141	0.6416	0.8557	−6.7828	3.3743
	Scale	0.1374	1.5568	0.2333	−1.5447	12.7500	−0.3781	0.8817	1.2598	−11.8850	7.7536
	NCIndex	0.2009	2.7211	0.2881	−1.5476	9.2260	−0.8035	1.4657	2.2692	−16.2520	9.9358
	Oslo Axess	0.0286	1.5985	0.1080	−1.5222	8.4866	−0.5680	0.8945	1.4625	−9.8320	5.8424

IQR, interquartile range.
Source: Own study.

rates of return is left-skewed, which was mirrored in the negative value of the skewness index. Similarly, half of the analyzed indices presented negative skewness in the distributions of their rates of return during the time before the pandemic outbreak. These were mainly those indices that recorded falling prices during this period. A similar reaction could be observed during the pandemic as all of the indices showed left-skewed distributions in their rates of return. However, the asymmetry was much stronger during the pandemic than during the whole period or to the pre-pandemic period for the majority of the indices. The left-skewed distributions of the rates of return meant that the returns grew slowly but declined rapidly. This is an undesirable situation from an investor's point of view as a rapid decline in returns means a rapid decline in possibilities of achieving high returns. Considering the fact that the vast majority of the indices presented stronger asymmetry during the pandemic than beforehand, it can be stated that the pandemic contributed to rapid declines in the investors' income in its early stages.

There were no significant differences in the rates of return that were achieved by the indices (which was confirmed by the significance test regarding the differences in the expected values); during the "crisis," however, all of the indices achieved higher average rates of return than during the period before the pandemic. The minimum rates of return were usually higher than the maximum in absolute terms.

Additionally, it can be observed that the spread of rates of return is much higher during times of market uncertainty.[3] For instance, the lowest rates of return were recorded in NewConnect (a decline of 16% in its index value within a single day), Nasdaq First North (a decline of more than 12% in its index value within a day), and German Scale (a decline of over 11% in its index value within a day). However, these markets also recorded the highest rates of return. This situation where the maximum positive and negative rates of return are achieved on the same markets may indicate market volatility and high investment risk. These observations were also confirmed by the values of the standard deviations of the rates of return and the value of the interquartile range. The behaviors of the rate-of-return distribution during the periods before and during the pandemic are shown in the diagrams in Figure 6.2.

Taking the hypothesis that refers to the impact of the pandemic on the distribution of the rates of return on the analyzed indices into account, it may be argued that the pandemic period did not have a negative influence on the returns that were expected by investors on ATSs. However, it led to an increase in the differentiations of the results that were achieved by certain exchanges, that is, to an increase in the level of the investment risk that was related to the indices that were listed on individual stock exchanges.

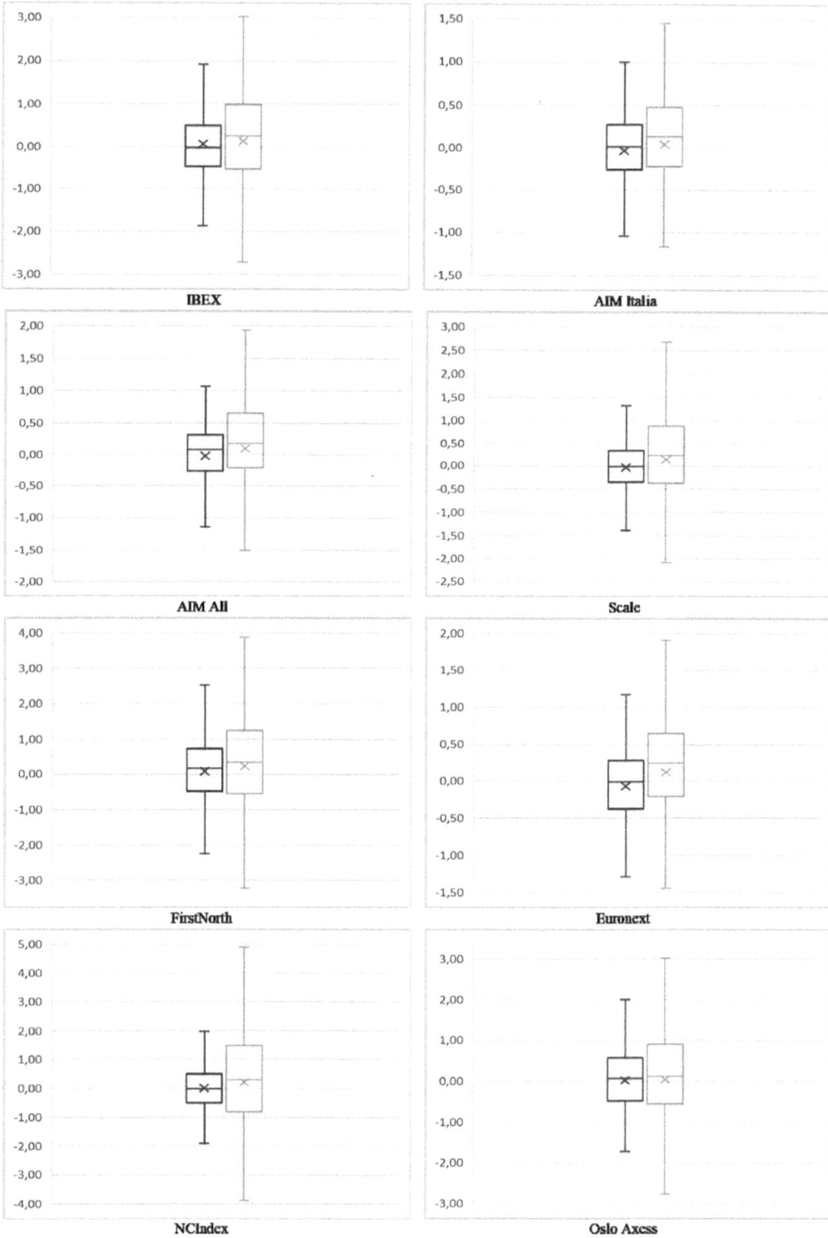

Figure 6.2 Box plots (without outliers) for the rates of return on ATS indices during the pre-pandemic period (left) and pandemic period (right). ATS, alternative trading system.

Source: Own study based on the data obtained from the Internet websites of individual exchanges from ATS.

Analysis of short- and long-term relationships between markets and crises in markets: research methodology

Adjusted correlation coefficient and significance tests

According to the definition that was proposed by the World Bank, one may speak of a contagion when market correlation becomes significantly stronger during a crisis than it is during normal calm periods. This definition refers to the financial volatility that is related to plenty of markets and results in considerable simultaneous price changes (Pericoli & Sbracia, 2003). Naturally, it cannot be stated that the pandemic led to market contagion; however, by employing the tools that were used for examining the "contagion effect," we can consider the influence that the pandemic spread on mutual relationships between markets of the same character. One of the tools that were applied for testing the financial market correlation changes was the Pearson correlation coefficient, which has been used for a long time (for example, Lee & Kim, 1993). In the work by Forbes & Rigobon (2002), however, it was indicated that this particular correlation coefficient is a positive variability function and may be the reason for overestimating the relationships between the rates of return during a crisis. Therefore, the authors proposed removing the influence of the heteroskedasticity of the variance from the correlation coefficient. Nowadays, there are two correlation measures that are employed in research on the market contagion effect. For the purpose of this research, the adjusted correlation coefficient that was suggested by Forbes and Rigobon (2002) will be applied:

$$\rho_k = \frac{\rho^h}{\sqrt{1+\left(\frac{\sigma_k^{2h}}{\sigma_k^{2l}}-1\right)\cdot\left(1-\left(\rho^h\right)^2\right)}}, \tag{6.1}$$

where

ρ_k is the adjusted correlation coefficient for stock market k,

σ_k^{2h} is the variance of returns on index from stock market k during the crisis period,

σ_k^{2l} is the variance of returns on index from stock market k during the pre-pandemic period, and

ρ^h is the conditional Pearson correlation coefficient for stock market k during the crisis period.

It should be noted that the adjusted correlation coefficient ρ_k was lower than the classic coefficient that was calculated during the crisis; therefore, the significance tests for the correlation coefficient change will refer to the adjusted coefficient during the pandemic period (ρ_k) and the relative correlation coefficient during the pre-pandemic period $\left(\rho^{s}\right)$. Hence, the testing will refer to the following hypothesis:

$$\begin{aligned} &H_0\text{: } \rho_k \le \rho^{s}; \\ &H_1\text{: } \rho_k > \rho^{s}. \end{aligned} \tag{6.2}$$

This test may be based on the FR_1 statistic with a normal distribution, which was proposed by Forbes and Rigobon (2002):

$$FR_1 = \frac{0.5 \cdot \ln\left(\dfrac{1+\hat{\rho}_k}{1-\hat{\rho}_k}\right) - 0.5 \cdot \ln\left(\dfrac{1+\hat{\rho}^{s}}{1-\hat{\rho}^{s}}\right)}{\sqrt{\dfrac{1}{T_k - 3} + \dfrac{1}{T_s - 3}}}. \tag{6.3}$$

If these tests show no grounds for rejecting H_0, this means that an increased correlation coefficient is the result of the mutual relationships between the rates of return. On the other hand, rejecting H_0 denotes the significant process of the rate of return contagion.

Time series stationarity and cointegration models

Although the method of estimating the cointegrating vectors (Longin & Solnik, 1995) is not directly related to the "contagion effect," it enables the long-term analysis of cross-market relationships. Hence, a hypothesis on whether the pandemic had an influence on the long-term relationships between the markets can be verified by employing this method.

The first step of examining a long-term relationship is to verify the stationarity of the analyzed time series. Due to the wide employment of cointegration tests, they will not be discussed in this chapter; further information can be found in the works by Dickey & Fuller (1981), Charemza & Deadman (1992), Enders (1995), and Min (2019). This chapter employs the Dickey–Fuller unit root test (Dickey & Fuller, 1981), according to which no grounds for rejecting the null hypothesis denote that the time series is nonstationary (has a unit root); hence, it is integrated by at least order 1.

Variables X and Y are cointegrated if it is possible to find a linear combination of those that will be stationary. Such equations are called cointegrating, and the vector of the equation's parameters is calles a cointegrating vector. An important fact is that cointegration is a method that is used to describe long-term equilibrium; this means that if variables $Y, X \sim I(1)$ are cointegrated with the cointegrating vector, then the relationship may be presented by the error–correction mechanism (ECM) (Johansen, 1998):

$$\Delta y_t = \alpha\left(y_t - \beta x_t\right) + \sum_{i=1}^{r} \gamma_i \Delta x_{t-i} + \sum_{i=1}^{r} \theta_i \Delta y_{t-i} + \varepsilon_t, \tag{6.4}$$

where residual $\varepsilon_t \sim I(0)$.

The error–correction model attempts to connect the descriptions of the long-run state of equilibrium with a short-run states of non-equilibrium. Hence, defining the cointegrating vectors in such a model may result in the assumption of long-run causal connections between the variables in the model (Welfe, 2003).

Changes in relationships between alternative markets: research results

Assessment of significance of market "contagion effect" during the pandemic

The adjusted correlation coefficient is asymmetric as it is based on the volatility of the rates of return on the indices of a given country. Additionally, this coefficient for each country was twice as low, on average, as the conditional correlation coefficient that was calculated for the pandemic period (for example, the Pearson coefficient between NCIndex and FirstNorth was 0.6391, but the adjusted correlation coefficient for these stock exchanges was 0.4522).

The values of the correlation coefficient during the pre-pandemic period were very low in absolute terms (for the pre-pandemic period, these coefficients were between -0.0768 [NCIndex and IBEX] and 0.2196 [FirstNorth and AIM All]). This may suggest that there was no significant short-term relationship between the rates of return on the AST indices that could be observed. However, these values increased during the crisis (for the pandemic period, the conditional correlation coefficients were between -0.1573 [NCIndex and Euronext] and 0.6391 [NCIndex and FirstNorth]). In order to evaluate whether the rise was an effect of the pandemic or of the stronger relationships, the values of the FR_1 test statistics were calculated.[4]

The market that was most affected by the pandemic crisis was the Polish alternative market, which reacted to the situations on the Italian, Spanish, and Scandinavian markets (which was confirmed by the high values of the respective test statistics of 2.5648 [$p < 0.01$], 1.9017 [$p < 0.05$], and 4.4795 [$p < 0.01$]). Presumably, this was a result of the rapid spread of the COVID-19 pandemic in these countries. The fact that the crisis caused NewConnect to develop in this particular direction may have been the effect of the sequence of confirmed COVID-19 cases in the individual countries – in Poland, the first cases of COVID-19 that were recorded after Italy, Spain, and Finland confirmed their cases. A significant level of contagion could also be observed between the Spanish alternative stock exchange and Nasdaq First North (2.1704 [$p < 0.05$]) as well as Euronext and the London AIM (1.2938 [$p < 0.1$]). In the cases of the other alternative stock exchanges, noticeable effects of the pandemic were apparent.

Furthermore, some countries recorded drops in the correlation coefficients between the rates of return on their indices (negative values) during the pandemic; this was related to the mutual relationships of the rates of return. Possibly, this resulted from the different operating methods that were employed by investors during the pandemic. Although the spread of the virus led to a greater volatility in the share prices and mobilized investors to boost their engagement, such index behavior may be related to the spheres of the business of the companies that were listed on these stock exchanges in the cases of ATSs. These were innovative companies that operated in the biotechnological and gaming industries as well as those companies that informed the market about actions that were related to the fight against the coronavirus.

Pandemic and long-term cross-market relationships

Two types of processes were chosen for the long-term analysis between markets: the closing prices and the opening prices of the markets on the following day. Thus, the long-term effect of the closing of the ATS markets on the previous day on the opening of the other analyzed markets will be studied.

In order to confirm "the common random walk" of the processes (in other words, their long-run relationships), the stationarity of these processes needs to be pre-examined. For this purpose, the unit root Dickey–Fuller test was conducted, and the order of integration of the processes was determined[5] – both during the pre-pandemic period and over the whole research period.

The analysis of the variables' order of integration gave conclusive results for the given time series. Based on the p-values for the ADF test, one can assume that all of the analyzed processes presented unit roots in the cases of their levels regardless of the time period. This means that the order of integrating the time series was at least 1. Simultaneously, the grounds for rejecting the null hypothesis in the ADF test for the first differences in the variables confirmed their stationarity. Hence. the processes were integrated at a level of order 1.

An analysis of the mutual correlograms between the variables enabled the determination of the initial level of the lag at a maximum that was equal to 2 for all of the analyzed processes.[6] Hence, it was essential to estimate the models of the relationships between the variables and examine the stationarity of their residuals in the next step (Engle & Granger, 1987).

This part of the research considered the relationships between each of the individual pairs of indices. This enabled an evaluation of the possible long-term equilibrium for the isolated variables (without the influence of other indices). Table 6.2 presents the unit root test *p*-values for the residuals in the models among the pairs of indices. If the residuals were stationary, then it may be assumed that the starting indices "walked together

Table 6.2 ADF Test *p*-Values for Residuals in Models between Indices on Markets from ATSs (Influence of Previous Day's Closing Prices on Opening Price on Given Day) and EC1 Parameter Value Together with Its Significance in Cointegrating Model between ATS Indices

	ADF test p-values							
Total period (*)	**IBEX**	**AIM_Italia**	**AIM_All**	**Scale**	**FirstNorth**	**Euronext**	**NCIndex**	**Oslo Axess**
IBEX	X	0.0245	0.0359	0.0275	0.2776	0.0467	0.0369	0.0484
AIM_Italia	0.0047	X	0.0025	0.0015	0.0003	0.0211	0.1565	0.0432
AIM_All	0.0216	0.0032	X	0.0005	0.0007	0.0102	0.0121	0.0184
Scale	0.1813	0.0026	0.0011	X	0.0028	0.0014	0.1063	0.0250
FirstNorth	0.0257	0.0001	0.0002	0.0002	X	0.0003	0.3695	0.0004
Euronext	0.2632	0.1076	0.0296	0.0026	0.0263	X	0.9547	0.2430
NCIndex	0.0014	0.0011	0.0004	0.0004	0.0221	0.0011	X	0.0000
Oslo Axess	0.1269	0.0297	0.1755	0.0292	0.1081	0.0436	0.1206	X
Pre-pandemic period (*)	**IBEX**	**AIM_Italia**	**AIM_All**	**Scale**	**FirstNorth**	**Euronext**	**NCIndex**	**Oslo Axess**
IBEX	X	0.5661	0.8701	0.7455	0.1081	0.8216	0.6397	0.1756
AIM_Italia	0.0429	X	0.1086	0.0185	0.0299	0.0196	0.3165	0.1070
AIM_All	0.1764	0.1916	X	0.0013	0.1364	0.0007	0.1041	0.1225
Scale	0.0467	0.0068	0.0010	X	0.1185	0.0194	0.1953	0.1344
FirstNorth	0.0005	0.0132	0.1743	0.1872	X	0.1110	0.1974	0.0001
Euronext	0.0219	0.0087	0.0003	0.0087	0.1096	X	0.2651	0.1049
NCIndex	0.0157	0.1758	0.0380	0.1838	0.1556	0.1019	X	0.0125
Oslo Axess	0.0120	0.3081	0.7174	0.6209	0.0007	0.6525	0.3406	X

ECM parameter value

total period (*)	IBEX	AIM_Italia	AIM_All	Scale	FirstNorth	Euronext	NCIndex	Oslo Axess
IBEX	X	-0.0092***	-0.0046***	-0.0036***	-	-0.0047***	-0.0107*	-0.0067**
AIM_Italia	-0.0072*	X	-0.0199**	-0.0206**	-0.0064	-0.0142**	-	-0.0036
AIM_All	-0.0075***	-0.0143**	X	-0.0521***	-0.0124***	-0.0231***	-0.0062**	-0.0049*
Scale	-	-0.0087	0.0006	X	-0.0137**	-0.0048	-	-0.0061***
FirstNorth	-0.0138*	-0.0221**	-0.0082*	-0.0080**	X	-0.0148***	-	-0.0175**
Euronext	-	-	-0.0533**	-0.0591***	-0.0111***	X	-	-
NCIndex	-0.0298**	-0.0235***	-0.0220***	-0.0221***	-0.0207***	-0.0235**	X	-0.0243***
Oslo Axess	-	-0.0084	-	-0.0049	-	-0.0074	-	X
pre-pandemic period	**IBEX**	**AIM_Italia**	**AIM_All**	**Scale**	**FirstNorth**	**Euronext**	**NCIndex**	**Oslo Axess**
IBEX	X	-	-	-	-	-	-	-
AIM_Italia	-0.0002*	X	-	-0.0128	-0.0080	-0.0119	-	-
AIM_All	-	-	X		-		-	-
Scale	-	-0.0146***	-0.0132***	X	-	-0.0134***	-	-
FirstNorth	-0.0255**	-0.0247**	-	-	X	-	-	-0.0265***
Euronext	-0.0088***	-0.0119**	-0.0119***	-0.0118***	-	X	-	-
NCIndex	-0.0277***	-	-0.0282***	-	-	-	X	-0.0278***
Oslo Axess	-0.0087**	-	-	-	-0.00178	-	-	X

(*)– the first column contains dependent variables
*– significance at the level of 10%, **– significance at the level of 5%, ***– significance at the level of 1%
Source: Own study.

randomly" in the sense that the difference between them was stationary. In other words, they were so correlated that they would not scatter in time even though there was a trend in each index. Hence, it will be possible to claim that these indices were cointegrated.

Table 6.2 also presents the results that were obtained from the estimation of the ECM parameter in a cointegrating equation after the correction of the specification for the given indices as well. The conducted analysis of the cointegration showed that long-term cross-market relationships exist. For example, Polish NewConnect is in a long-term relationship with the London market (the influence of the previous day's closing prices of AIM on the opening prices of NewConnect on a given day). The structure of NewConnect is built on the concept of London AIM; therefore, the majority of the solutions that are applied on these markets are similar. In this case, the negative value of the ECM parameter ensures the returning to the state of equilibrium of a pair of indices. Additionally, this value means that the daily changes in the NCIndex value may be explained by nearly 3% through the long-run relationship with AIM All. Similar long-run relationships can be observed between NewConnect and the Spanish and Norwich stock exchanges. It should also be noticed that big stock exchanges such as the London or Spanish markets did not cointegrate with any European stock exchange; they set the trends for other markets from ATSs. In the cases of these big markets, however, changes in the long-term relationships can be observed when analyzing the total research period. It is entirely visible that the pandemic influenced the long-term relationships on the stock exchanges. Even on the big alternative stock exchanges were companies affected by the climates of other countries – countries that before had no impact on the directions of their development. Only the Norwich stock exchange changed their direction of growth, becoming somehow independent of the other European ATSs. It can be also observed that the long-term relationships changed in the case of the German Scala, i.e., the German Scala index changed its direction on a long-term heading toward a state of equilibrium with the Scandinavian stock exchanges.

Conclusions

During the pandemic period, the organization of the process of issuing shares was technically more difficult because of the restrictions and major share prices fluctuations on the stock exchanges. On the other hand, the competition between the companies that aimed to gain funding on the capital market was less intense. However, another characteristic feature of the pandemic period was the appearance of a great number of new investors on the stock market. In order to compensate for the losses that resulted from the pandemic, these investors planned to increase their capital relatively quickly by investing in small stock markets. The success of such small markets was strictly related to the biotechnological and gaming companies as these companies recorded increases during the pandemic. According to experts, these exact sectors were the driving forces of the alternative markets.

As shown by the analysis, small stock exchanges did not fall into crisis because of the pandemic despite the initial market turmoil. Although there was a noticeable increase in the volatility of the rates of return during this period (which can be understood as an increase in investment risk), there was no significant change in the average rates of return that were achieved by ATSs. It should be emphasized that the distribution of the majority of the indices was much more left-skewed during the pandemic; this suggests that this period had an influence on the rapid decline in the investors' returns. Nevertheless, this might have been the result of a series of drops in the values of the indices at the beginning of the pandemic.

For Polish NewConnect and Scandinavian First North, the "contagion effect" was visible as a result of the "pandemic crisis." The Polish market was mostly affected by Italian, Spanish, and Scandinavian markets, whereas First North was mostly affected by the Spanish market. Nevertheless, there were no noticeable effects of the pandemic in the short-run relationships of the majority of the alternative stock markets. Furthermore, certain countries recorded declines in the correlation coefficient values between the returns of the indices during the pandemic period; in other words, the short-run relationships between these markets were weaker. However, the pandemic influenced the long-term relationships among the markets. Analyses of both the pre-pandemic and total periods displayed other long-term relationships among the small stock markets. This may imply a change in the long-run influences that the individual markets had on each other as a result of this situation. This is important for those who invest in risky stocks by analyzing the behavior of similar assets that are listed on leading markets. When the interconnections between stock markets change, such an analysis may be ineffective and may not guarantee returns that are in line with expectations.

It should be also noted that a global assessment of the pandemic's influence on the behavior of the alternative markets should be conducted after the pandemic ends. Since the pandemic period that was included in the above analysis was not long, one may expect that the results would change when the pandemic period was extended. Supposedly, the initial successes of small stock markets and the fact that they managed the current situation were only short-term effects. In order to see the whole picture, one should wait until the end of the COVID-19 pandemic; then, a further already planned analysis will surely be conducted.

Notes

1 *Analysis based on the data from Internet websites:* www.nasdaqomxnordic.com, www.cse.com.cy, www.oslobors.no; www.newconnect.pl; www.deutsche-

boerse.com, www.euronext.com, www.londonstockexchange.com, www.borsaitaliana.it, www.bolsamadrid.es.
2 https://biznes.wprost.pl/technologie/10341399/pandemia-byla-czasem-zniw-dla-branzy-gier-newconnect-z-ogromnym-wzrostem.html.
3 As the tests that were performed are standard statistical procedures, the results are not included in this chapter.
4 Due to editorial limitations, the test results can be made available on request.
5 Due to editorial limitations, the test results can be made available on request.
6 By virtue of editorial limits and the technical aspect of the analysis, this part is not included.

References

Ambros, M., Frenkel, M., Huynh, T.L.D., Kilinc, M. (2020) COVID-19 pandemic news and stock market reaction during the onset of the crisis: evidence from high-frequency data, *Applied Economics Letters*, 28 (19), 1–4, https://www.tandfonline.com/doi/epub/10.1080/13504851.2020.1851643?needAccess=true

Bollerslev, T., Engle, R.F., Nelson, D.B. (1994) *ARCH models*, in: Engle, R.F., McFadden, D. (eds), *Handbook of Econometrics*, vol. 4, Elesevier Science B.V., Amsterdam, The Netherlands, 2959–3038.

Charemza, W.W., Deadman, D.F. (1992) *New Directions in Econometric Practise*, Edward Elgar, Cheltenham.

Dempsey, M. (2020) *Investment Analysis. A Introduction to Portfolio Theory and Management*, Routledge, London.

Dibrell, D., Davis, P. Craig, J. (2008) Fueling innovation through information technology in SMEs, *Journal of Small Business Management*, 46(2), 203–218.

Dickey, D.A., Fuller, W.A. (1981) Likelihood ratio statistics for autoregressive time series with a unit root, *Econometrica*, 49, 1057–1072.

Enders, W. (1995) *Applied Econometric Time Series*, John Wiley & Sons, New York.

Engle, R.F., Granger, C.W.J. (1987) Co-integration and error correction: representation, estimation and testing, *Econometrica*, 55, 251–276.

Engle, R.F., Patton, A.J. (2001) What good is a volatility model?, *Quantitative Finance*, 1(2), 237–245.

FESE (2008) *Alternative Markets/Segments in Equity Analysis*, FESE Economics and Statistics Committee.

Forbes, K.J., Rigobon, R. (2002) No contagion, only interdependence: measuring stock market comovements, *The Journal of Finance*, 57(5), 2223–2261.

Gacki, M. (2020) *W czasach pandemii współodpowiedzialność zyskuje na znaczeniu*, wywiad z członkiem zarządu *Giełdy Papierów Wartościowych- Piotrem Borowskim*, https://polishbrief.pl/news/4776/borowski_w_czasach_pandemii_wspolodpowiedzialnosc_zyskuje_na_znaczeniu_wywiad.

Hadro, D., Pauka, M. (2018) *Reakcje cenowe w debiucie na NewConnect. Znaczenie asymetrii informacji*, Wydawnictwo Uniwersytetu Ekonomicznego we Wrocławiu, Wroclaw

He, P., Sun, Y., Zhang, Y., Li, T. (2020a) COVID–19's impact on stock prices across different sectors—An event study based on the chinese stock market, *Emerging Markets Finance and Trade*, 56(10), Special Issue: Research on Pandemics, 2198–2212.

He, Q., Liu, J., Wang, S., Yu, J. (2020b) The impact of COVID-19 on stock markets, *Economic and Political Studies*, 8, 275–288.

Johansen, S. (1988) Statistical analysis of cointegration vectors, *Journal of Economic Dynamics and Control*, 12, 231–254.

Lee, S.B., Kim, K.J. (1993) Does the October 1987 crash strengthen the co-movements among National Stock Markets?, *Review of Financial Economics*, 3, 89–102.

Longin, F.M., Solnik, B. (1995) Is the correlation in international equity returns constant: 1960–1990?, *Journal of International Money and Finance*, 14(1), 3–26.

Mendoza, J.M. (2008) Securities regulation in low-tier listing venues: the rise of the alternative investment market, *Fordham Journal Corporate & Financial Low*, 12(2), 257–328.

Michelacci, C., Suarez, J. (2004) Business creation and the stock market, *Review of Economic Studies*, 71(2), 459–481.

Min, C.-K. (2019) *Applied Econometrics. A Practical Guide*, Routledge, London.

Pericoli, M., Sbracia, M. (2003) A primer on financial contagion, *Journal of Economic Surveys*, Wiley Blackwell, 17(4), 571–608.

Vasileiou, E. (2020) Behavioral finance and market efficiency in the time of the COVID-19 pandemic: does fear drive the market?, *International Review of Applied Economics*, 35, 224–241.

Welfe, A. (2003) *Ekonometria. Metody i ich zastosowanie*, PWE, Warszawa

Websites

www.bolsamadrid.es
www.borsaitaliana.it
www.deutsche-boerse.com
www.euronext.com
www.londonstockexchange.com
www.nasdaqomxnordic.com
www.newconnect.pl
www.oslobors.no

7 Impact of COVID-19 pandemic on international trade in 2020 with regard to COVID-19-related medical products – case of Poland

Joanna Brzyska and Izabela Szamrej-Baran

Introduction

The end of the second decade of the 21st century turned out to be unique in the world economy. The SARS-CoV-2 virus spread to all of the inhabited continents; this was the reason that the WHO announced the COVID-19 pandemic on March 11, 2020 (WHO, 2020). At the time of this chapter's finalization, the number of infected people exceeded 246 million, with nearly 5 million deaths (CSSE JHU, 2021).

For the first time, economies almost all over the world were in lockdown due to the outbreak of the pandemic; it was an unprecedented occurrence; never before had economies been closed to such a large scale. Additionally, it took place in a world where globalization is very advanced (Mahyudin, 2019). At the beginning of 2020, a lockdown occurred in the regions of China where the COVID-19 pandemic developed; by March, the authorities of many nations decided to close their countries. They introduced export prohibitions and restrictions as an immediate response to the pandemic (BDI, 2020). The consequences of these actions were quite far-reaching. Many people lost their jobs, economic activity was significantly reduced, and many supply chains were disrupted (Harjoto and Rossi, 2021). As a result, the GDPs of a large number of countries decreased (Ibn-Mohammed et al., 2021). The closure of economies also had a major impact on international trade. In a world that is characterized by integrated and often just-in-time manufacturing processes, these caused marked reductions in the supplies of manufactured goods (Barlow et al., 2021). There was a drastic reduction in trade interconnectedness, connectivity, and density among the countries after the COVID-19 outbreak (Vidya, 2020; Wenjing et al., 2020).

A side effect of a lockdown is that it causes disruptions in international supply chains. Countries that have highly open economies and are heavily dependent on foreign trade were more negatively affected by the

DOI: 10.4324/9781003368687-7

pandemic than countries with less openness. Service-oriented economies in particular were negatively affected by the crisis (Fernandes, 2020). Due to Syed Sharfuddin, a new international order will be redrawn by the most powerful countries in a post-COVID-19 world, taking the lessons that have been learned in dealing with the current pandemic into account (Sharfuddin, 2020). Developing countries with low GDP growths, high debt, and increased dependence on oil and essential technologies will find it difficult to maintain independent foreign policies. Furthermore, the role of international institutions will be critically reviewed.

Moreover, it will play a major role in all aspects of life in commerce and e-governance as well as in education, health, and artificial intelligence. The COVID-19 pandemic has had a huge impact on the labor market; it has caused a revolution in the ways that companies and employees work. The lockdowns resulted in massive layoffs and increased unemployment in most countries; however, these redundancies did not affect all industries alike (Barlow et al., 2021; Dube et al., 2020a, 2020b). More at-risk jobs could be found in service-oriented economies (Fernandes, 2020). Countries with higher GDPs per capita that were the hardest hit by the coronavirus will have to make changes to their labor systems in order to minimize the fallout (Marti et al., 2021), although COVID-19 has had a significant positive impact on new job openings in the gig economy (Umar et al., 2020). Moreover, the importance of remote working has significantly increased (de Lucas Ancillo, 2020).

The objective of this chapter is to present and evaluate the impact of the COVID-19 pandemic on international trade. There were defined trends in Polish foreign trade as compared to selected economies and the world, with a particular focus on trade in COVID-19-related goods.

Methods of descriptive statistics were used in this chapter (in particular, dynamics and trend analyses). This study was conducted for the quarters of the years 2005–2020. In the third part of the chapter on medical supplies that are related to COVID-19, monthly data from the Eurostat database were used and then converted to quarterly data. The sources of data that are presented in this chapter are the WTO, OECD.Stat, Statistics Poland, and Eurostat databases.

Trends in international trade in goods

At the beginning of the 21st century, world trade was characterized by positive growth. At the end of 2008, it was abruptly interrupted by the outbreak of the global financial crisis. There was a large decline (25%); however, it was relatively short. It was one of the greatest collapses in world trade – comparable to the oil crisis of 1973 and the Great Depression of 1929 (Irwin and O'Rourke, 2011). The next decade was characterized by a systematic increase in world trade, which was interrupted by a slightly longer but smaller decline during the period of 2015–2016 (13%). Furthermore, there was again an upward trend in the second half of the second decade of the 21st century.

Poland's exports largely coincided with the trend of increasing world trade. However, the growth rate of Polish exports exceeded the growth rate of global trade. As a result, Poland's share in international trade increased from 0.9 to 1.4% during the period of 2005–2019.

The situation has changed in 2020; the pandemic outbreak triggered a decline in global trade. In the first quarter, there was a very large decrease in international trade (by as much as 7% than in the first quarter of 2019); in the second quarter, however, international exchange collapsed when the economies were closed. The rate of decline was more than three times higher than in the previous quarter. Numerous forecasts were rather pessimistic and pointed to a huge decline in world trade. According to the UNCTAD's nowcast, the decrease in international trade would be greater than during the crisis of 2008 – more than a quarter of the trade value (UNCTAD, 2020a; Baldwin, 2020). The WTO projected two scenarios of changes in trade volumes. In the optimistic version, the drop in 2020 would amount to 13%, while in the pessimistic scenario as much as a 32% drop (WTO, 2020a). The OECD also assumed two scenarios of projecting changes in the global exports of goods and services, making them dependent on a potential second outbreak. In the single-hit scenario, global exports in 2020 would drop by 6% and in the double-hit scenario by 7.6% (OECD, 2020a).

The pessimistic character of the forecasts can be quite easily explained. Nowadays, countries are very closely interlinked. During the age of globalization, intra-industry trade is of great significance; this in turn relies on international supply chains (Sajjad, 2021). It is enough to tear down just one link to stop all production and trade. Without specific components, it is impossible to produce final products. Therefore, the closure of the economies of most countries resulted in a sudden and significant reduction in production and, therefore, a large drop in international trade.

However, the pessimistic nature of these forecasts turned out to be slightly exaggerated. The second semester of 2020 brought a marked recovery in international trade. Already in the summer, foreign trade turnover increased significantly (by as much as 20% as compared to the spring quarter). In the autumn, the upward trend of trade was maintained; however, the growth rate slowed down quite significantly (so much so that it was not possible to reach the volume of global exports from 2019). The upward trend continued in the fourth quarter, indicating a recovery in trade. The dynamics of this growth slowed considerably, but the second wave of the COVID-19 pandemic (which took place in the fall of 2020) no longer had as strong of an impact on reducing global trade as the first wave did in the spring. Moreover, the declines in the first half of 2020 were greater than the increases in the second half of the year. As a result, the world's commodity market turnover was still lower than in 2019 during the third and fourth quarters of 2020. However, it should be noted that the difference was relatively small, which may seem quite surprising. This indicates the great strength of international trade and proves that, even under difficult pandemic conditions, it can recover quickly. The current forecast for trade development is much more optimistic. On the one hand, the experience and lessons learned from the first wave of the pandemic allow for a more flexible adaptation to the pandemic situation, while on the other hand mass vaccination has been an important activity that slowed down the development of the pandemic.

At the end of 2020, the WTO revised its forecast of changes in world trade, finding that the drop in goods trade would be less severe than predicted (9.2%). The WTO in turn predicted that global trade would grow by 7.2% in 2021 (WTO, 2020c). The OECD was slightly more cautious and forecasted a slightly lower growth (4.4%) (OECD, 2021). On the other hand, UNCTAD revised the decline in global exports to 9% for 2020 and predicted that, during the first quarter of 2021, the rebound in trade would continue (although it would slow down) (UNCTAD, 2021).

Poland's foreign trade trends were very similar to those of global trade, with the difference that they were slightly shifted in time and characterized by a little more intensity. While global exports fell by 10% in the first quarter of 2020, Poland's exports remained stable; it was only in the second quarter that it experienced a very high decline. Compared to the global trade, however, the dynamics of these changes were higher; in the second quarter, the decline of exports in Poland was nearly 18%, while in global exports it was 13%. In the third and fourth quarters of 2020, on the other hand, exports rebounded, with their rate of growth exceeding the global average.

Declines in foreign trade during the second quarter of 2020 were recorded by almost all countries (see Figure 7.1). China, the largest global supplier of goods to the world market, distinguished itself against this background. Indeed, China's exports remained at a similar level relative to the second quarter of 2019 and even increased slightly (0.1%). Among the EU countries, an upward trend was recorded only in Cyprus. Moreover, this also occurred in Chile, Paraguay, the Kyrgyz Republic, and Tanzania. Except for the last two countries, this was rather small (less than 5%). However, the high export growth dynamics in the Kyrgyz Republic (14%) and Tanzania (60%) were related not so much to the increase in the volume of exchange and booming trade as to the significant changes in the price of gold, which is an important group of goods in the exports of these countries. In the remaining countries, there was a downward trend.

Relatively small drops took place in Switzerland, Chinese Taipei, Ireland, Vietnam, New Zealand, and Brazil, where they did not exceed 10%. Stronger declines (between 10 and 20%) were noted in nearly half of the EU countries; however, the largest EU economies were not among them.

Figure 7.1 Changes in the world exports during the COVID pandemic (second quarter 2020 to second quarter 2019, %).

A 17% drop in foreign sales was recorded in Poland. Less than 20% reductions in exports were also observed in the Baltic states, Austria, Denmark, the Netherlands, Bulgaria, Croatia, Slovenia, and Sweden.

Important global exporters experienced a much more severe reduction in international trade. Exports by the United States fell by 30%, while those by Japan, the United Kingdom, and Germany fell by around 25%. In addition, oil-producing countries suffered huge declines; these were mainly caused by the changes in oil prices. For the first time, there was an unprecedented event, namely negative spot prices for these commodities.

When comparing the exports of selected countries at the beginning of 2020 with those of 2015[1] and 2019, one can see that the decreases after the COVID-19 pandemic outbreak were quite large, especially in the spring. While the value of world trade was 6% lower in the first quarter of 2020 than it was in the first quarter of 2019, a 6% growth was recorded as compared to the first quarter of 2015. However, the situation was completely different for global trade during the second quarter of 2020. Deep declines were not only noticed when compared to the same period of the previous year but also to five years earlier (although slightly smaller). During the third quarter of 2020, the situation improved, while during the last quarter the growth rate changed most favorably.

The worst situation among the analyzed countries was in Russia, where the downward trend in exports was the strongest (mainly due to low oil prices); only a slight improvement was noted in the third quarter. A large reduction in exports took place in France and India, but the situation improved over the second half of the year. There was a clear rebound in

Table 7.1 Indices of Dynamics of Exports in Selected Economies: 2015–2020

Country/ Region	*Q1 2020 (Q1 2015 = 100)*	*Q2 2020 (Q2 2015 = 100)*	*Q3 2020 (Q3 2015 = 100)*	*Q4 2020 (Q4 2015 = 100)*	*Q1 2020 (Q1 2019 = 100)*	*Q2 2020 (Q2 2019 = 100)*	*Q3 2020 (Q3 2019 = 100)*	*Q4 2020 (Q4 2019 = 100)*
World	106	89	110	121	93	79	96	103
China	93	112	119	128	86	100	108	117
European Union	115	89	114	125	95	76	98	106
France	103	72	100	111	89	64	90	99
Germany	109	83	106	118	94	75	96	106
India	106	77	111	119	87	64	95	96
Japan	104	86	101	119	96	76	88	103
Poland	134	110	144	156	99	83	109	116
Russia	99	77	100	117	87	69	77	84
United Kingdom	94	72	83	95	88	73	87	92
United States	105	75	95	106	96	70	87	94

Source: Own elaboration based on WTO database – https://data.wto.org/ (accessed: 03.02.2022).
USD, Seasonally Adjusted.

exports during the third quarter of 2020. In the fourth quarter, exports continued their upward trend – the greatest increases occurred in China and Poland. Although nearly half of the analyzed countries failed to reach the level of exports from a year earlier, increases over the level from five years earlier predominated (see Table 7.1).

Similar changes for exports occurred on the import side as well. During the first quarter of 2020, declines in imports to the analyzed countries were still moderate. Changes in imports also affected China. However, they were already much larger in the second quarter of 2020. These also occurred in Poland and were higher as compared to its exports. A huge drop in imports (by more than half) was recorded in India. However, the third quarter of 2020 brought a marked increase in trade to all of the analyzed countries except for Japan, where a rebound only occurred toward the end of the year. During the fourth quarter of 2020, most countries had already recorded an upward trend as compared to the same period a year earlier (as was the case on the import side). If we compare the volume of imports with that of five years ago, it increased in all of the analyzed countries, especially in Poland.

Changes in the sectoral composition of world trade in goods

The changes that were brought about by the COVID-19 pandemic did not merely consist of a reduction in international trade. They also resulted in significant changes in the structure of the trade. However, the reductions were not evenly distributed across all sectors; some sectors experienced deep declines, others had less trade reduction, and (contrarily) international trade increased in some sectors.

A large decrease in global trade occurred primarily in the trade in manufactured goods and resources and was significantly smaller in agricultural goods. The low rate of decline of the latter was mainly because agricultural products are considered essential goods for life and the greater tendency to purchase these goods due to the uncertainty about the future (Hayakawa and Mukunoki, 2020).

The biggest falls were noted in the automotive sector. Although the first quarter of 2020 brought an 8% reduction in trade, in the second quarter it decreased almost by half. At the same time, the drop in foreign trade in the automotive sector was even greater in Poland. Such large drops are mainly due to supply and demand shocks (Rio-Chanona et al., 2020). The closures of factories as a result of the lockdowns resulted in the suspension of production and interruption of supplies. On the other hand, consumers and investors began to look for and increase their savings during the time of the developing crisis and, as a result, postponed their decisions to buy vehicles – just like with many other manufactured goods (e.g., electrical machinery and precision instruments). An exception in this regard was the trade in office machinery, which grew throughout most of 2020. This can be explained by the fact that, in a very short period, there was a change from stationary to remote work on a very large scale. This was often associated with the need to purchase equipment that enabled remote working. In Poland, a high increase in the import of office machinery was recorded during this period.

The COVID-19 pandemic also led to a very high level of uncertainty in the resources market. In March 2020, an unprecedented occurrence took place, with negative oil prices on international markets (The World Bank, 2020). The lockdown of many economies resulted in a drop in demand for energy commodities and very large price fluctuations, which caused very high declines in the dynamics of trade in these products.

The group of goods that increased in trade during the COVID-19 pandemic in Poland was medical and pharmaceutical products. During the whole year of 2020, the growth of exports was very high (as was that of imports). It was a natural increase in demand for medical products – especially those that were meant for prevention, testing, and treatment.

International trade of COVID-19-related medical goods in Poland

In 2020, the coronavirus continued to spread throughout the globe. The rise in the number of cases and deaths led to an understandable increase in governments' interest in taking protective measures to stop the pandemic. A crucial concern was enabling those medical products that were essential to the fight against COVID-19. This resulted in a natural increase in demand for medical products, especially those that were meant for prevention, testing, and treatment. Some of these products were in critically short supply – the measures were difficult to access and their prices were very high. This was especially applicable to personal protective equipment – masks, gloves, and disinfectants but also various medical devices (ventilators, multiparametric patient monitoring devices, and infrared thermometers). For example, COVID-19 caused a remarkable shortage in the supply of face masks. At the beginning of the COVID-19 crisis, China was the main producer of surgical masks – supplying about half of the world's supply (OECD, 2020b); however, this was not enough to meet the demand in January 2020 – China manufactured about 20 million masks per day, yet needed around 240 million per day. So, they stopped exporting masks and imported 56 million masks during the first week of January; some masks were also donated to China by some countries (OECD, 2020c). In February 2020, China increased its production to around 116 million per day and started to export masks to other countries.

The trade of products that were described as critical and in severe shortage during the COVID-19 crisis equaled about $597 billion (or 1.7% of the total world trade in 2019) (WTO, 2020b). Many of these are manufactured in numerous countries, and trade is a way to ensure global supply. The ten largest supplying economies accounted for almost 75% of the total world exports of medical products; the top three (Germany, the United States, and Switzerland) supplied slightly more than one-third of the world's medical products (UNCTAD, 2020b).

In 2019, the imports and exports of medical products amounted to about $2 trillion (including intra-EU trade), which accounted for 5.3% of the total world trade of goods (WTO, 2020b). In 2020, the imports and exports of medical goods increased by 16% as compared to the previous year. In contrast, the total value of the world's merchandise trade contracted by 7.6% in 2020.

Over the past five years, the growth trend in the extra-EU trade of medical goods that were relevant to COVID-19 was even faster, with an average annual increase of 10–11%. In 2020, EU-extra exports and imports increased by 74% and 64%, respectively, as compared to 2015. When compared to 2019, however, there was less growth in the exports (5%) and imports (10%) of medical goods, although it should be noted that the total EU exports and imports declined (9.4 and 11.6%, respectively). Thus, the increases that were observed in the trade of medical goods became more significant and indicated the growing demand for these types of goods.

The increase in the value of the foreign trade of medical goods in Poland was significant in 2020. Between 2015 and 2020, imports of these products grew at an average annual rate that was faster than in the European Union (12.9%), reaching a level that was 83% higher in 2020 than it was in 2015. Exports also grew at a similar annual rate (12.2%) and were 78% higher in 2020 than they were in 2015. When comparing 2020 to 2019, Polish exports of medical goods that were related to COVID-19 increased by 19.5% and imports increased by 15%. It should be highlighted that, during the same period, Polish total exports decreased by 0.6%, and the country's imports decreased by more than 5%. An important distinction between the Polish and EU data was that the European Union had a foreign trade surplus during the years under review while Poland had a deficit.

Polish imports of medical goods that were related to COVID-19 were 20–40% greater than exports during the period of 2018–2020. Slight increases in demand for medical goods occurred during all quarters of 2020 as compared to the previous periods; especially high import values were recorded during the first and fourth quarters of 2020. In the second quarter, there was a decrease in the value of imports as compared to the previous quarter; this was caused by the fact that most global economies experienced lockdowns due to the pandemic. Nevertheless, the value of imports still increased by 7.4% in this quarter as compared to the second quarter of the previous year. This is a very significant result, especially when considering that Polish imports fell by 23% in the second quarter of 2020 as compared to the second quarter of 2019.

The indicators of the dynamics of the Polish exports of medical goods were at an even better position, especially during the last two quarters of 2020. There was a 24% increase in exports in the first quarter of 2020 (30% for imports), a 7% increase in the second quarter (7% for imports), a 22% increase in the third quarter (9% for imports), and a 23% increase in the fourth quarter (13% for imports) as compared to the corresponding quarters of the previous year.

In the group of medical goods that were related to COVID-19, several subgroups could be distinguished: test kits and equipment for diagnostic testing, protective garments, disinfectants and sterilization products, oxygen therapy equipment, medical consumables, vehicles, and other medical devices. These groups did not note the same changes in international trade. There was an increased demand for kits and equipment for testing for COVID-19 in 2020 – both in Poland and other countries. This was shown by the significant increases in the values of the Polish imports and exports of COVID-19-related medical goods. For the imports, the highest values were recorded during the second and fourth quarters of 2020. In the second quarter of 2020, there was more than a two-fold increase in the value of the imports as compared to the second quarter of 2019. For the whole of 2020, the value of the imports increased by more than 70% as compared to 2019; when compared to 2015, the increase in the imports in this section was more than 250%.

In all of the quarters of 2020, the values of the exports of test kits and equipment for diagnostic testing remained at similar levels (€280–310 million). The exports of products from this group were more than two times greater in the first and second quarters of 2020 than in the first and second quarters of 2017 and 2019 and more than four times greater than in the first and second quarters of 2018. Comparing the fourth quarter of 2020 to the same quarter in 2017, we can notice more than a five-fold increase in the values of these exports.

The second group was protective garments. In 2019, Poland was ranked tenth on the list of the top exporters of personal protective products (WTO, 2020b). The value of the exports of these products grew steadily until the first quarter of 2020 when it reached nearly €600 million – slightly higher than the value of the imports in that quarter. During the next quarter, this fell to €508 million (a 15% decline); however, it was still higher than during the same quarter of the previous year. It then grew at a quarterly rate of more than 15% until it reached its highest value during the entire considered period in the fourth quarter of 2020. The value of the imports grew the fastest during the second through the fourth quarters of 2020 (at a quarterly rate of about 16%). On an annual basis, the imports were growing progressively faster in the subsequent quarters of 2020 as compared to the corresponding quarters from a year earlier, starting with a growth of

8% in the first quarter, 15% in the second quarter, 23% in the third quarter, and more than 40% in the fourth quarter.

In the next group – disinfectants and sterilization products – there were no clear change patterns. Before 2020, these imports were generally lower during the first two quarters of each year and higher during the last two quarters; in 2020, however, this pattern did not occur. In the second quarter of 2020, there was a significant increase in the value of the imports, and in the following quarters, it remained high after a slight decrease. It should be mentioned here that the demand for disinfectants and sterilizers was huge; due to the limited supply, however, their prices were very high, and purchase limits appeared. In Poland, this enormous demand for disinfectants was complemented by the launch of additional domestic production (KGHM, ORLEN). This production was extensive enough to increase the export values, which were the highest in the entire dataset during the fourth quarter of 2020. The export value in this quarter was higher by an impressive 25% than the import value.

The fourth group covered oxygen therapy equipment: artificial respiration apparatus, pulse oximeters, and the like. The imports of such equipment oscillated between €150 and €200 million during the years 2017–2019; the only outlier during the examined period occurred in the second quarter of 2018, where the imports approached the €250-million level. The year 2020 differed from previous years. In the first quarter, the value of the imports was 10–25% higher than in previous years. In contrast, there was a significant collapse in the value of imports during the second quarter, which was likely caused by the lockdowns of economies. The following quarters showed significant increases in the value of the imports of products from oxygen therapy equipment. The data for the exports followed a similar trend. The values of the imports and exports were the highest in the reported period during the fourth quarter of 2020 and exceeded 62% and 73%, respectively, of the corresponding values for the previous year.

The fifth group – various medical devices (including CT scanners, Multichannel Pulswave Monitor devices, infrared thermometers, ultrasonic scanning apparatus, and the like) – were appliances whose purchases are usually planned and placed in the financial plan of a unit. Therefore, it was difficult to find homogeneous trends here. The most characteristic here was the significant reduction in the values of the imports and exports during the second quarter of 2020. For the export data, an increase in exports was recorded during the third and fourth quarters of 2020 for most of these devices. The value of the exports was the highest in the entire studied period during the fourth quarter of 2020.

The imports and exports of the sixth group (which included wadding, gauze, bandages, syringes and needles, paper bed sheets, plastic bags, soap, and the like) increased. In the fourth quarter of 2020, these imports reached a record value of nearly €1.8 billion. The Polish exports of this group were as much as two to three times higher than the imports.

Conclusions

The outbreak of the COVID-19 pandemic had a very large impact on global trade. During the first half of 2020, there were very large drops in trade. Fortunately, the first very pessimistic forecasts did not come true. Although declines that were greater than those during the 2008 financial crisis were expected, the reduction in trade was not so large. The second quarter was the worst; but by the third quarter, there was a significant rebound in exports. During the fourth quarter, the upward trend continued (although much more slowly).

The downward trend in foreign trade affected not all countries to the same extent. The biggest winner was China, which had already seen its exports fall during the first quarter. In the second quarter of 2020, however (as the rest of the world plunged), China's exports grew, and this trend strengthened in the following quarters. The foreign sales of the world's largest exporters (i.e., the United States, Japan, and Germany) fell by more than 25%, and those of Poland fell by 17%. The export growth during the second half of the year indicated a clear improvement in the trade situation, but it was not large enough to compensate for the declines from the first half of the year. The worst scenarios did not come true. Extensive experience from the first wave of the pandemic (and the lessons learned on its basis) allowed for the more flexible adjustment of the trade situation to the changing situation on the international market.

Despite the emergence of the second wave of the pandemic, foreign trade experienced a gradual recovery. During the second half of 2020, the situation in international trade began to improve, and turnover grew again (but not fast enough to compensate for the declines from the first half of the year). The worst-case scenarios did not materialize. The experience that was gained from the first wave of the pandemic (and the lessons that were learned from it) allowed trade to adapt more flexibly to the changing international market situation.

Not all groups were affected by declines to the same extent. Exports fell the most in the automotive, energy (mainly as a result of large drops in prices), and machinery sectors. Countries that specialized in exporting these goods were more strongly affected by the negative impact of the COVID-19 pandemic on exports. However, exports grew in the group of goods that allowed for remote work: office machinery and communication equipment. The same was true for goods that were intended to fight against the pandemic (medicinal and pharmaceutical products).

The share of medical products that were related to COVID-19 in global trade increased by nearly 50% in 2020. This phenomenon was observed in the European Union as well as in Poland. Oxygen therapy machines, test kits, and protective garments were characterized by particularly high export and import dynamics.

There were high declines in imports and exports of goods during the second quarter of 2020, while COVID-19-related medical product trade experienced only a slight slowdown; however, the values were still higher than in previous years in most cases. During the subsequent quarters of 2020, demand for these products increased significantly, resulting in high growth rates. The fight against the pandemic is still ongoing, so the continued trend of the growth of COVID-19 medical goods is expected in global trade.

Note

1 The years of 2019 and 2015 were chosen by the authors to make comparisons with the previous year and the five-year period. The choice of 2015 was also supported by the fact that, in 2015, the values of Polish exports were relatively low and constituted a good basis for comparisons.

References

Baldwin R. (2020) *Research-based policy analysis and commentary from leading economists*, https://voxeu.org/article/greater-trade-collapse-2020 (Accessed: 5 November 2021).

Barlow P., CI van Schalkwyk M., McKee M., Labonté R., Stuckler D. (2021) COVID-19 and the collapse of global trade: building an effective public health response, *The Lancet Planetary Health*, 5, pp. 102–107, https://doi.org/10.1016/S2542–5196(20)30291-6.

BDI Bundesverband der Deutschen Industrie (2020) Export controls and export bans over the course of the COVID-19 pandemic. Export restrictions impair ability to respond to the crisis, https://english.bdi.eu/publication/news/export-controls-and-export-bans-over-the-course-of-the-covid-19-pandemic/ (Accessed: 5 November 2021).

CSSE JHU. (2021) COVID-19 dashboard by the Center for Systems Science and Engineering at Johns Hopkins University, https://gisanddata.maps.arcgis.com/apps/opsdashboard/index.html#/bda7594740fd40299423467b48e9ecf6 (Accessed: 5 November 2021).

de Lucas Ancillo A., del Val Núñez M.T., Sorin Gavrila S. (2020) Workplace change within the COVID-19 context: a grounded theory approach, *Economic Research-Ekonomska Istraživanja*, 34:1, pp. 2297–2316, https://doi.org/10.1080/1331677X.2020.1862689.

Dube K., Nhamo G., Chikodzi D. (2020a) COVID-19 cripples global restaurant and hospitality industry, *Current Issues in Tourism*, 24:11, pp. 1487–1490, https://doi.org/10.1080/13683500.2020.1773416.

Dube K., Nhamo G., Chikodzi D. (2020b) Impact of COVID-19 on the global network of airports. In: *Counting the Cost of COVID-19 on the Global Tourism Industry*. Springer, Cham, pp. 109–133 https://doi.org/10.1007/978-3-030-56231-1_5.

Fernandes N. (2020) Economic effects of coronavirus outbreak (COVID-19) on the world economy. IESE Business School Working Paper No. WP-1240-E, Available at SSRN: https://ssrn.com/abstract=3557504 (Accessed: 5 November 2021) http://doi.org/10.2139/ssrn.3557504.

Harjoto M.A., Rossi F. (2023), Market reaction to the COVID-19 pandemic: evidence from emerging markets, *International Journal of Emerging Markets*, 18:1, pp. 173–199,ahead-of-print, https://doi.org/10.1108/IJOEM-05-2020-0545.

Hayakawa K., Mukunoki H. (2021) Impact of COVID-19 on international trade: evidence from the first shock *Journal of the Japanese and International Economies*, 60, p. 101135, https://doi.org/10.1016/j.jjie.2021.101135.

Ibn-Mohammed T., Mustapha K.B., Godsell J., Adamu Z., Babatunde K.A., Akintade D.D., Acquaye A., Fujii H., Ndiaye M.M., Yamoah F.A., Koh S.C.L. (2021) A critical analysis of the impacts of COVID-19 on the global economy and ecosystems and opportunities for circular economy strategies, *Resources, Conservation & Recycling*, 164, January 2021, p. 105169, https://doi.org/10.1016/j.resconrec.2020.105169.

Irwin D.A., O'Rourke K.H. (2011) Coping with shock and shifts: the multilateral trading system in historical perspective. National Bureau of Economic Research, Working Paper 17598, Cambridge, http://www.nber.org/papers/w17598.

Mahyudin A. (2019) Globalisation, economic growth, and spillovers: a spatial analysis. *The Journal of Applies Economic Research*, 13:3, pp. 255–267, https://doi.org/10.1177/2347631119841257.

Marti L., Puertas R. (2021) European countries' vulnerability to COVID-19: multicriteria decision-making techniques, *Economic Research-Ekonomska Istraživanja*, 34:1, pp. 3309–3320, https://doi.org/10.1080/1331677X.2021.1874462.

OECD (2020a) *OECD Economic Outlook*, Volume 2020, No. 107, OECD Publishing, Paris, https://doi.org/10.1787/0d1d1e2e-en.

OECD (2020b) *The face mask global value chain in the COVID-19 outbreak: evidence and policy lessons*, 4 May, http://www.oecd.org/coronavirus/policy-responses/the-face-mask-global-value-chain-in-the-covid-19-outbreak-evidence-and-policy-lessons-a4df866d/#boxnote-d1e71 (Accessed: 5 November 2021).

OECD (2020c) *COVID-19 and international trade. Issues and actions*, 12 June, http://www.oecd.org/coronavirus/policy-responses/covid-19-and-international-trade-issues-and-actions-494da2fa/#back-endnotea0z4 (Accessed: 5 November 2021).

OECD (2021) *Trade in goods and services forecast*, https://data.oecd.org/trade/trade-in-goods-and-services-forecast.htm (Accessed: 5 November 2021).

Rio-Chanona R.M. del, Mealy P., Pichler A., Lafond F., Farmer J.D. (2020), Supply and demand shocks in the COVID-19 pandemic: an industry and occupation perspective, *Oxford Review of Economic Policy*, 36:Supplement_1, pp. S94–S137, https://doi.org/10.1093/oxrep/graa033.

Sajjad A. (2021) The COVID-19 pandemic, social sustainability and global supply chain resilience: a review, *Corporate Governance*, 21:6, pp. 1142–1154, https://doi.org/10.1108/CG-12-2020-0554.

Sharfuddin S. (2020) The world after Covid-19, The Round Table. *The Commonwealth Journal of International Affairs*, 109:3, pp. 247–257, https://doi.org/10.1080/00358533.2020.1760498.

The World Bank (2020) *The Economy in The Time of COVID-19*, April 2020 (Accessed: 5 November 2021).

Umar M., Xu Y., Mirza S.S. (2020) The impact of COVID –19 on Gig economy, *Economic Research-Ekonomska Istraživanja*, 34:1, pp. 2284–2296, https://doi.org/10.1080/1331677X.2020.1862688 (Accessed: 5 November 2021).

UNCTAD (2020a) *Global trade update*, https://unctad.org/en/PublicationsLibrary/ditcmisc2020d2_en.pdf (Accessed: 5 November 2021).

UNCTAD (2020b) *How COVID-19 is changing the world: a statistical perspective*, Committee for the Coordination of Statistical Activities, https://unstats.un-.org/unsd/ccsa/documents/covid19-report-ccsa.pdf (Accessed: 5 November 2021).

UNCTAD (2021) *Global trade update*, https://unctad.org/system/files/official-document/ditcinf2021d1_en.pdf (Accessed: 5 November 2021).

Vidya C.T., Prabheesh K.P. (2020) Implications of COVID-19 pandemic on the global trade networks, *Emerging Markets Finance and Trade*, 56:10, pp. 2408–2421, https://doi.org/10.1080/1540496X.2020.1785426.

Wenjing D., Shujin Z., Mingyong L. (2020) The impact of COVID-19 on China's trade and outward FDI and related countermeasures, *Journal of Chinese Economic and Business Studies*, 18:4, pp. 355–364, https://doi.org/10.1080/14765284.2020.1855395.

WHO (2020) *WHO announces COVID-19 outbreak a pandemic*, https://www.euro.who.int/en/health-topics/health-emergencies/coronavirus-covid-19/news/news/2020/3/who-announces-covid-19-outbreak-a-pandemic (Accessed: 5 November 2021).

WTO (2020a) *Trade falls steeply in first half of 2020*, https://www.wto.org/english/news_e/pres20_e/pr858_e.htm. (Accessed: 5 November 2021).

WTO (2020b) *Trade in medical goods in the context of tackling COVID-19*. Information note, 3 April, https://www.wto.org/english/news_e/news20_e/rese_03apr20_e.pdf (Accessed: 5 November 2021).

WTO (2020c) *Trade shows signs of rebound from COVID-19, Recovery still uncertain*. Press Release 862, https://www.wto.org/english/news_e/pres20_e/pr862_e.htm (Accessed: 5 November 2021).

8 Public support for enterprise operation in Poland in conditions of crisis caused by SARS-COV-2 pandemic

Katarzyna Sieradzka and Radosław Luft

Introduction

The SARS-COV-2pandemic descended on the world in 2019. The crisis has affected everybody: households, enterprises, institutions, and national governments. The emergence of the pandemic triggered a crisis situation in the real economy, as well. GNPs, consumption, and investments have declinedwhile unemployment, inflation, budget deficits, and public debt have soared. The steps that were taken by the particular governments (primarily as parts of a variety of fiscal policies) have been designed to limit social and economic consequences,first of all by protecting workplaces and enterprises. The Polish government prepared and approved the so-called anti-crisis and financial shields for businesses that have sufferedfrom the COVID-19 crisis.

This paper aims to analyze and assess the instruments of enterprise support in Poland during the COVID-19 pandemic. The following Research Hypothesis H1 is advanced: *Financial support is a major factor of support for enterprise operations under the conditions of the crisis that was caused by the COVID-19 pandemic.*

The results of research into 350 enterprises that are active in Polish economy and exploratory factor analysis are applied to verify the hypothesis. The data areanalyzed by means of Statistica 12 software.

Theoretical background

The crisis denotes a situation where the fundamental values, interests, and objectives of social groups, organizations, enterprises, and states or life, property, civil rights, and liberties are jeopardized. From an economic point of view, a crisis means an economic collapse under the effect of wrong investments and decisions (Rothbard, 2010; Czech et al., 2020, p. 10) and a dramatic contraction of economic activities in both enterprises and entire economies. Economic crises are unpredictable even though their presence is natural. In broader terms, a crisis is associated not only with

DOI: 10.4324/9781003368687-8

slower economic growth but also with widened income inequalities, the escalating instability of the financial sector, environmental issues, andthe contraction of social and human capital (Horodecka, 2017, pp. 211–238).

Disasters and crises worldwide contribute not only to tangible and financial losses but also to a sense of insecurity and continuing stress (Economou et al., 2013, pp. 308–314). Threats are classified as extreme with very high (even disastrous) impacts and intensities, including natural disasters, epidemics, and wars (Ficoń, 2007). The COVID-19 pandemic is an instance of extreme danger that has led to an economic, social, and environmental crisis.

The outbreak of the COVID-19 epidemic that was caused by the SARS-CoV-2 coronavirus in China has been widely commented on and analyzed by researchers, governments, and public opinion. The rapid global spread of the virus caused the World Health Organization (WHO) to categorize it as a pandemic (Maier, Brockamnn, 2020, 742–746). It is the fifth pandemic in the 21st century (WEF, 2020). It is described as the most severe crisis since the Second World War (Boccaletti et al., 2020). The COVID-19 pandemic is often referred to as a black swan event (Antipova, 2020; Platje, 2020; Brzeziński et al., 2021, p. 916), although this view is not shared by the author of the term (Taleb, 2007; Avishai, 2020) nor by many others (McGillivray, 2020; Drake, 2021; Simianer, Reimer, 2021) who point out that the pandemic had been forecasted (Jones et al., 2008; Morse et al., 2012; Walsh, 2017).

It is emphasized that the global economy is facing at least three major crises. A pandemic-induced health crisis has rapidly ignited an economic crisis with yet-unknown consequences for financial stability, and all of this is playing out against the backdrop of a climate crisis that cannot be addressed by "business as usual" (Mazzucato, 2020). Government responses to the COVID-19 pandemic have indicated some tensions and decision-making problems in the search for a consensus between economic and health objectives (Jones et al., 2008; Correia et al., 2020; Laurent, 2020; Ma et al., 2020). The effects of COVID-19 are said to be far graver than those of the 2008–2009 credit crunch (Grzeszczak et al., 2020, p. 4) and comparable to the Great Depression of the 1930s (OECD, 2020); therefore, it can be called a great compression (Harvey, 2020, p. 8). Carmen and Vincent Reinhart claimed that the world economy was not going to return to its pre-pandemic condition while the effects of the stimulation and repair packages were unsatisfactory (Reinhart, 2020).

The persistent SARS-CoV-2 endemic has given rise to a recession in both the United States, the eurozone, and the whole global economy. Many governments have introduced severe restrictions on social and economic activities and barriers to travel. The realization of the European Union state authorities' decisions in response to the spread of the COVID-19 virus has considerably and adversely affected the economic situations in particular countries. In light of the National Office of Statistics GUS (2021) figures, the Polish GNP in 2020 shrank by 2.8% as compared to 2019 (after a 4.5% rise in 2019), domestic demand fell by 3.7%, investments dropped by 8.4%, and private consumption fell by 3.0%. However, the recession in Poland is seen as one of the shallowest in Europe – the European Union's GNP diminished by 6.3%–and of the eurozone'sdropped by 6.8%. The recession was most severe in Greece and Spain, where their GNPs decreased by 10% and 11%, respectively. The OECD forecast (2021) that the GNP growth in Poland would amount to 5.3% in 2021, 5.3% in 2022, and 3.3% in 2023. Consumption and investments are to be the main drivers of growth. The OECD forecast points to higher economic activity in the world economy: a 5.6% increase in 2021, 4.5% in 2022, and 3.2% in 2023.

The crisis that was triggered by the spread of the SARS-CoV-2 virus is exceptional since it did not originate in the capital market. It is both demand- and supply-based (Fornaro, Wolf, 2020). The following long-term consequences of COVID-19 have been indicated (Osiński, 2021):

- impairment of long-term economic dynamics and lower real natural rates of interest;
- greater risk of entrenched excessive debts of public and private sectors;
- entrenched environment of low interest rates and consequent risks;
- enhanced 'moral hazard' as a source of systemic risk;
- structural changes in financial markets that boost the likelihood of their instability;
- greater risk of financing a substantial part of the commercial real estate market;
- greater cyber risks.

COVID-19 has posed some enormous challenges to small- and medium-sized enterprises (SMEs) all around the world. 'SMEs have suffered more because of their lack of resilience and flexibility in the face of large environmental shocks. Moreover, SMEs tend to be more vulnerable to external environmental tremors because of a lack of liquid and nonliquid resources compared to large firms' (Trawnih et al., 2021, p. 1). The lockdown measures that were imposed by governments across the globe caused significant harm to SMEs during the COVID-19 pandemic to the point of questioning their survival (Papadopoulos et al., 2020). A number of impediments to enterprise operation have been identified, including the following (OECD, 2020a): interrupted chains of supply, cash flow problems, and the impossibility of keeping deadlines. The resulting lower demand for imported goods and services, a growing reluctance to take risks in financial markets (OECD, 2020b), and reduced business confidence will have a substantial effect on enterprises and their chains of supply (OECD, 2020c). Some digital transformation issues (a challenge to small businesses) are raised as well (Hossain et al., 2020; Papadopolous et al., 2020).

The chief burden of counteracting the consequences of the pandemic rests on the states, with governments launching simulation packages ($2.2 in the United Statesand €1.1 billion in Germany), and on central banks (e.g., the Federal Reserved System [an unlimited program of share buy-outs], or the ECB [a plan of asset purchasing worth €750 billion with the option of expanding it]). The European Unionhas aided the efforts of its member states while the IMF and World Bank have offered easier access to financing for developing states (Wnukowski, Wąsowski, 2020). The following characteristics of the European aid packages are pointed out (Piłat et al., 2021):

- high homogeneity of proposed aid;
- guarantees account for more than 60% of the overall value of aid – aid packages equal to 20–40% of GNP;
- universal use of domestic development institutions (in the capacity of lenders or credit guarantors);
- subsidies are primarily taken advantage of by SMEs;
- broad range of fiscal policy solutions (including reduced rates of taxation and more flexible methods and times of settlements).

The research into the support programs for business in OECD countries (OECD, 2020d) has indicatedthat governments have commonly applied programs that are designed to maintain jobs, financial liquidity, subsidies, and tax reliefs. Financial support (first of all, credit guarantees, credits, and loans to SMEs) is a substantial part of the aid.

A comparative analysis of the aid packages in European states (Piłat et al., 2021) has identified their homogeneity. However, these vary across the markets to which they apply, the characteristics of a given economy, and the weights or locations of the sectors that have been most affected by the pandemic. They are suited to the legal and financial system of a given country. Job protection through wage subsidies or exemptions from contribution payments (e.g., Italy) or outpayments of most wages (the United Kingdom) is characteristic of European programs. SMEs and the self-employed have been helped in all of the reviewed European countries. In Spain and the Netherlands, the range of guarantees and tax solutions to large enterprises has been limited, whereas SMEs can take the advantage of subsidy instruments. The pandemic has mostly affected the following sectors in all of these countries: tourism and hotels, catering, entertainment, sports, and education. Some sectors that are specific to certain countries require particular assistance, like gardening in the Netherlands or fishing in Sweden. Subsidies and modifications to tax legislation are most frequently offered to entrepreneurs in the most severely affected industries (e.g., lower VAT rates for tourism in the United Kingdom).

To alleviate the economic effects of the COVID-19 pandemic crisis, the government in Poland prepared and passed an aid package in 2020 that consisted of sixanti-crisis shields and a financial shield. The support totaled PLN 162.9 billion in 2020 and was distributed via the following institutions: the Polish Development Fund (PLN 62.6 billion), Bank Gospodarstwa Krajowego (PLN 54.2 billion), the National Insurance Company (PLN 18.6 billion), the Ministry of Development, Labor, and Technology (PLN 27.4 billion), and the Industrial Development Agency (PLN 0.152 billion) (Dębkowska et al., 2021, p. 4).

As initially announced by the government, the support program for the Polish economy projected outpayments of more than PLN 212 billion. It was stressed that too little spending was earmarked directly for the protection of jobs and income guarantees for workers and other groups. A considerable part of the program tended to assure the liquidity of the financial sector and introduce bank guarantees to preserve business solvency (Męcina, Potocki, 2020, p. 7). In the face of rising public expectations, the postulates of entrepreneurs and trade unions, and political suggestions, the government continued to initiate more aid in the form of successive anti-crisis shields. The total support was estimated to be more than PLN 300 billion in 2020–2021, including PLN 212 billion for job and economy protection and PLN 100 billion under the financial shield (www.gov.pl).

A Lewiatan Confederation study in March 2020 (Męcina, 2020a, pp. 37–40) suggested that most firms suffered distinctly adverse effects fromthe first shock of the pandemic. The research confirmed thatthe smaller the firm, the more serious the consequences were felt to be. A full 69% of businesses reaffirmed their intentions of firing workers. More than 60% declared that the government instruments would help finance the costs of idle time and limit redundancies. Another Lewiatan study from-July 2020 (Męcina, 2020b, pp. 28–34) concerned the conclusions that entrepreneurs drew from the pandemic. Asked about their opinions about the government's actions during the pandemic, the entrepreneurs pointed to the clear and comprehensible information from the government on the one hand and the absence of a clear strategy of economic support for the coming months and leaving businesses to their own devices on the other; this highlightedthe limited government dialog with the business community. As far as the most useful anti-crisis shield instruments were concerned, Marć, Skowron (2020), Męcina (2020b), and Dębkowska et al. (2021) pointed out that a great majority of the entrepreneurs underlined the exemptions from or reductions of national insurance contributions. The most common difficulties with obtaining the anti-crisis shield aid were vague interpretations of the law, long times of application handling, narrow criteria of access, and complicated procedures combined with the unavailability of detailed information.

Government help has been forthcoming as the crisis that was caused by the SARS-CoV-2 pandemic exacerbated. Enterprises can take the advantage of diverse forms of support that help counteract the adverse effects of the pandemic. A review of the specialist literature has led to the following research hypothesis: *Financial support is a major factor of support for enterprise operations under the conditions of the crisis that was caused by the COVID-19 pandemic.*

Research methodology

The results of the authors' national study using computer-assisted telephone interviewswith a randomly generated sample of 350 SMEs are presented. Assuming α = 95% and β = 6%, the results are representative of the general population. The empirical research employed an original survey questionnaire that consisted of twoparts: particulars and questions. The former characterized the sample with the following objective criteria: the legal organization, sector, and region of an enterprise. As a result, the following were notable:

1 Limited liability companies (197) and joint-stock companies (79) constituted an overwhelming majority of the studied firms (that is, more than 78% of all of the entities).
2 In addition, most of the enterprises were clearly active in the commercial and service sector (146), with consumer goods businesses forming the smallest grouping (11).
3 Entities from the Mazovian (56) and Silesian (51) regions were the most numerous;these accounted for more than 30% of the study.

Six questions were posed in the latter partthat concerned enterprise operations during the COVID-19 pandemic crisis. The results ofthe question about the selected support instruments are discussed in this paper. The respondents were expected to assign significance levels to the following observable variables: V.1 – exemption from ZUS national insurance contributions; V.2 – idle time benefits; V.3 – reduced working hours or remote working; V.4 – financial shield; V.5 – subsidies to wages and national insurance contributions; V.6 – extension of children care allowance; V.7 – microloans; V.8 – preferential settlements of tax losses; V.9 – extension of time to introduce PPK employee capital plans fromthree to ninemonths; V.10 – suspension of compulsory periodical medical testing; V.11 – temporary deferral of real estate tax payment; V.12 – subsidies to credit interest; V.13 – protection against takeovers by investors from outside the European Union; and V.14 – resignation from simplified contributions. These were ranked on a scale from 1 to 10, where 1 stood for a low significance and 10 stood for a high significance.

The significance of the selected support instruments was measured and evaluated by means of descriptive statistics (arithmetic mean and standard deviation). In order to explain any interrelations among the observable variables, exploratory factor analysis was applied to identify those causes (factors) that underlay the observable variables (Wolak-Tuzimek, Duda,

2021, p. 317). A number of variables with a similar variance were assumed to clearly correlate with a certain latent value that was represented by a factor. In order to identify the number of factors (which was key to the continuing analysis), Cattell's scree test was undertaken; this helped specify the number of factors until the graph changed into a 'factor scree.'

Results

The results are presented for 350 enterprises that took the advantage of various forms of support during the crisis that was caused by the SARS-CoV-2 pandemic. In order to establish the significance of the particular sources of aid, position (arithmetic mean) and variability (standard deviation) measures were used;these show around which values the distribution of the variables concentrate and measure the dispersion of the studied variables.

An analysis of the descriptive statistics of the observable variables that described some support instruments at the time of the COVID-19 pandemic implies that the average assessments for all of the studied variables were above 2.80 and within a range of <2.86: 5.78> – evidence that all of the variables have been assessed as average and in an inconsistent manner. V.7, V.13, and V.6 were granted the maximum average values; that is, 5.78, 5.71, and 5.51, respectively. On the other hand, V.8, V.10, and V.9 generated the lowest minimum values; namely, 2.86, 2.89, and 2.97, respectively, on average. The standard deviations of the selected variables were within a range of<1.40:2.72>. The least varied responses were given for the *temporary deferral of real estate tax payment*and *suspension of compulsory periodical medical testing* variables. The standard deviation was 1.40 in both cases, whereas the responses were the most varied for *microloans* (2.72) and *extension of children care allowance* (2.58). A comparison of the central tendency measures points to a certain dependence: the assessments were less varied for the variables that were given high evaluations and more diverse for the low-assessed variables.

An exploratory factor analysis was then employed to explain the mutual relationships among the observable variables. Cattell's scree test served to identify anumber of factors. Unfortunately, its review failed to clearly show how many separate factors the sharply declining curve turned into a mild factor scree that would determine the number of factors that were eligible for continued analysis. The Kaiser criterion was used in addition; therefore, only those factors with corresponding eigenvalues that were above onewere subject to further analysis. This additional criterion demonstrated the sharply falling curve changes into a mid-factor scree where the three factorswere separated. The remaining factors had low eigenvalues and, therefore,were rejected. A model that consisted of three factorswas, thus, selected for continuing analysis.

Table 8.1 Matrix of Eigenvalues and Matrix of Factor Loads for Selected Instruments of Support

Factor	*Eigenvalue*	*Percentage of total variance*	*Accumulated eigenvalue*
F. 1	4.62	32.97%	4.62
F. 2	3.56	25.42%	8.18
F. 3	2.46	17.60%	10.64

Factor loads (normalized Varimax)
Main components (loads in bold are greater than 0.7)

Variable	*Factor 1*	*Factor 2*	*Factor 3*
V. 1	0.11	−0.54	0.09
V. 2	0.22	**−0.85**	−0.02
V. 3	0.18	**−0.89**	0.02
V. 4	0.93	0.17	−0.06
V. 5	0.95	0.17	−0.10
V. 6	0.95	0.18	−0.11
V. 7	0.95	0.16	−0.10
V. 8	−0.15	−0.11	**−0.90**
V. 9	−0.13	−0.12	**−0.91**
V. 10	−0.14	−0.11	**−0.87**
V. 11	0.23	**−0.77**	0.12
V. 12	0.19	**−0.87**	0.03
V. 13	0.06	−0.51	0.12
V. 14	0.89	0.11	−0.08

Source: Authors' own compilation.

Table 8.1 contains a matrix of the eigenvalues for the identified factors and a matrix of the loads for the factors that described the support instruments and had a value of 0.7.

Table 8.1 suggests that the subsequent eigenvalues and, thus, the parts of the variance that are explained for the three factors, were as follows:

- For Factor 1– 4.62 or 32.97% of the overall variance;
- For Factor 2– 3.56 or 25.42% of the overall variance;
- For Factor 3– 2.46 or 17.60% of the overall variance;

whereas the accumulated eigenvalue for the three factors was 10.64. This means that the system of factors explains as much as 75.99% of the overall variance.

In order to improve and generate the so-called simple factor structure, the matrix of the factor loadings was subject to Varimax rotation to simplify the interpretation of the factors by minimizing the number of variables that were required to explain a given factor. Table 8.1 shows the correlation between the observable variables and the factors that were introduced to the model. The minimum correlation that qualified as being significant was assumed to be 0.7. The analysis implies the following:

- Factor 1 was loaded by five variables: V.4 (financial shield), V.5 (subsidies to wages and national insurance contributions), V.6 (extension of children care allowance), V.7 (microloans), and V.14 (resignation from simplified contributions).
- Factor 2 was loaded by four variables: V.2 (idle time benefits) V.3 (reduced working hours or remote working), V.11 (temporary deferral of real estate tax payment), and V.12 (subsidies to credit interest).
- Factor 3 was loaded by three variables: V.8 (preferential settlements of tax losses), V.9 (extension of the time to introduce PPK employee capital plans fromthree to ninemonths), and V.10 (suspension of compulsory periodical medical testing).

As suggested by the literature (STATISTICA PL, 1997, p. 3543), the factor names in Figure 8.1 were derived from the variables of maximum factor loadings. Thus, Factor 1 was termed *'financial support,'* Factor 2 – 'work-*support,'* and Factor 3 – *'support for realization time.'* The resultant model of the selected support instruments is depicted in Figure 8.1.

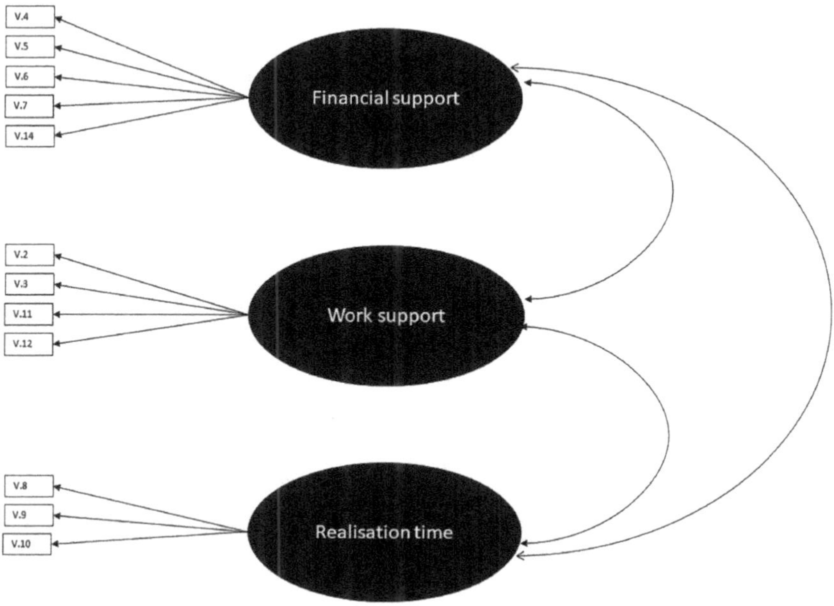

Figure 8.1 The factor model of support instruments.
Source: The authors' own compilation.

In Figure 8.1, the particular observable variables (positions on the scale) are represented with rectangles while the latent variables (factors) are depicted with ovals. The cause-and-effect (regressive) relationships are expressed with unidirectional arrows, and the correlation dependencies are marked with bidirectional arrows. The application of the exploratory factor analysis allowed for grouping the 14 variables into three key categories of support instruments. These factors were *'financial support,'* *'work support,'* and *'realization time,'* which were correlated.

The first two factors (i.e., *'financial support'* and *'work support'*) explicated 58% of the total variance. Factor 1was the most important as it was loaded by five variables: V.4 (financial shield), V.5 (subsidies to wages and national insurance contributions), V.6 (extension of children care allowance), V.7 (Micro-loans), and V.14 (Resignation from simplified contributions). The financial aspect can therefore be said to act as the crucial form of support among the surveyed enterprises. Thiswas reaffirmed with the average assessments of the tested variables, which were within a range of <4.94;5.78> (with the significance of microloans appreciated the most). The support for work was also highly valued by the enterprises. The assessments of the variables that loaded Factor 2 averaged <5.13;5.44>, with 5.44 for V.11 (temporary deferral of real estate tax payment). Factor 3 (*realization time*) explicated 17.60% of the total variance while the variables that constituted this factor range between <2.86 and 2.97> and were granted the minimum assessments by the respondents.

Discussion

The specialist literature suggests that the sector of SMEs has been gravely affected by the consequences of the COVID-19 pandemic (Hossain et al., 2020; Papadopoulos et al., 2020; Trawnih et al., 2021). This is due to their limited capacity for responding to both demand and supply shocks (OECD, 2020 a; b; c). A study of 756 SMEs in Poland (Gajewska et al., 2020) proved that 63% of medium-sized manufacturing firms reduced their activities and 51% cut employment while 35% signaled incomes falling by more than 50% in connection with the socioeconomic changes that resultedfromthe COVID-19 pandemic.

An international study of 5,206 enterprises in 23 countries during the period of April–August 2020 (Stephan et al., 2021) showed that 61% of the entrepreneurs saw the very existence of their businesses under threat due to the significant decrease in trading activitieseven though layoffs had only taken place in 28% of the SMEs at that time. This means that the jobs of 3,162 entrepreneurs and their 41,578 employees were, nevertheless, at risk. The respondents also reported problems with non- or late-paying customers (28%) and problems with paying for the upkeep of their business (27%). About two-fifths of the entrepreneurs (42%) increased remote working or introduced workingfrom home for their employees. A third

(33%) continued work at their business premises, and a fifth (20%) were already working from home before the pandemic. The time of pandemic had an extensive effect on the skill of adapting businesses to the existing conditions: 68% adjusted their businesses to the situation and 40% saw opportunities for development during the pandemic.

The burden of counteracting the pandemic's effects rested on national governments, which launched stimulation packages to alleviate the adverse social and economic effects. They attempted to mitigate the economic consequences by supporting enterprises. Research into business support programs (OECD, 2020, 2021; BGK, 2021) showed that most of these consistedof credit guarantees and direct loan instruments, compensations for SMEs, and direct equity or co-invested equity programs in various forms to support companies without increasing indebtedness.

Another study (Stephan et al., 2021) indicated that 62% of the examined enterprises applied for government support during the pandemic, such as jobretention schemes or deferred tax and rate payments. Most of the enterprises that sought public aid operated in New Zealand (97.8%), Poland (87.6%), France (82.1%), and Italy (80%).

The authors' research upheld the importance of public financial support for enterprise operations under the conditions of the crisis that was caused by the COVID-19 pandemic. Two key factors were highlighted: financial support and work support (which explained 58% of the overall variance). The financial support factors were comprised of microloans, financial shields, subsidies to wages and national insurance contributions, resignationsfrom simplified contributions, and extensions of children care allowances. Work support (i.e., the introduction of remote work, idletime benefits, temporary deferral of real estate tax payments, and subsidies to credit interest) proved to be important as well, like the organizational issues named 'realization time,' which encompassed extensions of the time to introduce PPK employee capital plans, suspensions of compulsory periodical medical testing, and the preferential settlements of tax losses.

Conclusions and recommendations

The COVID-19 pandemic began its active global spread in early 2020. The situation was particularly difficult in Italy, Spain, China, Iran, South Korea, and the United States. It developed very fast, bringing grave changes that affected various areas of society, state, and business as a consequence (Starostin et al., 2020, p. 531; Duda et al., 2021, p. 140). The COVID-19 pandemic has caused huge turbulence in the global markets. Enterprises have faced a number of restrictions, prohibitions, and limitations that have often prevented their activities. Tourism, entertainment activities, and catering firms have suffered most painfully (Sieradzka, 2021, p. 43). Governments took extraordinary steps to contain the epidemic, like overall isolation and large-scale restrictions on business activities. Aid and remedy packages were announced to support enterprises and workers. Fiscal and monetary policy measures were applied. As part of mitigating the economic crisis that was caused by the COVID-19 pandemic, the Polish government introduced a package of aid measures that included business support instruments, known as anti-crisis shields. An additional package (financial shields) was launched to preserve the financial liquidity of firms.

The authors applied exploratory factor analysis to design a factor-based model of enterprise support instruments under the conditions of the crisis that was caused by the SARS-CoV-2 pandemic. The resultant multidimensional structure grouped a number of variables into three main categories (factors); namely, *'financial support,' 'work support,'* and *'realization time.'* Financial support was the crucial form of support during the crisis, as demonstrated by the number of variables that loaded the factor model and the above-average assessments for some variables.

The results and statistical analysis validatedResearch Hypothesis H1*: Financial support is a major factor of support for enterprise operations under the conditions of the crisis that was caused by COVID-19.*

The authors' results can be useful in the process of enterprise management as a guide to which tools should be employed to mitigate the consequences of the crisis that was caused by the COVID-19 pandemic. The research showed that financial instruments were the most important factors that supported enterprises. In addition, the skill of properly utilizing work support and organizational support factors was essential. This was particularly important to SMEs, which often avoided their realization (e.g., of reduced working hours or the introduction of remote work).

References

Antipova, T., (2020), *Coronavirus Pandemic as Black Swan Event* [in:] Antiopva T. (eds.), *Integrated Science in Digital Age 2020. ICIS 2020*, Vol. 136, pp. 356–366.

Avishai, B., (2020), *The Pandemic isn't a black swan but a portent of a more fragile global system*, The New Yorker, April 21, https://www.newyorker.com/news/daily-comment/the-pandemic-isnt-a-black-swan-but-a-portent-of-a-more-fragile-global-system

Boccaletti, A., Ditto, W., Mindlin, G., Atangana, A., (2020), *Modeling and forecasting of epidemic spreading: the case od COVID-19 and beyond*, Chaos Solutions Fractals, Vol. 135, pp. 109794.

Brzeziński, Ł., Hadas, Ł., Cyplik, P., (2021), *The transformation of the business model of SMEs due to COVID-19 pandemic*, European Research Studies Journal, Vol. XXIV, Issue 2B, pp. 915–924.

Correia, S., Luck, S., Verner, E., (2020), *Pandemics depress the economy, public health interventions do not: evidence from the 1918 flu*, March 2020. Working Paper, pp.1–56, https://papers.ssrn.com/sol3/papers.cfm?abstract_id=3561560

Czech, K., Karpio, A., Wielechowski, M., Woźniakowski, T., Żebrowska-Suchodolska, D., (2020), *Polska gospodarka w początkowym okresie pandemii COVID-19*, Wyd. Szkoły Głównej Gospodarstwa Wiejskiego, Warszwa.

Dębkowska, K., Kłosiewicz-Górecka, U., Szymańska, A., Ważniewski, P., Zybertowicz, K., (2021), *Tarcza antykryzysowa. Koło ratunkowe dla firm i gospodarki?*, Polski Instytut Ekonomiczny, Warszawa.

Drake, J., (2021), *Was COVID-19 a black swan event?*, Forbes November 11, https://www.forbes.com/sites/johndrake/2021/11/11/was-covid-19-a-black-swan-event/?sh=5d16dc7bd36a

Duda, J., Wolak-Tuzimek, A., Wójtowicz, Ł., (2021), *Instruments of competition applied by large enterprises at time of crisis triggered by COVID-19 pandemic*, European Research Studies Journal, Vol. XXIV, Issue 2, pp. 139–151.

Economou, M., Madinos, M., Peppou, L., Patelakis, A., Stefanis, C., (2013), *Major depression in the Era of economic crisis: a replication of a cross-sectional study cross Greece*, Journal of Affective Disorders, Vol. 145, Issue 3, pp. 308–314.

Ficoń, K., (2007), *Inżynieria zarządzania kryzysowego. Podejście systemowe.* Wydawnictwo Bel Studio, Warszawa.

Fornaro, L., Wolf M., (2020), *Coronavirus and macroeconomic Policy*, VOXeu, CEPR Policy Protal, https://voxeu.org

Gajewska, A., Oleszczuk, P., Smoleń, D., Gocłowska, M., Morawski, I., Osica, O., Garlicki, J., (2020), *Polski mikro, mały i średni biznes w obliczu Pandemii COVID-19*, PwC, https://www.pwc.pl/pl/pdf/polski-mikro-maly-sredni-biznes-w-obliczu-pandemii.pdf.

Grzeszczak, J., Leśniewicz, F., Śliwowski, P., Święcicki, I., (2020), *Pandenomics. Zestaw narzędzi fiskalnych i monetarnych w dobie kryzysów*, Polski Instytut Ekonomiczny, Warszawa.

GUS, (2021), *Produkt Krajowy Brutto w 2020 roku – szacunek wstępny*, https://stat.gov.pl/

Harvey, C., (2020), *The economic and financial implications of COVID-19*, https://www.darden.virginia.edu/sites/default/files/inline-files/COVID-19%20Presentation_Cambell%20Harvey.pdf

Horodecka, A., (2017), *Polityka gospodarcza w świetle przemian współczesnej myśli ekonomicznej. Perspektywy polityki gospodarczej*, Prace i Materiały Instytutu Rozwoju Gospodarczego Szkoły Głównej Handlowej, Warszawa.

Hossain, M., Akhter, F., Sultana, M., (2020), *SMEs in COVID-19 crisis and combating strategies: a systematic literature review (SLR) and a case from emerging economy*, Operations Research Perspectives, Vol. 9, January 15, https://www.ncbi.nlm.nih.gov/pmc/articles/PMC8752191/

Jones, C., Phillipon, T., Venkateswaran, V., (2008), *Optimal mitigation policies in a pandemic: social distancing and working from home*, NBER Working Paper Series, No. 26984, pp. 1–40.

Jones, K.E., Patel, N.G., Levy, M.A., Storeygard, A., Balk, D., Gittleman, J.L., Daszak, P., (2008), *Global trends in emerging infectious diseases*, Nature, Vol. 451, Issue 7181, pp. 990–993.

Laurent, L., (2020), *Politics & Policy: europe freezes its economy in order to fight the coronavirus*, Bloomberg, March 16.

Ma, C., Rogers, J., Zhou, S., (2020), *Global economic and financial effects of 21st century pandemics and epidemics*, Covid Economics. Vitted and Real Time Papers, SSRN Electronic Journal, Issue 5, pp. 56–78, CEPR Press.

Maier, B.F., Brockmann, D., (2020). *Effective containment explains subexponential growth in recent confirmed COVID-19 cases in China*, Science, Vol. 368, Issue 6492, pp. 742–746.

Marć, Ł., Skowron, B., (2020), *Pomiar pulsu przedsiębiorstw. Badanie COVID-19 Business Pulse Servey (COV-BPS) – Polska*, World Bank Group, PARP.

Mazzucato, M., (2020), *Coronavirus andthe capitalism: how will the virus change the way the Word Works?*, World Economic Forum, https://www.weforum.org/agenda/2020/04/coronavirus-covid19-business-economics-society-economics-change

McGillivray, G., (2020), *Coronavirus is significant, but i sit a true black swan event?*, The conversation, April 30, https://theconversation.com/coronavirus-is-significant-but-is-it-a-true-black-swan-event-136675

Męcina, J., (2020a), *Koronawirus. Raport z działań Lewiatana. Stan na 30 kwietnia 2020*, Konfederacja Lewiatan, Poland, https://lewiatan.org/pliki/raporty-roczne/Konfederacja_Lewiatan_raport_roczny2020.pdf

Męcina, J., (2020b), *Impuls dla Polski 2020–2022*, Konfederacja Lewiatan, Poland, https://lewiatan.org/pliki/raporty-i-badania/Impul_dla_Polski_30_IX.pdf

Męcina, J., Potocki P., (2020), *Wpływ COVID-19 na gospodarkę i rynek procy w Polsce – wyciąg z raportu badawczego*, Ekspertyza 11, Open Eyes Economy Summit, https://oees.pl

Morse, S.S., Mazet, J.A., Woolhouse, M., Parrish, C.R., Carroll, D., Karesh, W.B., Zambrana-Torrelio, C., Lipkin, W.I., Daszak, P., (2012), *Prediction and prevention of the next pandemic zoonosis*, Lancet, Vol. 380, pp. 1956–1965.

OECD, (2020), *Economic outlook*, Issue 1, https://www.oecd-ilibrary.org/economics/oecd-economic-outlook/volume-2020/issue-1_0d1d1e2e-en

OECD, (2020a), *COVID-19: SME policy responses*, Paris, https://oecd.dam-broadcast.com/pm_7379_119_119680-di6h3qgi4x.pdf

OECD, (2020b), *Global financial markets policy responses to COVID-19*, Paris, https://read.oecd-ilibrary.org/

OECD, (2020c), *OECD economic outlook*, Paris, https://www.oecd-ilibrary.org/

OECD, (2020d), COVID-19 *Government financing support programmes for business*, https://www.oecd.org/finance/COVID-19-Government-Financing-Support-Programmes-for-Businesses.pdf

Osiński, J., (2021), *Długookresowe skutki COVID-19 a stabilność systemu finansowego*, Oberwator-finansowy.pl.

Papadopoulos, T., Baltas, K.N., Balta, M.E., (2020), *The use of digital technologies by small and medium enterprises during COVID-19: implications for theory and practice*, International Journal of Information Management, Vol. 55.

Piłat, A., Rozkrut, M., Samołyk, O., Ropiak, P., Walewski, M., (2021), *Przegląd pakietów pomocowych oferowanych przez wybrane państwa europejskie w odpowiedzi na kryzys COVID-19*, Bank Gospodarstwa Krajowego, Warsaw, https://www.bgk.pl/

Platje, J., Harvey, J.A., Rayman-Bacchus, L., (2020), *COVID-19 – reflections on the surprise of both an expected and unexpected event*, Central European Review of Economics and Management, Vol. 4, Issue 1, pp. 149–162.

Reinhart, C., Reinhart, V., (2020), *The pandemic depression. The global economy will never be the same*, Foreign Affers, Vol. 99, No.5, https://www.foreignaffairs.com/

Rothbard, M.N., (2010), *Wielki Kryzys w Ameryce*, Instytut Ludwika von Misesa, Kraków.

Sieradzka, K., (2021), *The conditions of development of innovative business undertakings at the time of the COVID-19 pandemic*, Central European Review of Economics and Finance, Vol. 3, pp. 43–53.

Simianer, H., Reimer, C., (2021), *COVID-19: a "black swan" and what animal breeding can learn from it*, Animal Frontiers, Vol. 11, Issue 1, pp. 57–59.

Starostin, V., Samokhodkin, E., Elzon, A., (2020), *Changing consumer and brand behavior in the early stages of the COVID-19 pandemic in Russia*, European Research Studies Journal, Vol. 23, Issue 4, pp. 531–543.

StatSoft, STATISTICA PL (1997). *Tom III:Statystyki II, praca zbiorowa*, StatSoft, Kraków.

Stephan, U., Zbierowski, P., Perez-Luno, A., Klausen, A., (2021), *Entrepreneurship during the COVID-19 pandemic: a global study of enterpreneurs' challenges, resilience and well-being*, KBS Covid-19 Research Impact Papers, No. 4.

Taleb, N.N., (2007), *The Black Swan. The impact of the highly improbable*, Random House, New York.

Trawnih, A., Yaseen, H., Al.-Adwan, A.S., Alsoud, A.R., Jaber, O.A., (2021), *Factors influencing social media adoption among SMEs during COVID-19 crisis*, Journal of Management Information and Decision Sciences, Vol. 24, Issue 6, pp. 1–18.

Walsh, B., (2017), *The world is not ready for the next pandemic*, The Times, May 15, Vol. 189, No. 18, https://time.com/magazine/us/4766607/may-15th-2017-vol-189-no-18-u-s/

Wnukowski, D., Wąsowski, M., (2020), *Skutki pandemii COVID-19 dla gospodarki światowej*, Biuletyn PISM, No.84, https://pism.pl

Wolak-Tuzimek, A., Duda, J., (2021), *The Concept of Corporate Social Responsibi ity as a Source of an Enterprise's Competitive Advantage*, [in:] Bukowski S.I., Hyż A., Lament M. (eds.),*Competitiveness and Economic Development in Europe: prospects and Challenges*,Routledge, Taylor & Francis Group, London.

World Economic Forum, (2020), *A visual history of pandemics*, https://www.weforum.org/agenda/2020/03/a-visual-history-of-pandemics

9 Effects of COVID-19 pandemic on productivity

Can destruction bring creation?

Agnieszka Szczepkowska-Flis and Anna Kozłowska

Introduction

Could the COVID-19 pandemic and its consequences be a catalyst for positive economic change as far as innovation and productivity growth are concerned? This question can be considered to be controversial in light of the experiences of previous epidemics and the various scenarios of the development of the economic situation (Keogh-Brown et al., 2009; McKibbin, Fernando, 2020). The findings have indicated that the effects of the last four epidemics (SARS, MERS, Ebola, and Zika) were significant and permanent decreases in productivity, amounting to about 4% (Dieppe, Celic, Okou, 2020, p. 100). Economists have pointed out that in the case of the COVID-19 pandemic, the loss in productivity may be more severe because of the global reach of the pandemic, unprecedented preventive measures (lockdowns), and other solutions that were introduced to slow down the spread of the virus (Dieppe, Celic, Okou, 2020, p. 100; McKibbin, Fernando, 2020; Sudipta, Kaushik, 2020; Weder di Mauro, 2020). Although the effect of the COVID-19 pandemic will be a short-term one- or two-year economic shock according to some forecasts (Salterio, 2020; Karabag, 2020; McKibbin, Fernando, 2020), the most pessimistic variant (demand–supply "doom loop" [Fornaro, Wolf, 2020]) cannot be ruled out. The recession can turn into a depression with low production, high unemployment, and stagnation in productivity.

As cited by various authors, the sources of the negative consequences of the pandemic on productivity essentially lie in two interrelated areas: innovation and technological progress, and structural changes at the levels of industries, sectors, and economies. In this context, many authors have emphasized the destructive impact of the COVID-19 pandemic on investments, including R&D spending and new knowledge creation, global supply chains and related international knowledge transfer, and reallocations of resources and labor market alignment (worker-firm matches) (Salterio, 2020; Shen et al., 2020; Fornaro, Wolf, 2020; di Mauro, Syverson, 2020; Dieppe, Celic, Okou, 2020, p. 98; Sudipta, Kaushik, 2020; Boone, Haugh, Pain, Salins, 2020, pp. 37–44; Dieppe, Matsuoka, 2020, p. 358). In the long run, this means not only a slowdown in technological

DOI: 10.4324/9781003368687-9

progress and productivity growth but also a stiffening of the economic structure in which the transfer of production factors from less to more efficient uses is significantly limited.

In the discussion on the socio-economic effects of the COVID-19 pandemic, views are also presented according to which the current crisis may paradoxically be a period of a higher pace of knowledge creation, an accelerated diffusion of technology, and a catalyst for increasing productivity actions (adaptive innovations [di Mauro, Syverson, 2020][1]). According to OECD experts, for example, the extensive use of information technology and remote work during the COVID-19 pandemic may not only reduce operating costs but also contribute to the growth of human capital and the improvement of labor productivity (OECD, 2020). As some economists have pointed out, an additional strengthening of these pro-efficiency impulses may exert strong pressure on resource reallocation and business rotation. The pressure will arise as soon as the government protection packages have expired (di Mauro, Syverson, 2020; Dieppe, Matsuoka, 2020, p. 365).

The main research problem that is undertaken in this chapter is the search for an answer to the following question: Can the disruptions (supply and demand shock) that were caused by the COVID-19 pandemic be a catalyst for positive changes in the economic system that lead to overcoming the productivity stagnation that can be observed in many economies in the long run? This research problem is part of the ongoing global debate on the effects of the COVID-19 pandemic on productivity. Our approach in solving this problem allows us to combine the seemingly contradictory views of economists into a coherent theoretical structure.

The aim of our research is not to forecast *ex ante* changes in productivity but rather to analyze the current processes in the context of Schumpeter's theory of development and the works of other economists on creative destruction and the role of market selection in economic processes. The ability to transform natural depression into an abnormal liquidation that is not accompanied by an improvement in productivity and the distinction between simple destruction and creative destruction provide the fundamental analytical framework for our concept of "inverse creative destruction." As in J.A. Schumpeter's works, destruction does not have to be a consequence of creation but vice versa – destruction and the accompanying processes can be creative, thus influencing the trajectory of productivity growth – both during a period of abnormal liquidation and after its completion. The concept of "inverse creative destruction" does not stand in opposition to other analyses of the economic effects of the COVID-19 pandemic, but rather creates an alternative theoretical framework for the interpretation of events.

An integral part of our study is an empirical analysis on the impact of creation and destruction on changes in labor productivity in Polish manufacturing during the COVID-19 pandemic. The interpretation of the results of the econometric analysis in the context of "inverse creative destruction" was preceded by a discussion of the research methodology. Our scheme and the indicators of creative destruction that were used have the value of general applicability. The method of the measurement of creation and destruction based on evometrics is a good alternative to those indicators that are commonly used in empirical research (job creation, job destruction, firm exit, firm entry, etc.) – especially when there is no access to data at the micro-level. To our knowledge, the approach that we propose in order to analyze the effects of the COVID-19 pandemic on productivity (both in theoretical and empirical terms) has not been used by other authors thus far.

Simple destruction vs creative destruction in COVID-19 pandemic

According to the theory of J.A. Schumpeter, economic development runs in a cyclical manner – manifested by alternating periods of revival and depression. The sources of development processes are innovations that, by activating the mechanism of creative destruction, lead to two interrelated phenomena (Wäckerle, 2014, p. 146):

- "Wave of creation:" typical of revival when new enterprises, production methods, goods and services, sales techniques, technical and organizational solutions, etc., appear on the market.
- "Wave of destruction:" typical of depression, the essence of which is market selection and the accompanying reallocation of resources toward new more effective uses (those elements of the economic structure that do not fit the conditions that are created by innovations during the revival are eliminated from the market).

Although both processes have different consequences, their coexistence is a necessary condition for development processes. According to J.A. Schumpeter, depression is the economy's natural response to revival; the destruction that occurs during this period is a normal process of absorption and elimination. Exogenous factors, random events, systemic errors, speculation, panic, etc., may turn destruction into an abnormal liquidation, which also affects potentially effective companies and solutions during a prolonged depression (crisis) ("scarring" effect) (Ouyang, 2005).

The research that has been conducted in many economies, sectors, and industries on the role of creative destruction in economic processes has revealed that firm rotation as well as market selection and the reallocation of resources are sources of aggregate productivity growth (Baldwin, Gu, 2002; Foster, Haltiwanger, Krizan, 2002; Foster, Haltiwanger, Syverson, 2005; ter Wengel, Rodriguez, 2006; Geroski, 1989; Bartelsman, Dhrymes, 1998; Jensen, McGuckin, Stiroh, 2001). As other studies have indicated, however, the market-cleansing effect does not work pro-effectively during severe economic crises – the probability of the survival of companies does not depend on their productivity but on the sizes of their sales, the sizes of their assets, and creditworthiness, or (as in the current COVID-19 crisis) their financial liquidity (Lee, Lee, Beak, 2017; Kılınç, 2018; Bosio et al., 2020). In this context, it is necessary to distinguish between creative destruction and simple destruction (Levinsohn, Petropoulos, 2001). Although destruction is devoid of elements of creation and is accompanied by firm rotation in both cases, the criteria and, thus, the effects of market selection on economic systems are utterly different. In the first case, destruction that is caused by innovation (creation) is identified with selection that is based on efficiency and such a reallocation of resources that leads to productivity improvement and the better use of production factors. The bases of selection in simple destruction (identified with abnormal liquidation in this study) are features other than efficiency, which means that the result of "reallocation" is the unproductive release of resources (particularly, the labor force), thus leading to a decline in production and productivity stagnation.

The processes that have taken place during the current economic crisis that was caused by the COVID-19 pandemic appear to be in line with the description of simple destruction. The unprecedented uncertainty that has been caused by the random event, the lockdown (which is a pure form of economic destruction), and the resulting first wave of business closures and suspensions can be considered to be characteristics of an abnormal liquidation. The adjustments that have been undertaken by companies in response to this pure destruction, however, are of a creative nature, which allows us to see the present situation as some analogy to Schumpeter's creative destruction (for which, the correct analytical scheme may be the concept of "inverse creative destruction"). The concept is derived from Schumpeter's idea; however, while preserving the essence of the processes of creation and destruction, it differs from the original in two fundamental respects. First, the factor that disturbs the economic system is not innovation (as per J.A. Schumpeter), but the lockdown that was caused by the COVID-19 pandemic; this implies the reverse order of the two processes. Destruction is not a consequence of creation; contrarily, it is destruction that triggers creative processes, thus affecting the trajectories of changes in productivity. Second, state intervention during the COVID-19 pandemic has not only disrupted economic processes (lockdowns), but also, through the anti-crisis instruments that have been aimed at protecting companies and workplaces, has acted as an "institutional selection" that has distorted the operation of market selection.

The analytical basis of "inverse creative destruction" is formed by a three-level hierarchical structure of the economic system: the level of enterprises, the level of industries, and the level of the sector (mesoeconomic perspective). Referring to the method of the decomposition of aggregate productivity change that is used by many economists (Baily, Bartelsman, Haltiwanger, 2001, p. 422; Griliches, Regev, 1992, p. 7; Sekkat, 2010), we consider its three components:

- Within-firm effect (internal restructuring): resulting from organizational changes, the introduction of new technologies, R&D activity, or changes in the proportions of the production factors that are used in enterprises.
- Between-firm effect (selection effect): expressing the result of the market-selection mechanism among enterprises that operate within an industry.
- Inter-industry effect (reallocation effect): due to the reallocation of resources among the industries of a given sector.

The first two of the above-mentioned effects determine changes in the productivity that can be observed at the level of individual industries. According to R.A. Fisher's theorem, the basis for the selection mechanism that operates within the sector is the differentiation of the productivity levels between industries: The greater the heterogeneity of the productivity, the stronger the pressure on resource reallocation and the greater the share of the inter-industry effect in changes of aggregate productivity (Andersen, 2004b; Metcalfe, 1998, pp. 62–65).

The impulse that triggers "inverse creative destruction" (lockdown) and anti-crisis measures defines a two-dimensional analytical space in which there are four basic variants of the functioning of the economy:

- Variant I: lockdown without anti-crisis instruments;
- Variant II: lockdown with anti-crisis instruments;
- Variant III: unfreezing economy while continuing anti-crisis assistance; and
- Variant IV: unfreezing economy without anti-crisis aid.

Freezing the economy (Variant I) is a catalyst of market selection. It accelerates the liquidation of companies in which the risk of collapse was visible well in advance of the lockdown – analogous to the "shadow of death" effect (Griliches, Regev, 1992; Troske, 1996). At the same time, the process of abnormal liquidation begins, which is a factor that triggers the "scarring" effect that is typical of the period of simple destruction during which the basis for the selection of companies is not efficiency but disruptions in the current financial liquidity that prevent further economic activity.[2] The increasing risk of bankruptcy (of destruction) is a disciplining tool that forces managers to accelerate the adoption of new technologies and organizational solutions – adaptive innovations (speciation) (intra-firm effect) (Levinthal, 1998).

The research results indicate that, while the intra-firm effect causes productivity improvement, the "scarring" effect works in the opposite direction (Sekkat, 2010; Griliches, Regev, 1992; Yaşar, Rejesus, Mintemur, 2004; Baldwin, Gu, 2002; Foster, Haltiwanger, Krizan, 2002; Foster, Haltiwanger, Syverson, 2005; ter Wengel, Rodriguez, 2006; Geroski, 1989; Bartelsman, Dhrymes, 1998; Jensen, McGuckin, Stiroh, 2001).[3] The final effect that is visible after the period of pure lockdown at the level of individual industries is the result of their combined impact.

The activation of anti-crisis instruments in the economy during a lockdown (Variant II) results in the following:

- The disappearance of the "scarring" effect and enabling potentially effective enterprises to survive in the market.
- Replacing the "shadow of death" effect with the "zombie" effect, which refers to enterprises that, without government intervention, would have to leave the market due to poor performance, freeing resources, and enabling their effective reallocation (di Mauro, C. Syverson, 2020).
- Weakening the intra-firm effect by reducing the pressure to introduce creative adaptations.[4]

Undoubtedly, there are arguments in favor of massive state intervention during a lockdown; as di Mauro, Syverson (2020) rightly emphasized, however, long-term support (institutional selection) that is devoid of any efficiency criteria may generate misallocations of resources, limit the creation of new more productive companies, and expand efficient entities. In this context, the scale of the "zombie" effect may be of key importance for the changes in productivity that can be observed in industries – not only during the lockdown with anti-crisis measures but also during the unfreezing of the economy with anti-crisis aid (Variant III). The negative consequences of such solutions may exceed the potential positive effects of adaptive innovations – the full use of which may be postponed in time.

Terminating anti-crisis aid while limiting epidemic restrictions (Variant IV), in turn, implies strong market-selection processes among enterprises. Assuming that the basis of selection is efficiency, the probability of a firm's survival in the market is a positive function of adaptive innovations and other anti-destruction measures. The positive impact of the inter-firm effect is reinforced by the intra-firm effect, and the result of the processes that can be observed in industries is an increase in productivity.[5]

Assuming that a lockdown is a factor that additionally strengthens the barriers to the mobility of production factors among industries, the first two variants of the functioning of the economy *ex definitione* exclude the role of the inter-industry effect in any changes in aggregate productivity; this may have particularly negative implications in emerging and developing economies (Dieppe, Matsuoka, 2020, p. 362). Unfreezing the economy with anti-crisis assistance (Version III) does not provide adequate fuel to stimulate the reallocation of resources between industries; moreover, the indicated threats may preserve the existing (perhaps ineffective) economic structure due to the "zombie" effect. Two solutions are possible in this situation: the implementation of Variant IV, or institutional selection based on criteria that promote efficiency-oriented reallocation and innovative activity of enterprises.

During the COVID-19 pandemic, governments have implemented different economic policies, interventions, and timelines; therefore, some of the variants may not have occurred in some economies/sectors/industries (or the events may have followed a different sequence). Therefore, the concept of "inverse creative destruction" sets only the theoretical framework for the interpretation of the phenomena that has occurred during the COVID-19 pandemic – the details of which can only be provided by empirical research that is conducted for various economies, industries, and sectors that are treated as case studies at this stage of the research.

Data and concept of empirical research

An econometric study was conducted for manufacturing in Poland for the period of February 2010 to June 2020.[6] Two sub-periods were distinguished in the analysis: from February 2010 to February 2020 (the period before the COVID-19 pandemic), and from March to June 2020 (the COVID-19 pandemic period). We used monthly data that were published by the Central Statistical Office.

As the dependent variable, we used the change in labor productivity (*DAPL*); the independent variables were as follows:

- innovation effect (creation) (*EI*): in line with multi-level version of G.R. Price's equation (Andersen, 2004a, pp. 37–39) that reflected consequences of intra- and inter-firm effects for labor productivity in industries;
- selection effect (destruction) (*ES*): expressing consequences of inter-industry effect for labor productivity.

Labor productivity (*APL*) was calculated as the quotient of the real sold production of industry (*SP*)[7] and the average employment in the enterprise sector (*L*). Both categories were seasonally adjusted using the Census X-13 ARIMA procedure.

To estimate the selection and innovation effects, we used evometrics (evolutionary econometrics[8]) (Andersen, 2004a). The values of the innovation (*EI*) and selection effects (*ES*) were calculated based on the labor productivity in individual industries of manufacturing according to the following equation:

$$\Delta APL_t = \frac{\sum_j u_{jt}\left(w_{jt} - w_t\right)\left(APL_{jt} - APL_t\right)}{w_t} + \frac{\sum_j u_{jt} w_{jt} \Delta APL_{jt}}{w_t} = ES_t + EI_t, \tag{9.1}$$

where

$w_{jt} = \frac{SP_{jt}}{SP_{jt-1}}$ – absolute reproduction coefficient of industry *j* in year *t*;

ΔAPL_{jt} – change of labor productivity in industry *j* in year *t*;

u_{jt} – share of industry *j* in sold production in manufacturing in year *t*;

$w_t = \sum_j u_{jt} w_{jt}$ – weighted average reproduction coefficient in manufacturing in year *t*;

$APL_t = \sum_j u_{jt} APL_{jt}$ – weighted average labor productivity in manufacturing in year *t*.

The empirical study was conducted in two steps. The aim of the first step was to test whether "inverse creative destruction" as the mechanism of the economy's response to the COVID-19 pandemic was reflected in the data. Two versions of the *ex post* forecast were estimated – adopting different assumptions for each of them:

- Version I: a forecast that was prepared on the *ceteris paribus* assumption: the COVID-19 pandemic did not take place, and the factors and the mechanism of their impact on labor productivity (based on creative destruction) remained unchanged.
- Version II: a forecast that was prepared on the assumption that the COVID-19 pandemic changed the values of the factors that determined changes in labor productivity but did not change the mechanism of their impact.

The basis of the former was autoregressive model AR (*p*), while the latter was prepared using autoregressive distributed lag (ARDL) model (*p*, *q*, *z*) in which two independent variables were included: the *ES* and the *EI*. Both models were estimated for changes in labor productivity during the period from February 2010 to February 2020. The values of the forecast of the changes in labor productivity (*DAPL*) for the period from March to June 2020 were used to calculate the levels of labor productivity (*APL*) during this period.

The aim of the second step was to determine whether the COVID-19 pandemic caused a change in the mechanism of the influence of creation and destruction on the changes of labor productivity. In this step, the ARDL model was used in which a binary variable D1 was included in addition to the explanatory variables (*EI*, *ES*, and their lags) and the autoregressive component, which was assigned a value of 1 during the months of March to June 2020 (i.e., during the COVID-19 pandemic in Poland). Based on the estimated model parameters, a multiplier analysis was performed.

The general form of ARDL (*p*, *q*) model is described by the following equation:

$$y_t = c + \alpha_1 y_{t-1} + \ldots + \alpha_p y_{t-p} + \beta_0 x_t + \beta_1 x_{t-1} + \ldots + \beta_q x_{t-q} + \varepsilon_t, \qquad (9.2)$$

where
c – constant;
y – endogenous variable;
x – exogenous variable;
$\alpha_1, \beta_0, \beta_1, \beta_2$ – regression coefficients; and
ε – residuals.

The multiplier analysis allowed us to determine the short-run and long-run influences of the exogenous variables on the endogenous variable (Verbeek, 2004, pp. 310–311; Hill, Griffiths, Lim, 2011, pp. 378–382; Davidson, MacKinnon, 1999, pp. 568–569; Johnston, DiNardo, 1997, pp. 244–245, 273). The effect of the change in x for the current changes in y is reflected in short-run multiplier $m_s = \beta_0$. If the change in x persists in subsequent periods, its long-run impact on variable y is described by the following long-run multiplier:

$$m_l = \frac{\sum \beta}{1 - \sum \alpha}. \qquad (9.3)$$

Moreover, if the estimated parameters of the model that is described by Equation (9.2) meet the following conditions:

- the absolute value of the sum of the estimates of parameters $\alpha_1 + \ldots + \alpha_p$ is less than 1 ($|\Sigma\alpha| < 1$), and
- the long-term multiplier is statistically significant,

then the model has a long-run equilibrium that is described by the following equation:

$$y^{\star} = C + m_l x^{\star}, \tag{9.4}$$

where
$y\star$ – long-run level of endogenous variable;
$x\star$ – long-run level of exogenous variable;
$C = \frac{c}{1 - \sum \alpha}$ – long-run constant.

The parameters of the regression equations were estimated using ordinary least squares. The Akaike criterion (Gujarati, 2004, p. 537) was used for selecting the lags of the variables in the AR and ARDL models. The statistical significance of the regression parameter estimates was determined using the Student's *t*-test at a level of $\alpha = 0.05$. The normality assumption was tested using the Lilliefors test (Abdi, Molin, 2007). The assumption of homoscedasticity was verified with the Breusch, Pagan, and Godfrey tests (Gujarati, 2004, pp. 411–413; Hill, Griffiths, Lim, 2011, pp. 303–305; Greene, 2012, pp. 276–277). The LM Breusch and Godfrey test was used to verify the hypothesis about the lack of the autocorrelation of the residual component (Gujarati, 2004, pp. 472–474; Hill, Griffiths, Lim, 2011, pp. 354–355). The statistical significance of the long-run multiplier was tested with the Wald test (Baltagi, 2011, pp. 26–29).

The results that were obtained during the empirical analysis are presented in the next part of the study, along with their interpretation in the context of the concept of "inverse creative destruction."

Results of empirical analysis

The regression analysis was preceded by ADF unit root tests (Baltagi, 2011, pp. 379–383). The test results showed that all of the variables were stationary.

The results of the estimation of regression parameters, which were the basis for the forecasts of labor productivity, are presented in Table 9.1 – Columns A and B.

A comparison of the empirical values of *APL* and the values that were calculated based on Version II of the forecast shows that, during the COVID-19 pandemic, the mechanism that was responsible for shaping labor productivity changed (Figure 9.1). The stronger-than-forecast declines in *APL* that were observed from March to April 2020 suggest that, during this period, the mechanism of creative destruction was replaced by simple destruction. On the other hand, the increases in labor productivity that were recorded from May to June 2020 (stronger than the forecasts

Table 9.1 Results of Parameter Estimation

Column:	*A*	*B*	*C*
Independent variables	*AR(2) model – Forecast Version I Time range: 02.2010–02.2020 Dependent variable: DAPL*	*ARDL(2, 2, 2) model – Forecast Version II Time range: 02.2010–02.2020 Dependent variable: DAPL*	*ARDL(1, 1, 1, 1, 1) model with binary variable Time range: 02.2010–06.2020 Dependent variable: DAPL*
$DAPL_{t-1}$	−0.7714 [0.0827]	−0.6007 [0.0924]	−0.5604 [0.0915]
$DAPL_{t-2}$	−0.4487 [0.0826]	−0.3654 [0.0903]	−0.2063 [0.0485]
EI	X	0.3701 [0.0229]	0.3683 [0.0230]
EI_{t-1}	X	0.1554 [0.0414]	0.1362 [0.0408]
EI_{t-2}	X	0.0880 [0.0422]	X
ES	X	−0.1769 [0.0255]	−0.1706 [0.0254
ES_{t-1}	X	−0.0915 [0.0300]	−0.0868 [0.0293]
ES_{t-2}	X	−0.0540 [0.0306]	X
$D1 \times EI$	X	X	0.1179 [0.0618]
$D1_{t-1} \times EI_{t-1}$	X	X	0.4181 [0.0840]
$D1 \times ES$	X	X	0.1739 [0.2274]
$D1_{t-1} \times ES_{t-1}$	X	X	1.1706 [0.2366]
C	0.2804 [0.1195]	−0.1706 [0.0742]	−0.1226 [0.0715]
	Number of observations: 119 $R^2 = 0.43$; $\hat{}R^2 = 0.42$; F-statistic = 43.7; $p = 0.00$	Number of observations: 119 $R^2 = 0.84$; $\hat{}R^2 = 0.83$; F-statistic = 72.1; $p = 0.00$	Number of observations: 123 $R^2 = 0.88$; $\hat{}R^2 = 0.87$; F-statistic = 82.0; $p = 0.00$

Source: Own calculations.

indicated) may have indicated the transformation of the mechanism of simple destruction into "inverse creative destruction." These statements imply that the mechanism of "inverse creative destruction" was necessary – not only for overcoming simple destruction but also providing the economy with greater dynamism than that which resulted from creative destruction. This conclusion was partially confirmed by the comparative analysis of the empirical APL values with the forecast in Version I (Figure 9.1).

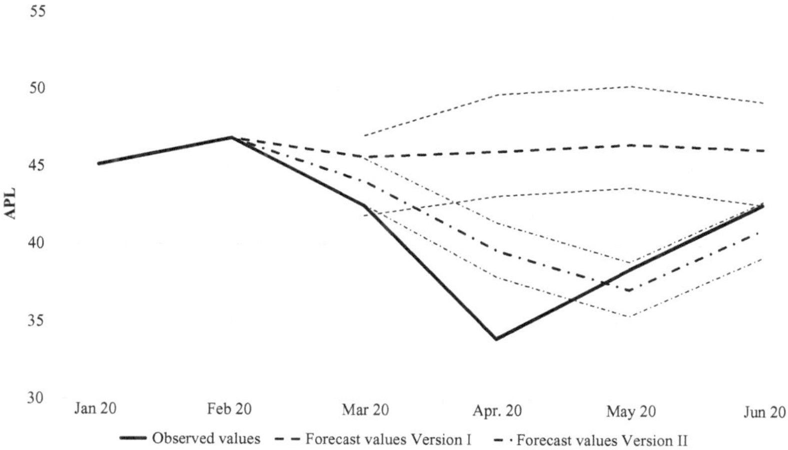

Figure 9.1 Shows the actual and forecasted levels of labor productivity with 95% confidence intervals for each version of the forecast.
Source: Own calculations.

The labor productivity that was recorded in June 2020 reached a level that was close to the value that was specified in the lower confidence interval of the first version of the forecast. Assuming that the dynamics of the *APL* changes that were observed starting in May 2020 will continue in the coming months, the level of labor productivity will exceed the values that were forecast for the economy functioning under normal conditions, that is, without the COVID-19 pandemic. Such a scenario would overcome the productivity stagnation trap that is visible in the first version of the forecast, which may suggest that, from the point of view of efficiency, the processes that have taken place during the unprecedented situation of the COVID-19 pandemic may be a catalyst for positive economic changes in the long run. The results of the multiplier analysis that was based on the ARDL model with binary variable D1 that was prepared in the second step of our research (Table 9.1 – Column C) confirm these conclusions.

The autoregressive part of the model is a stationary process, and the long-term multipliers that were estimated for the periods before and during the COVID-19 pandemic meet the adopted criterion of statistical significance. This means that, during both distinguished sub-periods of the analysis, there were long-run equilibria between the dependent variable and each independent variable. The long-run equilibria before and during the COVID-19 pandemic are described by Equations (9.5) and (9.6), respectively, as follows:

– For changes in labor productivity before COVID-19 pandemic:

$$DAPL = -0.07 + 0.29^{\star} EI - 0.15^{\star} ES; \tag{9.5}$$

– For changes in labor productivity during COVID-19 pandemic:

$$DAPL = -0.07 + 0.45^{\star} EI + 0.57^{\star} ES. \tag{9.6}$$

The multiplier analysis leads us to two basic conclusions: First, both in a normally functioning economy and during the period of the COVID-19 pandemic, the combined long-run impact of the intra- and inter-firm effects (*EI*) resulted in an increase in labor productivity growth (which was stronger during the second of the periods); and second, while the processes of the reallocation of resources among industries (*ES*) led to a reduction in labor productivity growth during the period before the COVID-19 pandemic, the current crisis changed the strength of this impact and (most importantly) its direction. Thus, the results of the multiplier analysis led to the following conclusion: The processes that took place during the COVID-19 pandemic not only strengthened the pro-efficient impact of the *EI* but also became a catalyst for positive long-run changes in the economy through strong productivity-based pressure on the reallocation of resources.

Due to the limitation of an empirical study to one sector and one country, the short time span of the analysis for the period of the COVID-19 pandemic, and the *APL* index that was used (which is only a rough measure of productivity), the results cannot be the basis of a full empirical verification of our concept of "inverse creative destruction." Nevertheless, our study opens up a promising direction for further research on the role of innovations and selection under conditions of abnormal liquidation.

Conclusions and recommendations

A key element of the concept of "inverse creative destruction" is the adaptive innovations that were implemented by enterprises as an escape from simple destruction during the COVID-19 pandemic. Excluding adaptive innovations from economic processes implies that changes in productivity would only be the result of incorrect selection. The negative effects of market selection in the form of the "scarring" effect would be amplified by the "zombie" effect, which is a derivative of institutional selection that is devoid of an efficiency criterion. Under such conditions, the most optimistic version of the events after the COVID-19 pandemic from the point of view of productivity would be a return to the previous growth path. In this context, adaptive innovations seem to be a necessary condition – not only for reversing the tendencies that are typical of simple destruction, but also for breaking the productivity stagnation that can be observed in many countries for years to come.

It should be emphasized that adaptive innovations resulted mainly from the implementation of available technical and organizational solutions that were developed before the COVID-19 pandemic, so they cannot be considered to be innovations in the Schumpeterian sense. Can actions that are based on the current production–possibility frontier ensure the economic dynamics that result from the long-run equilibrium equation that is estimated for the COVID-19 pandemic period? How long can "inverse creative destruction" be a fuel for productivity growth without the support of a pro-efficiency mechanism of institutional selection?

In light of these questions, the necessity for conducting state policy to support R&D activity and the implementation of innovations during the COVID-19 pandemic (and after its completion) is obvious. Few, however, see the need to link the tools that are used by the state to protect companies and jobs with a criterion that is based on efficiency. A state policy that is devoid of this element may lead to perpetuate an ineffective technologically obsolete economic structure (Askenazy, Erhel, 2015; Kılınç, 2018; Peters, Walsh, 2019; Faccio, McConnell, 2020) and, in the context of our results, deprive the economy of the long-term benefits that result from resource reallocation processes.

Notes

1 The authors use the term "induced innovation"; i.e., induced by the pandemic. However, the understanding of induced innovation in the economic literature is different. J.R. Hicks defined induced innovations as inventions that are caused by a change in the relative prices of production factors and aimed at limiting the use of a relatively more expensive factor in the new conditions (Kulawik, 2016). According to H.D. Kurz (2012, p. 80), complementary innovations in another sector (i.e., induced innovations) are necessary for an invention to take the form of an innovation implemented in one sector. Therefore, the term "adaptive innovations" is used in this study.

2 During the COVID-19 crisis, the "scarring" effect has affected both well-established companies (exporters whose operations are widely recognized as being highly effective) and the most productive entities in the initial stage of activity (Bosio et al., 2020).

3 The direction of the "shadow of death" effect on productivity depends on the relationship between firms' financial conditions and their productivity.

4 According to orthodox Schumpeterian, the propensity to implement adaptive innovations in response to falling profits and shrinking demand is the risk of the bankruptcy/liquidation of a business (Erixon, 2016).

E. Erixon (2016, p. 94) uses the term "orthodox Schumpeterian" to refer to a group of economists who, referring to the considerations of J.A. Schumpeter concerning Kondratieff long waves, emphasize "the role of negative external conditions as a driving force in innovation processes."

5 In the absence of anti-crisis aid, the probability of the "zombie" effect is minimal, as such companies are subject to destruction. Assuming that efficiency is the basis for the selection, the "scarring" effect will not occur in the analyzed variant.

6 The period of the analysis was determined by the availability of the statistical data.

7 The sold production of industry was expressed in constant prices from January 2010 using the consumer price index.

8 E.S. Andersen proposed the method of quantifying creative destruction and named it "evometrics." The method is derived from biological sciences and was used by G.R. Price to describe the mechanism of evolutionary processes; hence, its name – "evolutionary econometrics."

Literature

Abdi, H., Molin, P., (2007) Lilliefors/Van Soest's Test of Normality, in: *Encyclopedia of Measurement and Statistics*, N.J. Salkind (ed.), Sage Publications, Thousand Oaks, CA, 540–544.

Andersen, E.S., (2004a) Evolutionary Econometrics: From Joseph Schumpeter's Failed Econometrics to George Price's General Evometrics and Beyond, www.business.aau.dk/evolution/esapapers/esa04/evometrics.pdf

Andersen, E.S., (2004b) Population Thinking, Price's Equation and the Analysis of Economic Evolution, *Evolutionary and Institutional Economics Review*, 1/1, 127–148.

Askenazy, P., Erhel, C., (2015) The French Productivity Puzzle, *IZA Discussion Paper*, 9188.

Baily, M.N., Bartelsman, E.J., Haltiwanger, J., (2001) Labor Productivity: Structural Change and Cyclical Dynamics, *Review of Economics and Statistics*, 83/3, 420–433.

Baldwin, J.R., Gu, W., (2002) Plant Turnover and Productivity Growth in Canadian Manufacturing, *OECD Science, Technology and Industry Working Papers*, 2002/2.

Baltagi, B., (2011) *Econometrics*, Springer-Verlag, Berlin.

Bartelsman, E.J., Dhrymes, P.J., (1998) Productivity Dynamics: U.S. Manufacturing Plants, 1972–1986, *Journal of Productivity Analysis*, 9/1, 5–34.

Boone, L., Haugh, D., Pain, N., Salins, V., (2020) Tackling the Fallout from COVID-19, in: *Economics in the Time of Covid-19*, Baldwin, R., Weder di Mauro, B., (eds.), CEPR Press, London, 37–44.

Bosio, E., Djankov, S., Jolevski, F., Ramalho, R., (2020) Survival of Firms During Economic Crisis, *World Bank Policy Research Working Paper*, 9239, https://ssrn.com/abstract=3599546

Davidson, R., MacKinnon, J.G., (1999) *Foundations of Econometrics*, Oxford University Press, New York.

Dieppe, A., Celic, S.K., Okou, C., (2020) What Happens to Productivity During Major, Adverse Events, in: *Global Productivity. Trends, Drivers, and Policies*, Dieppe, A., (eds.), World Bank, Washington, DC, 97–154.

Dieppe, A., Matsuoka, H., (2020) Sectoral Sources of Productivity Growth, in: *Global Productivity. Trends, Drivers, and Policies*, Dieppe, A., (ed.), World Bank, Washington, DC, 357–389.

di Mauro, F., Syverson, C., (2020) The COVID Crisis and Productivity Growth, https://bfi.uchicago.edu/wp-content/uploads/BFI_White-Paper_Syverson_6.2020.pdf

Erixon, L., (2016) Is Firm Renewal Stimulated by Negative Shocks? The Status of Negative Driving Forces in Schumpeterian and Darwinian Economics, *Cambridge Journal of Economics*, 40/1, 93–121.

Faccio, M., McConnell, J.J., (2020) Impediments to the Schumpeterian Process in the Replacement of Large Firms, *NBER Working Papers*, 27871.

Fornaro, L., Wolf, M., (2020) Covid-19 Coronavirus and Macroeconomic Policy, *Working Papers*, 1168, Barcelona Graduate School of Economics, Barcelona, Spain.

Foster, L., Haltiwanger, J., Krizan, C.J., (2002) The Link Between Aggregate and Micro Productivity Growth: Evidence from Retail Trade, *NBER Working Papers*, 9120.

Foster, L., Haltiwanger, J., Syverson, C., (2005) Reallocation, Firm Turnover, and Efficiency: Selection on Productivity or Profitability?, *NBER Working Papers*, 11555.

Geroski, P.A., (1989) Entry, Innovation and Productivity Growth, *Review of Economics and Statistics*, 71/4, 572–578.

Greene, W.H., (2012) *Econometric Analysis*, Pearson Education, Boston, MA.

Griliches, Z., Regev, H., (1992) Productivity and Firm Turnover in Israeli Industry: 1979–1988, *NBER Working Papers*, 4059.

Gujarati, D.N., (2004) *Basic Econometrics*, McGraw-Hill, New York.

Hill, R.C., Griffiths, W.E., Lim, G.C., (2011) *Principles of Econometrics*, John Wiley & Sons, Hoboken, NJ.

Jensen, J.B., McGuckin, R.H., Stiroh, K.J., (2001) The Impact of Vintage and Survival on Productivity: Evidence from Cohorts of U.S. Manufacturing Plants, *Review of Economics and Statistics*, 83/2, 323–332.

Johnston, J., DiNardo, J., (1997) *Econometric Methods*, McGraw Hill, New York.

Karabag, S.F., (2020) An Unprecedented Global Crisis! The Global, Regional, National, Political, Economic and Commercial Impact of the Coronavirus Pandemic, *Journal of Applied Economics and Business Research*, 10/1, 1–6.

Keogh-Brown, M., Wren-Lewis, S., Edmunds, W.J., Beutels, P., Smith, R.D., (2009) The Possible Macroeconomic Impact on the UK of an Influenza Pandemic, University of Oxford, Oxford, *Economics Series Working Papers*, 431.

Kılınç, U., (2018) Productivity Slowdown and Misallocation in the Post-Recession: What Prevents Recovery?, *Journal of Technology Transfer*, 43/6, 1542–1570.

Kulawik, J., (2016) Environmental Regulations and Innovations versus Competitiveness, *Zagadnienia Ekonomiki Rolnej*, 1/346, 3–21.

Kurz, H.D., (2012) *Innovation, Knowledge and Growth. Adam Smith, Schumpeter and the Moderns*, Routledge, New York.

Lee, H.N., Lee, J.-D., Beak, C., (2017) Productivity Dynamics and the Cleansing Effect of Two Recessions: Evidence from the Manufacturing Sector in Korea, *Pacific Economic Review*, 22/4, 677–701.

Levinsohn, J., Petropoulos, W., (2001) Creative Destruction or Just Plain Destruction?: The U.S. Textile and Apparel Industries since 1972, *NBER Working Papers*, 8348.

Levinthal, D.A., (1998) The Slow Pace of Rapid Technological Change: Gradualism and Punctuation in Technological Change, *Industrial and Corporate Change*, 7/2, 217–247.

McKibbin, W., Fernando, R., (2020) The Global Macroeconomic Impacts of COVID-19: Seven Scenarios, *CAMA Working Papers*, 19/2020, http://dx.doi.org/10.2139/ssrn.3547729

Metcalfe, S., (1998) *Evolutionary Economics and Creative Destruction*, Routledge, London.

OECD (2020) *Productivity Gains from Teleworking in the Post COVID-19 Era: How can Public Policies Make it Happen?*, https://read.oecd-ilibrary.org/view/?ref=135_135250-u15liwp4jd&title=Productivity-gains-from-teleworking-in-the-post-COVID-19-era

Ouyang, M., (2005) The Scarring Effect of Recessions, *University of California Department of Economics Working Papers*, 050609.

Peters, M., Walsh, C., (2019) Declining Dynamism, Increasing Markups and Missing Growth: The Role of the Labor Force, Society for Economic Dynamics, *2019 Meeting Papers*, 658.

Salterio, S.E., (2020) *Accounting for the Unaccountable – Perspectives on the Economic Effects of the Coronavirus 19 Pandemic*, http://dx.doi.org/10.2139/ssrn.3581243

Shen, H., Fua, M., Panb, H., Yua, Z., Chena, Y., (2020) The Impact of the COVID-19 Pandemic on Firm Performance, *Emerging Markets Finance and Trade*, 56/10, 2213–2230.

Sekkat, K., (2010) *Market Dynamics and Productivity in Developing Countries: Economic Reforms in the Middle East and North Africa*, Springer-Verlag, New York.

Sudipta, A., Kaushik, B., (2020) The Impact of Coronavirus into the Global Economic Prospects, *The Journal of Indian Management*, 10/2, 1–4.

ter Wengel, J., Rodriguez, E.R., (2006) Productivity and Firm Dynamics: Creative Destruction in Indonesian Manufacturing, 1994–2000, *Bulletin of Indonesian Economic Studies*, 42/3, 341–355.

Troske, K.R., (1996) The Dynamic Adjustment Process of Firm Entry and Exit in Manufacturing and Finance, Insurance, and Real Estate, *Journal of Law and Economics*, 39/2, 705–735.

Verbeek, M., (2004) *A Guide to Modern Econometrics*, John Wiley & Sons, Hoboken, NJ.

Wäckerle, M., (2014) *The Foundations of Evolutionary Institutional Economics. Generic Institutionalism*, Routledge, London.

Weder di Mauro, B., (2020) Macroeconomics of the Flu, in: *Economics in the Time of Covid-19*, Baldwin, R., Weder di Mauro, B., (eds.), CEPR Press, London, 31–36.

Yaşar, M., Rejesus, R.M., Mintemur, I., (2004) Is There Evidence of Creative Destruction in the Turkish Manufacturing Sector? Lessons from a Cross-Industry Analysis of Aggregate Productivity Growth, *Applied Economics*, 36/17, 1927–1945a.

10 Factors of large enterprise competitiveness at initial stage of economic crisis

Anna Wolak-Tuzimek and Joanna Duda

Introduction

Regardless of its operations, each enterprise strives for market success; this is attained when an enterprise realizes its objectives effectively and gains an advantage over its competitors.

This advantage acquires special importance during times of crises. After Ritter and Pedersen (2020, p. 216), a crisis can be defined as "an unstable or crucial time or state of affairs in which a decisive change is impending" and "a situation that has reached a critical phase." The best known and remembered historical crises include the global economic crisis of 1929–1933, which originated with the overcapitalization at the New York Stock Exchange. This resulted in a huge surge in unemployment (ca. 33% in the US and 30% in Germany). Another was the financial crisis that continued for two years between 2007 and 2009. The high demand for the high-risk mortgage crediting that was being extended by American banks was its chief cause. The crunch led to the collapse of Lehman Brothers and the consequent loss of jobs, homes, and savings by millions of people worldwide.

The background to the present crisis is utterly different, as it was caused by a pandemic; however, its extent has still been global (like with the preceding crises). Market analysts increasingly take to comparing its consequences to the 1930s global crisis. Forbes reports unemployment worldwide rose the most rapidly since 1929–1933. Its rate in the US was 14.5%, in the Eurozone, 11.5%, and in Poland, 5.5%, respectively (https://www.forbes.pl/raport-forbes).

A crisis brings both threats and opportunities (Chisholm-Burns, 2010), and accelerates the implementation of new solutions. A crisis motivates entrepreneurs to change their business models. Ritter T and Pedersen C. advanced and proved the hypothesis that the crisis that was triggered by the coronavirus affected changes to the business models of enterprises (2020, pp. 214–224). Continuing this line of thinking, we have decided to determine whether the current crisis had an impact on the changes to the factors of enterprise competition and have posited hypothesis H1: The economic crisis that was caused by COVID-19 influenced changes in the factors of enterprise competitiveness.

DOI: 10.4324/9781003368687-10

Factors of enterprise competitiveness – review of literature

Competitiveness is one of the main factors that define the development potential of economic entities. Foundations of the competitiveness theory have been laid by Krugman (1994), who questioned the usefulness of the concept based on the theory of comparative advantage. Competitiveness is now taken to mean the economic power of an enterprise as compared to its competitors in the global market, where products, services, people, and innovations move freely in spite of geographic borders (Chao-Hung, Li-Chang, 2010, p. 563); an enterprise's ability to discover changes in its environment and inside by continuing improving market competitiveness criteria in comparison to its rivals (Nemethné Gál, 2010, p. 10); the ability to design, make, and sell products and services that are better than those that are offered by competitors in terms of pricing and quality criteria (Ambastha, Momaya, 2004, p. 45); enterprises' abilities to realize their objectives by means of better prices, quality, terms of delivery and payment, and other parts of a transaction that is important to buyers. The competitiveness of a given enterprise is expressed via its profits, market share, and significance in a sector or economy. By achieving these objectives, an enterprise is capable of maintaining or raising its competitiveness in the market. The specialist literature contains a number of interpretations of the concept, yet a universally accepted definition of enterprise competitiveness does not exist. Therefore, the notion may carry different meanings to diverse researchers or business stakeholders (Dzikowska, Gorynia, 2012, p. 5).

At present, competitiveness is regarded to be a fundamental part of economic life and a basic regulator in the allocation of all economic resources. It is increasingly considered to be a parameter that is equally as important as enterprise profitability. This stems from (and is part of) competition.

Competition drives the development of creativity of all human actions in all areas of life. It mobilizes enterprises to use their resources as efficiently as possible and constitutes a constant part of the market economy. Michael Porter defined competition as rivalry among competitors that consists of winning of the best possible position by way of price competition, advertising, the launching of new products, guarantees, etc. Rivalry occurs where one or more competitors are either under the pressure of a situation or see opportunities for improving their own standings (Porter, 1985, p. 34). An enterprise's capacity for operation in a given market is the essence of competitiveness. The term is employed universally in reference to different types of economic units, sectors of a national economy, products, resources, abilities, management systems and their features, information, structures, procedures, and strategies. Competition may be studied at diverse levels. Research into the competitiveness of enterprises and the national economy are of paramount importance. The competitiveness of the economy has been examined by a number of authors (e.g., Fyliuk et al., 2019; Botrić, Broz, 2016; Sachs, 2000), who has laid theoretical foundations for defining key aspects of competitiveness, instrumental factors, assessment ratios, etc. Competition among enterprises should be seen as the most important expression of competitiveness (Krugman, 1994). Enterprises are key links of the real economy. The directions and rates of development of national economies and living standards depend on enterprise behavior. Aiming for development that is closely associated with growing competitiveness is a major objective of an enterprise. It can therefore be said that an enterprise that is willing to develop attempts to enhance its competitiveness. The following components of an enterprise's competitiveness can be distinguished: its market share, importance in a sector or an economy, share of export revenue in total revenue, and profitability of invested capital. The realization of these objectives allows an enterprise to maintain or improve its competitiveness in the market. Enterprise competitiveness can also be addressed from the perspective of the environment's impact. In this connection, competitiveness can be understood as a system that consists of the following elements: competitiveness potential, competitive advantage, instruments of competing, and competitive standing. The foregoing characteristics define the levels of enterprise competitiveness.

Competitiveness potential means all of the tangible and intangible resources of an enterprise that are necessary for operation in the market arena of competition (Stankiewicz, 2005, p. 89).

According to M. Gorynia (2001, pp. 170–172), competitive potential encompasses not only broadly defined enterprise resources but also its culture, organizational and legal structure, strategic vision, and specific behavior.

It has its source in market and other internal (dependent on an enterprise) and external (independent) conditions. Competitive advantage arises from the utilization of competitiveness potential to create an attractive market offer and effective instruments of competing. A number of authors (e.g., Maráková et al., 2021; Wolak-Tuzimek, Duda, 2021; Wolak-Tuzimek, Luft, 2021; Sigalas, 2015; Sigalas et al., 2013; Arend, 2003; Ma, 2000) have claimed that the term is difficult to define unambiguously. It depends on a range of factors; consequently, its various types can be distinguished. The factors that lie at the source of the advantage are of key significance. For example, Porter (1990, p. 74) identified the following sources of competitive advantage: the making of top-quality products, the ability to run minimum costs of production, the manufacturing of products with different useful values, and offering a wide range of products. Competitive standing is the result of competing against other competitors. This is the effect of an enterprise's competition strategy (Ensign, 2001, p. 21). Competitive standing is most commonly measured with market share, numbers of customers, financial position, numbers, and the types of terms and conditions that are supported. The growth of innovation has been a key goal of enterprises that have desired to enhance their competitive standing in the markets (Sieradzka, 2013, p. 2734).

The competitiveness of an economic entity is determined by internal factors (tangible and intangible, human and financial resources), outcome-based factors (products, distribution, economic conditions of market exchange), and external (subjective and qualitative) factors to a substantial degree.

Internal factors form the potential of enterprise competitiveness. Their appropriate use decides one's capabilities for competing and affects the present and future competitive standing of an enterprise. Outcome-based factors (or instruments of competing) serve intensive fighting for a competitive position against one's rivals. The external factors of competitiveness, meanwhile, comprise subjective factors that were called the driving forces of competition by M. E. Porter and qualitative factors (i.e., the macro-environment).

The literature offers three major approaches to competitiveness measurements at the level of an enterprise – those that were proposed by P.J. Buckley et al. (1988), W.Y. Man et al. (2002), and A. Ambasth and K. Momay (2004). The model of competitiveness that was compiled by W.Y. Man et al. applies to the competitiveness of small- and medium-sized enterprises (which excludes this method from being applied to the research that is presented here). On the other hand, A. Ambasth's and K. Momay's model concerns the relationships among the processes of strategic management, human resources management, operations management, technology management, and enterprise competitiveness. The model includes a number of unmeasurable variables, which are very difficult to analyze by means of statistical methods.

The theory of three aspects of competitiveness that was advanced by P.J. Buckley et al. (1988) defined three dimensions of competitiveness: outcome-based competitiveness (the competitive standing of an enterprise), competitive potential, and the competitive process. The potential concerns expenses in operational activities, while outcome-based competitiveness relates to operational performance. The competitive process is, in turn, connected to enterprise management. The authors proposed a separate set of factors that were meant to measure each dimension. The dimension of outcome-based competitiveness encompasses the results of enterprise processes that can be measured with percentage market share or level of profitability, for example. As far as competitive potential is concerned, Buckley et al. (1988, p. 177) proposed the following factors of competitiveness: comparative advantage, cost level, productivity, work productivity, price level, quality of products, and access to resources (capital, qualified workforce, and raw materials). The process of management (the third dimension of competitiveness) includes quantitative and qualitative indicators; for example, benefits from ownership privileges, involvement in international business, marketing capabilities, relationships in the management process, or benefits of scale and scope.

Methods

The results of a Poland-wide study that was conducted in January 2018 and March 2020 using *computer-assisted telephone interview* (CATI) on a sample of 1600 large enterprises that were generated by random choice are presented in this article. In all, 264 enterprises answered all of the questions in the survey questionnaire in 2018, whereas the number of examined entities fell to 253 in the latter round of the study.

Assuming $\alpha = 95\%$ and $\beta = 6\%$, the results that were produced in 2018 and 2020 were representative of the general population.

The empirical study employed an original survey questionnaire that consisted of two parts: particulars and questions. Some objective criteria were adopted in the latter to characterize the sample, such as the organizational and legal status of the enterprise, its sector of operations, and the regions where it had offices.

An analysis of the surveyed enterprises indicated the following:

1 "Limited liability company" was the principal legal and organizational format in both of the enterprise groups. In 2018, these entities accounted for 72.35% of all of the businesses; in 2020, this number was 68.79%. The fewest enterprises in the study were "limited partnerships," with their shares constituting 2.27% and 2.37% of all of the entities, respectively.
2 Most of the enterprises engaged in trade and services (in 2018 – 104 firms; in 2020 – 118 firms) and industrial and chemical production (78 and 74 entities, respectively). The fewest enterprises in the study were active in consumer goods; that is, 2.27% (2018) and 2.37% (2020) of all of the firms.
3 The enterprises in the study were mostly based in Mazowieckie (56 firms in 2018; 46 in 2020) and Śląskie (36 firms in 2018; 34 firms in 2020). The fewest enterprises were registered in the Opolskie (1.89% in 2018) and Lubuskie (2.37% of all of the businesses in 2020) regions.

The other part of the survey asked six questions, and the responses were recorded on ten-point ordinal scales (where "1" meant a low significance, and "10," a high significance). This paper discusses the results that concerned three questions. The respondents were requested to assign significance to the individual observable variables that determined competitive standing, competitive potential, and instruments of competing. In all, 34 observable variables were taken into account and were divided according to the dimensions of enterprise competitiveness. In 2018, the competitive standing of an enterprise was measured by using five observable variables (market share [V1], financial position [V2], recognition of enterprise and its products in the market [V3], customer satisfaction [V4], implementation of Corporate Social Responsibility (CSR) [V5]), competitive potential was measured by using 16 observable variables (the financial liquidity of the enterprise [V6], profitability of enterprise [V7], equity level in the enterprise [V8], customer loyalty [V9], extensive distribution network [V10], appropriate management of IT infrastructure [V11], quality of managerial staff [V12], creativity of workers [V13], condition of plant and machinery [V14], research and development activities [V15], technical standard of products [V16], mastery of technology [V17], creation of strong product brand [V18], availability of materials [V19], standard of servicing [V20], and implementation of CSR [V21]); and instruments of competing were measured by using 13 observable variables (quality of product/service [V22], quality of servicing [V23], product brand [V24], advertising [V25], public relations [V26], image of enterprise [V27], highly qualified staff [V28], product pricing [V29], innovativeness of products [V30], size of product range [V31], matching of product structure to structure of consumer demand [V32], availability of products [V33], and implementation of CSR [V34]). In 2020, the competitive standing of each enterprise was measured by using five observable variables (market share [V1], financial position [V2], recognition of enterprise and its products in the market [V3], customer satisfaction [V4], and implementation of CSR [V5]); competitive potential was measured by using 16 observable variables (financial liquidity of enterprise [V6], profitability of enterprise [V7], equity level in enterprise [V8], customer loyalty [V9], method of distribution [V10], integrated IT system [V11], quality of managerial staff [V12], creativity of workers [V13], condition of plant and machinery [V14], research and development activities [V15], technical standard of products [V16], mastery of technology [V17], creation of strong product brand [V18], availability of materials [V19], standard of servicing [V20], and implementation of CSR [V21]); and instruments of competing were measured by using 13 observable variables (quality of product/service [V22], quality of servicing [V23], product brand [V24], advertising [V25], public relations [V26], image of enterprise [V27], highly qualified staff [V28], product pricing [V29], innovativeness of products [V30], size of product range [V31], matching of product structure to structure of consumer demand [V32], availability of products [V33], and implementation of CSR [V34]).

The research hypothesis was verified by means of exploratory factor analysis, a statistical method that serves to detect the optimum group of key factors, explicating correlations among observable variables (Thurstone, 1931). Factor analysis decomposes observable variables into a new set of uncorrelated variables that include shared and specific factors. It is designed to replace tested variables with fewer variables – factors on which the tested variables are linearly dependent and that explain dependencies and correlations among them as effectively as possible (Stanisz, 2007, p. 166).

As part of the factor analysis procedure, those factors that contributed most to the explication of the variability were successively defined. The input space was rotated to this end according to the *varimax* criterion. A regression line was defined in space that maximized the variance (variability) of the first factor while minimizing the variance around it. A factor that is separated in such a way has a maximum eigenvalue (variance); that is, it explains most of the variability of a studied phenomenon. Subsequent factors were defined that determined most of the remaining variability that was not covered by the previous factor. The number of factors to be determined was defined with the aid of the following:

- Kaiser criterion (1960): According to this, those factors with eigenvalues that are above 1 or loaded with at least a single variable can be retained;
- Cattell's scree test (1966): This illustrates eigenvalues as a linear graph. The selection of the number of factors is limited to finding a point (a number of components) where a plot begins to 'flatten out.' If a declining line turns horizontal, this is the so-called scree's end. Components to the right of the scree end point represent negligible variance and mostly random noise.

Results

The number of factors that were eligible for the analysis was determined on the basis of the Kaiser criterion and Cattell's scree test. Eleven factors were selected for continuing the analysis in the case of the data that were collected from the respondents in 2018, and nine factors were selected for that of 2020 (Figure 10.1).

More factors (11) and a greater concentration of factors with eigenvalues that were within a range of <1.05; 3.39> can be noted for the responses that were given in 2018. Fewer factors (9) were chosen for the responses

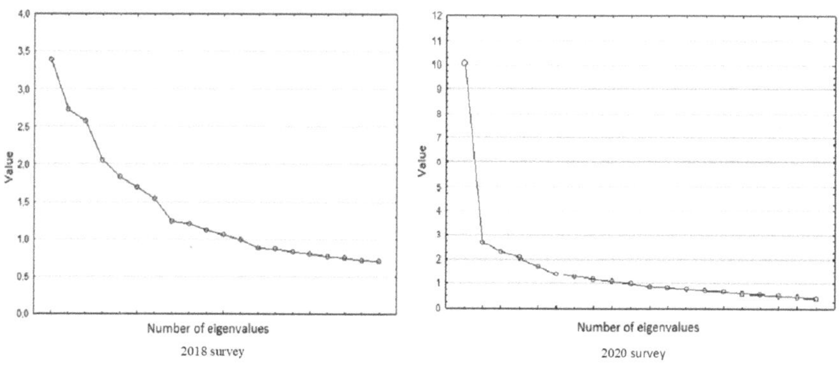

Figure 10.1 Scree diagram for eigenvalues for factors of enterprise competitiveness.

Table 10.1 Eigenvalue Matrix for Factors of Enterprise Competitiveness in Poland

Factor	*Characteristic value*		*Percentage of general variance*		*Accumulated characteristic value*		*Accumulated percentage*	
	I	*II*	*I*	*II*	*I*	*II*	*I*	*II*
F.1	3.39	10.05	9.97	29.57	3.39	10.05	9.97	29.57
F.2	2.73	2.67	8.02	7.86	6.12	12.72	17.99	37.43
F.3	2.58	2.30	7.57	6.77	8.69	15.02	25.56	44.20
F.4	2.06	2.05	6.05	6.03	10.75	17.07	31.61	50.23
F.5	1.83	1.70	5.39	4.99	12.58	18.77	37.00	55.22
F.6	1.69	1.39	4.97	4.09	14.27	20,16	41.97	59.31
F.7	1.54	1.26	4.54	3.72	15.81	21.42	46.51	63.03
F.8	1.24	1.16	3.64	3.42	17.05	22.58	50.15	66.45
F.9	1.21	1.06	3.55	3.13	18.26	23.64	53.70	69.58
F.10	1.12		3.30		19.38		57.00	
F.11	1.05		3.10		20.43		60.10	

I – Results of 2018 survey. II – Results of 2020 survey.
Source: Authors' own compilation.

that were gained in 2020, with the eigenvalue of the first factor equaling 10.05; this means that it explained 29.57% of the total variance. The remaining eigenvalues for this group of factors fell within a range of <1.06; 2.67>.

A comparative analysis of the data in Table 10.1 that concerned a matrix of eigenvalues for the enterprise competitiveness factors in respect to the responses that were provided in 2018 and 2020 shows that the factors that were mentioned in the 2020 responses were more reliable, as they explicated 69.58% of the overall variance. With regard to the responses that were generated in 2018, on the other hand, more factors explicated only 60.10% of the total variance. This means the responses that were given in 2020 were more consistent and accurate. As such, they can be used for purposes of a further analysis of COVID-19's effects on the factors of enterprise competitiveness.

The matrix of factor loads was subject to a Varimax rotation to produce a simple factor structure. Table 10.2 shows the matrices of the factor loads for those factors that describe enterprise competitiveness, that is, the correlation between the observable variables and the factors that were defined. The minimum correlation (0.6) was assumed to qualify as being significant. Values that were above 0.6 are shown in bold to highlight the variables that loaded the particular factors.

In 2018, the first factor (F.1) explicated 9.97% of the total variance and was represented by Variables 25 and 26 (i.e., advertising and public relations, respectively). The second factor (F.2) explained 8.02% of the overall variance and was represented by Variables 18 and 24, that is, creation

Table 10.2 Matrix of Factor Loads for Factors of Enterprise Competitiveness

Factor loads (normalized Varimax) principal components (loadings greater than 0.6)																				
Variable	*2018*											*2020*								
	F.1	*F.2*	*F.3*	*F.4*	*F.5*	*F.6*	*F.7*	*F.8*	*F.9*	*F.10*	*F.11*	*F.1*	*F.2*	*F.3*	*F.4*	*F.5*	*F.6*	*F.7*	*F.8*	*F.9*
1	0.00	0.11	0.05	**0.66**	0.17	−0.07	−0.11	0.16	−0.09	0.01	0.01	−0.11	0.42	0.28	−0.03	0.08	0.01	0.01	0.30	−0.03
2	0.11	−0.10	−0.06	0.26	0.54	−0.23	−0.04	−0.04	0.06	0.36	0.02	0.20	**0.78**	0.13	0.01	−0.09	0.10	0.01	0.01	0.11
3	0.01	−0.02	0.00	**0.81**	0.01	0.12	0.14	−0.05	0.05	0.02	−0.06	0.14	0.36	0.51	0.02	0.20	−0.05	0.02	0.08	−0.29
4	−0.01	−0.02	−0.02	**0.77**	−0.09	0.07	0.02	−0.10	0.04	−0.02	0.00	−0.06	0.33	0.38	0.12	0.09	−0.36	0.42	−0.04	0.03
5	0.06	0.00	−0.06	0.14	−0.14	**0.67**	−0.04	−0.14	−0.06	0.24	0.10	**0.82**	0.17	0.09	0.17	−0.06	0.03	0.03	0.22	0.02
6	−0.11	0.08	0.08	0.10	**0.74**	0.07	0.02	0.10	0.02	0.07	0.09	0.07	**0.86**	−0.04	0.09	0.19	0.09	0.12	0.05	0.05
7	−0.01	0.00	−0.03	−0.04	**0.74**	−0.12	0.16	−0.15	0.04	0.03	−0.04	0.08	**0.88**	−0.10	0.08	0.15	0.05	0.14	0.12	0.07
8	0.26	−0.10	0.16	−0.13	0.60	0.21	−0.01	0.06	0.03	−0.19	−0.05	0.07	0.26	−0.06	0.10	0.07	**0.81**	0.12	−0.01	0.08
9	0.39	0.00	−0.19	0.03	0.18	0.02	0.28	0.30	0.21	−0.03	0.19	−0.06	0.22	0.35	0.20	0.40	−0.22	0.47	0.07	0.12
10	0.27	0.60	−0.18	0.11	−0.02	0.10	0.08	−0.08	0.00	0.13	0.27	0.01	0.19	0.15	0.12	**0.69**	0.02	−0.09	0.17	0.01
11	−0.15	0.22	−0.49	0.08	−0.13	0.05	0.04	0.27	−0.31	−0.01	0.12	0.20	0.21	0.20	0.05	0.19	0.01	−0.02	0.14	**0.72**
12	−0.16	−0.11	0.06	0.14	0.19	0.09	**0.75**	−0.05	−0.09	0.13	0.03	0.10	−0.06	**0.61**	0.10	0.05	−0.21	0.29	0.06	0.18
13	0.19	0.20	0.06	−0.20	0.02	0.06	**0.64**	0.02	−0.05	0.10	−0.15	0.11	0.05	**0.66**	0.24	0.21	−0.03	0.30	0.17	0.14
14	−0.05	−0.11	**0.74**	0.13	0.07	−0.08	0.09	0.05	−0.08	0.05	−0.02	0.15	0.06	0.13	**0.69**	0.17	0.03	0.10	0.17	−0.23
15	−0.01	−0.01	**0.77**	−0.05	−0.05	0.00	0.05	−0.01	0.09	−0.01	0.12	0.08	0.05	0.26	**0.72**	0.18	−0.12	−0.15	−0.02	0.02
16	0.02	−0.03	**0.60**	−0.02	0.14	0.04	−0.15	0.25	0.03	0.45	−0.03	0.12	0.01	0.01	**0.82**	0.03	0.14	0.14	0.15	0.01
17	−0.13	−0.11	0.31	0.07	0.01	0.07	0.23	0.26	−0.07	**0.61**	0.07	0.05	0.10	−0.01	**0.79**	−0.12	−0.04	0.13	0.11	0.34
18	−0.02	**0.68**	0.02	−0.06	0.10	0.05	−0.19	0.09	0.02	−0.01	0.05	0.21	0.06	0.24	0.48	0.08	0.07	0.08	0.58	0.17
19	−0.20	0.00	−0.16	−0.12	0.00	0.19	0.00	−0.07	0.57	−0.08	0.45	0.37	−0.01	−0.07	0.22	0.45	0.22	0.47	−0.03	0.04
20	0.00	0.20	0.06	−0.02	0.03	0.02	−0.01	0.03	0.03	0.09	**0.78**	0.13	−0.01	0.10	0.48	0.21	0.10	0.09	0.08	0.49
21	0.13	0.12	0.08	0.06	0.10	**0.75**	0.01	0.03	−0.07	−0.18	0.05	**0.88**	0.14	0.07	0.16	0.03	0.01	0.06	0.19	0.13
22	−0.04	0.08	0.02	−0.05	0.04	−0.01	0.06	−0.14	0.12	**0.74**	0.02	−0.01	0.20	0.31	0.11	−0.04	0.04	**0.76**	0.08	0.08
23	−0.08	0.20	−0.26	0.06	0.00	−0.03	0.23	0.01	0.37	0.33	−0.40	0.14	−0.01	0.10	0.02	−0.02	0.14	**0.81**	0.25	−0.10

(continued)

Table 10.2 Continued

Factor loads (normalized Varimax) principal components (loadings greater than 0.6)																				
Variable	*2018*											*2020*								
	F.1	*F.2*	*F.3*	*F.4*	*F.5*	*F.6*	*F.7*	*F.8*	*F.9*	*F.10*	*F.11*	*F.1*	*F.2*	*F.3*	*F.4*	*F.5*	*F.6*	*F.7*	*F.8*	*F.9*
24	−0.09	**0.65**	−0.17	0.13	−0.16	0.09	0.08	−0.05	0.09	−0.01	0.08	0.14	0.16	0.29	0.15	−0.01	0.20	0.14	**0.66**	0.27
25	**0.79**	0.07	−0.06	−0.03	0.06	0.09	0.03	0.10	0.04	−0.04	0.00	0.26	0.07	0.05	0.05	0.33	−0.11	0.11	**0.73**	−0.09
26	**0.78**	−0.18	0.11	0.00	−0.03	0.07	0.06	0.11	−0.07	−0.05	−0.07	0.24	0.12	−0.05	0.16	0.034	−0.23	0.11	**0.66**	0.08
27	0.27	−0.08	−0.02	0.15	−0.04	−0.14	0.54	0.31	0.16	−0.04	0.08	0.16	0.34	0.10	0.11	0.05	−0.26	0.45	0.57	0.16
28	−0.40	0.58	0.05	−0.11	−0.01	−0.09	0.19	−0.05	0.13	−0.02	−0.12	0.18	0.07	0.55	0.10	0.02	0.20	0.37	0.35	0.23
29	0.13	0.22	0.25	−0.05	0.06	−0.05	0.03	0.00	0.43	0.25	0.08	0.08	0.06	0.12	0.03	0.58	0.02	0.09	0.32	0.26
30	0.02	0.04	0.09	0.10	0.06	−0.13	−0.06	0.18	**0.72**	0.04	−0.08	0.10	0.06	0.17	0.51	−0.01	0.07	0.26	0.51	0.13
31	0.34	0.17	0.04	−0.09	0.01	−0.02	−0.08	**0.64**	0.10	0.04	−0.18	0.35	−0.03	0.27	0.13	0.25	0.24	−0.03	0.56	−0.13
32	0.32	−0.39	0.28	0.00	−0.15	−0.01	0.16	0.51	0.11	0.00	0.11	0.13	−0.10	**0.62**	0.26	0.09	0.18	−0.02	0.43	0.16
33	0.03	−0.07	0.00	0.02	0.00	0.12	0.07	**0.74**	0.02	−0.03	0.07	0.04	0.10	0.25	0.06	0.47	0.29	0.09	0.41	0.39
34	0.01	0.04	−0.16	−0.04	0.01	**0.70**	0.10	0.36	0.04	−0.01	−0.08	**0.80**	0.01	0.13	0.08	0.14	0.04	0.09	0.19	0.12

Values above 0.6 are shown in bold to highlight the variables loading the particular factors.
Source: Authors' own compilation.

of strong product brand and product brand, respectively. The third factor (F.3) explicated 7.57% of the total variance and was represented by Variables 14, 15, and 16, namely the condition of plant and machinery, enterprise development activities, and technical standards of products, respectively. The fourth factor (F.4) explained 6.05% of the total variability and was represented by Variables 1, 3, and 4, that is, market share, knowledge of an enterprise and its products in the market, and customer satisfaction, respectively. The fifth factor (F.5) explained 5.39% of the total variance and was represented by Variables 6 and 7 (or financial liquidity and profitability of an enterprise, respectively). The sixth factor (F.6) explicated 4.97% of the total variance and was represented by Variables 5, 21, and 34. This was the implementation of CSR – a factor that is present in three dimensions of enterprise competitiveness (i.e., competitive standing, competitive potential, and instruments of competing). The seventh factor (F.7) explained 4.54% of the total variance and was represented by Variables 12 and 13, which were quality of management staff and creativity of workers, respectively. The eighth factor (F.8) explained 3.64% of the total variability and was represented by Variables 31 and 33, namely product range and availability of products, respectively. The ninth factor (F.9) explicated 3.55% of the total variance and was represented by Variable 30 (innovativeness of products). The tenth factor (F.10) explained 3.30% of the total variance and was represented by Variables 17 and 22, that is, mastery of technology and quality of product/service, respectively. The eleventh factor (F.11) explicated 3.10% of the total variance and was represented by a single variable (20 – the standard of servicing) (Duda, Wolak-Tuzimek, 2019, p. 124).

Based on the survey that was conducted in the initial phase of the crisis that was caused by the appearance of COVID-19, nine factors that were loaded by specific observable variables were determined. The first factor (F.1) explained 29.57% of the total variance and was represented by Variables 5, 21, and 34, that is, the implementation of CSR, which was present in the three dimensions of enterprise competitiveness. The second factor (F.2) explicated 7.86% of the total variance and was represented by Variables 2, 6, and 7, namely, financial standing, liquidity, and profitability of enterprise, respectively. The third factor (F.3) explained 6.77% of the total variance and was represented by Variables 12, 13, and 32, that is, quality of management staff, creativity of workers, and matching of products to structure of consumer demand, respectively. The fourth factor (F.4) explicated 6.03% of the total variance and was represented by Variables 14, 15, 16, and 17, that is, condition of machinery, development activities, technical standard of products, and mastery of technology, respectively. The fifth factor (F.5) explained 4.99% of the total variance and was represented by a single variable (10; i.e., method of distribution). The sixth factor (F.6) explicated 3.72% of the total variance and was represented by a single variable (8 – equity in enterprise). The seventh factor (F.7) explained 3.72% of the total variance and was represented by Variables 22 and 23, that is, quality of product/service and quality of servicing, respectively. The eighth factor (F.8) explicated 3.42% of the total variance and was represented by three variables (24, 25, and 26, namely, product brand, advertising, and public relations, respectively. The ninth factor (F.9) explained 3.13% of the total variance and was represented by a single variable (11; i.e., integrated IT system).

As suggested by the literature, the factor names were derived from the names of variables with maximum factor loads or from a shared characteristic.

In all, 11 factors that were loaded by 23 observable variables were indicated on the basis of the data that were provided by the respondents in 2018. The responses that were obtained in 2020 gave rise to 9 factors that were loaded by 21 observable variables. In both cases, most of the variables were related to the competitive potential of enterprises. The respondents pointed to eight variables in the dimension of competitiveness that were instruments of competing in 2018 and to seven variables in 2020. With reference to those variables that concerned competitive standing, the respondents identified four and two variables, respectively.

A comparison of our results from 2018 and 2020 that was generated on the application of exploratory factor analysis shows that the following can be noted:

1 Both of the groups of respondents defined six shared factors, that is, marketing communication, enterprise innovativeness, financial condition, CSR, human capital, and quality.
2 Five more factors were determined based on data that were received in 2018: brand, effects of marketing actions, product range, product innovativeness, and standard of servicing.
3 Three additional factors were determined based on the data that were received in 2020: method of distribution, equity in enterprise, and integrated IT system.

This situation is characterized in Table 10.3.

The analysis continued to decompose the factors into variables that were assigned to the particular dimensions of enterprise competitiveness. Observable variables were determined in such a way that had statistically significant effects on competitive standing, competitive potential, and instruments of competing. A comparative analysis of the results that were generated during both years implies the following:

1 The "Implementation of CSR" variable affected the competitive standing of the enterprises in both of the years under examination.
2 Nine shared variables (financial liquidity of enterprise, profitability of enterprise, quality of managerial staff, creativity of workers, condition

Table 10.3 Matrix of Enterprise Competitiveness Factors During Studied Years

Factor name		*2020 survey*								
		CSR	*Financial standing of enterprise*	*Human capital*	*Enterprise innovation*	*Method of distribution*	*Equity in enterprise*	*Quality*	*Marketing communication*	*Integrated IT system*
2018 survey	Marketing communication								X	
	Brand									
	Enterprise innovation				X					
	Effect of marketing actions									
	Financial standing of enterprise		X							
	CSR	X								
	Human capital			X						
	Product range									
	Product innovativeness									
	Quality							X		
	Standard of servicing									

Source: Authors' own compilation.

of plant and machinery, research and development activities, technical standard of products, mastery of technology, and implementation of CSR) had impacts on the competitive potential of enterprises, as did creation of strong product brand and standard of servicing in 2018 and equity levels in enterprise, method of distribution, and integrated IT system in 2020.
3 In 2018 and 2020, quality of product/service, product brand, advertising, public relations, and implementation of CSR were instruments of competing.

In the initial period of the economic crisis, the respondents designated three factors that were absent from the previous study, that is, method of distribution, enterprise equity, and integrated IT system (when loaded by the individual observable variables of the same names). These variables were related to one dimension of competitiveness, that is, competitive potential of enterprises.

The analysis demonstrated a difference in the structure of enterprise competitiveness factors that were applied prior to and at the initial stage of the economic crisis that was caused by COVID-19, which validates our research hypothesis.

Conclusion and recommendations

The current worldwide crisis that was caused by the COVID-19 pandemic has had an immediate impact on enterprises, which have been forced to adjust to changing market conditions. The selection of competitiveness factors that are used by enterprises to develop their advantage over their competition has changed as well.

The data that were obtained in surveys of 264 (2018) and 253 (2020) large enterprises that were active in the Polish economy have helped us show that there were statistically significant differences in the structures of competitiveness factors prior to and during the initial phase of the economic crisis. **Research Hypothesis** H1 (the economic crisis that was caused by COVID-19 affected changes of enterprise competitiveness factors) has thereby been validated.

The applied exploratory factor analysis led to the following conclusions:

1 The responses that were provided in 2020 were more consistent and accurate. Nine factors (CSR, financial condition of enterprise, human capital, innovativeness of enterprise, method of distribution, equity in enterprises, quality, marketing communication, and integrated IT system) were identified as factors that should now be employed by enterprises in order to improve their competitiveness in the market.
2 In light of the results that were produced in 2018, 23 variables influenced 11 factors of enterprise competitiveness, while the data that

were generated in 2020 suggested that 21 variables affected 9 factors. Most of the factors were competitive potential resources in both cases.

3 An analysis of the results that were produced in 2018 (before the crisis) and during the beginning of the crisis (March 2020) detected three new factors of competing, that is, method of distribution, equity in enterprise, and integrated IT system.

The modification of the factors of competition seems to be a response to the changes in the market. Under the official state of pandemic, it was found that the previously used competitive factors did not produce the expected effects. Therefore, entrepreneurs should apply new competitive factors such as method of distribution, equity level in enterprise, and integrated IT system. The total isolation prevented physical contact in the chain of supply (with suppliers and clients). Access to stationary outlets was more difficult or impossible. Therefore, suppliers, clients, and consumers took to e-commerce, buying products on the Internet. For this reason, enterprises should begin offering their products online with deliveries to homes or businesses. Enterprises are now implementing integrated IT systems that make teleworking substantially more efficient. These are ERP IV systems that include new functionalities that take advantage of new IT technologies like cognitive agent software, big data, the Internet of Things, computing clouds, and fog computing. This helps to realize the mechanisms of business globalization and the integration of links among market partners, cooperating organizations (banks, national insurance, broadly defined administration), and social portals to a greater extent.

The role of equity in enterprises has changed as well. In a number of sectors, the total lockdown in March 2020 caused enterprises to lose their incomes overnight, whereas fixed costs (like personnel overheads) remained constant. Banks considerably restricted lending, as the risk of business collapse increased. The restrictions on bank crediting expanded the share of equity in the financing of operations and development. Those enterprises without adequate equity levels commonly lost their financial liquidity and ended their businesses. The use of equity to borrow in order to boost investment capabilities above assets in hand could also be reduced. For these reasons, entrepreneurs should increase the proportions of the equity levels in their enterprises.

Literature

Ambastha, A. and Momaya, K. (2004) Competitiveness of firms: Review of theory, frameworks, and models. *Singapore Management Review*, 26(1), 45–61.

Arend, R.J. (2003) Revisiting the logical and research considerations of competitive advantage. *Strategic Management Journal*, 24(3), 279–284.

Botrić, V. and Broz, T. (2016) Competitiveness, trade with the EU and labour markets: Challenges for the Western Balkans. *South East European Journal of Economics and Business*, 11(2), 20–32.

Buckley, J.P., Pass, L.C. and Prescott, K. (1988) Measures of international competitiveness: A critical survey. *Journal of Marketing Management*, 4(2), 175–200.

Cattell, R. (1966) The scree test for the number of factors. *Multivariate Behavioral Research*, 1(2), 245–276.

Chao-Hung, W. and Li-Chang H. (2010) The influence of dynamic capability on performance in the high technology industry: The moderating roles of governance and competitive posture. *African Journal of Business Management*, 4(5), 562–577.

Chisholm-Burns, M.A. (2010) A crisis is a really terrible thing to waste, *American Journal of Pharmaceutical Education*, 74(2), 19.

Duda, J. and Wolak-Tuzimek, A. (2019) *Competitiveness Factors of Large Enterprises in Polish Economy*, In: J. Duda, I. Skalna (eds), *Functioning and Development of Enterprises – Contemporary Challenges*, Kraków: Wydawnictwo AGH, 127–145.

Dzikowska, M. and Gorynia, M. (2012) Teoretyczne aspekty konkurencyjności przedsiębiorstwa– w kierunku koncepcji eklektycznej? *Gospodarka Narodowa*, 4(248), 1–30.

Ensign, P.C. (2001) Value chain analysis and competitive advantage: Assessing strategic linkages and interrelationships. *Journal of General Management*, 27(1), 18–42.

Forbes, www.forbes.pl/raport-forbes (11.04.2023)

Fyliuk, H., Honchar, I. and Kolosha, V. (2019) The interrelation between economic growth and national economic competitiveness: The case of Ukraine. *Journal of Competitiveness*, 11(3), 53–69.

Gorynia, M. (2001) *Międzynarodowa konkurencyjność polskich przedsiębiorstw*, In: J. Kotowicz-Jawor (ed.), *Przedsiębiorczość i konkurencyjność*, Warszawa: Polskie Towarzystwo Ekonomiczne, 169–198.

Kaiser, H.F. (1960) The application of electronic computers to factor analysis. *Educational and Psychological Measurement*, 20(1), 141–151.

Krugman, P. (1994) Competitiveness: A dangerous obsession. *Foreign Affairs*, 73 (2), 28–44.

Ma, H. (2000) Competitive advantage and firm performance. *Competitiveness Review: An International Business Journal*, 10(2), 15–32.

Man, W.Y., Lau, T. and Chan, K.F. (2002) The competitiveness of small and medium enterprises. A conceptualization with focus on entrepreneurial competencies. *Journal of Business Venturing*, 17(2), 123–142.

Maráková, V., Wolak-Tuzimek, A. and Tuckova, Z. (2021) Corporate social responsibility as a source of competitive advantage in large enterprises. *Journal of Competitiveness*, 13(1), 113–128.

Nemethné Gál, A. (2010) Competitiveness of small and medium sized enterprises – a possible analytical framework. *Hungarian Electronic Journal of Sciences HEJ: ECO100115-A*, 1–14. http://heja.szif.hu/ECO/ECO-100115-A/eco100115a.pdf

Porter, M.E. (1985) *Competitive Advantage, Creating and Sustaining Superior Performance*. New York: The Free Press.

Porter, M.E. (1990) *The Competitive Advantage of Nations*. New York: The Free Press.

Ritter, T. and Pedersen, C. (2020) Analyzing the impact of the coronavirus crisis on business models. *Industrial Marketing Management*, 88, 214–224.

Sachs, J. (2000) Globalization and patterns of economic development. *Review of World Economics*, 136(4), 579–600.

Sieradzka, K. (2013) Innovativeness of enterprises in Poland, *Acta Univarsitatis Agriculturae et Silviculturae Mendelianae Brunensis*, LXI(7), 2729–2735.

Sigalas, C. (2015) Competitive advantage: The known unknown concept. *Management Decision*, 53(9), 2004–2016.

Sigalas, C., Economou., V.P. and Georgopoulos, N.B. (2013) Developing a measure of competitive advantage. *Journal of Strategy and Management*, 6(4), 2004–2016.

Stanisz, A. (2007) *Przystępny kurs statystyki z zastosowaniem Statistica pl – na przykładach z medycyny*, t. 3: *Analizy wielowymiarowe*, Kraków: Statsoft.

Stankiewicz, M.J. (2005) *Konkurencyjność przedsiębiorstwa. Budowanie konkurencyjności przedsiębiorstwa w warunkach globalizacji*, Toruń: TNOiK.

Thurstone, L.L. (1931) Multiple factor analysis, *Psychological Review*, 38, 406–427.

Wolak-Tuzimek, A. and Duda, A. (2021) *The concept of corporate social responsibility as a source of an enterprise's competitive advantage*. In S.I. Bukowski, A. Hyż, M. Lament (eds.), *Competitiveness and Economic Development in Europe: Prospects and Challenges,* New York: Routledge, 312–320.

Wolak-Tuzimek, A. and Luft, R. (2021) *Effect of Integrated IT Systems on Enterprise Competitiveness at Time of "Industry 4.0"*. In: J. Duda, A. Gąsior (eds.), *Industry 4.0. A Glocal Perspective,* New York: Routledge, 78–94.

11 Impact of the COVID-19 pandemic on competitive potential of large enterprises

Anna Wolak-Tuzimek and Vanda Maráková

Introduction

Competitiveness is one of the many characteristics of every enterprise; however, a minimum of two enterprises that conduct the same or similar activities must exist for one to be competitive in relation to the other (Duda and Wolak-Tuzimek, 2019, p. 115). Competitiveness has become the subject of market analysis and discussions as well as an integral element of economies, sectors, and enterprises that are engaged in market exchange. It is a very broad phenomenon, and its definitions have resulted from the views of authors. It may denote a complex capacity for effective competition in the market and a gaining of economic benefits as compared to one's competitors (Shevchenko et al., 2019, p. 16), the ability to achieve or maintain a competitive advantage, possibly synonymous with competitive ability (Ahmedova, 2015, p. 1105), being profitable and holding a dominant market standing (Sieradzka and Luft, p. 135), and an enterprise's actions to preserve an existing "good" competitive standing as compared to other firms (Šproch and Nevima, 2021, p. 111).

The competitiveness of an enterprise can be perceived as a system that consists of subsystems, each contributing to the enterprise's success in its competitive environment. Concepts of competitiveness as a model have been proposed by J.B. Barney (1991), M.J. Stankiewicz (2005), and M. Gorynia (2010), among others. A subsystem (dimension) of competitiveness is competitive potential, which is most commonly identified with the resources, competencies, and specific skills that are available to an enterprise. Its elements contribute to the achievement of competitive advantage, which arises when a firm is capable of securing the same benefits as its competitors at lower prices and above-average profits (Liu and Huang, 2009, p. 89); it is a relative efficiency in transforming the performance of key success factors into the firm's profitability (Ryu and Won, 2018, p. 118).

Factors of competitive potential and sources of competitive advantage in the market economy most frequently comprise the financial standing of an enterprise (Wen-Cheng et al., 2011) and its human capital (Cherkesova et al., 2016), Corporate Social Responsibility (CSR) (Maráková et al.,

DOI: 10.4324/9781003368687-11

2021; Abernathy et al., 2017), and organizational structure (Petison and Johri, 2006). Also, business innovations have become a crucial tool for firms to succeed (Pansuwong, 2020; Sieradzka, 2013) and gain integrated IT systems (Wolak-Tuzimek and Luft, 2021).

The emergence of the COVID-19 pandemic has caused a global economic slowdown, affecting trade, investments, growth, and levels of employment. It jeopardizes the economic welfare of individuals and institutions (Sneader and Singhal, 2020). A number of firms have been gravely affected by disturbances in the international chains of supply. Furthermore, the lockdowns have separated businesses from their customers. Enterprises have been forced to operate under the new conditions and use other factors in order to be competitive in the market.

It is the objective of this paper, therefore, to examine the impact of the COVID-19 pandemic on the competitive potential of large enterprises.

Results that were obtained from Polish enterprises prior to the pandemic (January 2018) and during its initial phase (March 2020) are presented. Exploratory factor analysis serves to construct two-factor models of enterprise competitive potential, which are subsequently compared.

Competitive potential of enterprise: review of literature

The competitive potential of an enterprise is a multi-dimensional concept that encompasses both the internal elements of a business and its environment (in particular, business support systems).

The term is primarily interpreted as a cluster of skills, abilities and capacities, powers and productivities (of a worker, a plant, machinery, and technology) (Sobolewski and Narojczyk, 2018, p. 38), an enterprise's resources and competencies (Bednarz, 2013, p. 26), and all of the tangible and intangible resources of an enterprise that are necessary for operating in market competition (Stankiewicz, 2005, p. 89). Competitive potential is composed of not only broadly defined resources but also the corporate culture, legal and organizational structure, strategic vision, and behavior that is specific to an enterprise (Gorynia, 2010, p. 75). It consists of processes and resources that are related to all areas of enterprise operation that are involved in production, marketing, finance, and human resource management. It includes those resources that are owned by and available to an enterprise (Kusa, 2007, p. 470).

M. Stankiewicz distinguished nine functional and resource domains that made up the competitive potential of an enterprise: research and development, production, quality management, procurement logistics, marketing, finance, employment, organization and management, and overall intangible resources. The individual domains consist of skills and resources that are components of competitive potential; these affect the creation and durability of competitive advantage (Stankiewicz, 2005, p. 118).

Most definitions of competitive potential include the notion of resources. The treatment of resources as the foundations of enterprise efficiency and competitiveness is most visible in the research and theoretical current that is known as a resource-based view of a firm or a resource-based theory of a firm. The current assumes that the competitive advantage of an enterprise depends on its resources. In general, the theory regards an organization as actively seeking hard-to-copy, rare, valuable, and unique configurations of resources and skills and being capable of creating, reproducing, and multiplying them.

J.B. Barney (1997, p. 143) stated that enterprise resources were factors that are controlled by an entity and used to develop and introduce its strategies or anything that can be treated as the strengths and/or weaknesses of an enterprise. These may help the enterprise attain a competitive advantage if they show the following characteristics (Barney, 1991, p. 112):

- they are strategically valuable, which means they can become foundations for using opportunities or counteracting threats;
- they are rare among current and future competitors;
- they are hard to imitate and copy by competitors;
- they cannot be substituted with other resources.

An enterprise's resources decide its competitiveness and constitute its chief sources of competitive advantage – owing to such characteristics as strategic value, rarity, and difficulty of imitation and substitution. Enterprises compete for resources that are unique and inaccessible to others. It should be noted, however, that the possession of resources in itself (treated as the assets that are available to an enterprise) is insufficient. Competitiveness is decided not by a quantity of resources but by their quality and the skill of their appropriate use. S. Łobejko and Z. Pierścionek (2011, p. 36) believed that competitive resources and skills must be unique, constitute major contributions to the values that are perceived by their customers, allow for the development of new products and services and expansion of their ranges.

Characteristic varieties of resources (referred to as competencies and/or abilities) are commonly addressed on a separate basis. Competencies form a specific part of all resources.

The specialist literature distinguishes competencies from abilities. There are two approaches in this respect: one treats both concepts as equivalent (though not synonymous), while abilities are among three components of competencies according to the other. The first approach defines competencies as the skill of maintaining coordinated resource allocation in such a way as to assist a firm in reaching its objectives. On the other hand, abilities mean recurrent action models that are relative to use of resources to create, manufacture, and/or launch products. The latter approach treats competencies as a whole that consists of three components: knowledge, abilities, and attitudes.

More and more researchers today are interested in exploring the field of developing the entrepreneurial knowledge, skill sets, and competencies that are required for the successful launch and management of a firm. Mitchelmore and Rowley (2010) proposed a list of key competencies, including 50 entrepreneurial skills, business and management skills, human relation skills, conceptual and relationship skills, and attitude or feature skills (Nikitina et al., 2020, p. 62).

Due to the multi-dimensional nature of the competitive potential of enterprises, a variety of factors are utilized in its comprehensive assessment. Those factors that determine competitive potential include an enterprise's philosophy, know-how, distribution channels, firm image, customer attachment to products, enterprise strategy, quality of management, finance management, research and development, marketing management staff, its possibility of acquiring state-of-the-art solutions, access to key resources, standard of operational and strategic management technology, the innovativeness of the staff, the tendency to improve qualifications, knowledge of the firm and its products in the market, the reputation (image) of the firm, the liquidity ratios, profitability ratios, and equity capital level in the enterprise, the commitment of third-party capital compared to equity, quality assurance systems in place, customer loyalty, a well-developed network of distribution, the proper management of the IT infrastructure, the quality of the managerial staff, the creativity of the staff, the condition of the plant and machinery, the creation of a strong product brand, the availability of materials, service standard, the convenient location of the enterprise, and the implementation of the corporate social responsibility concept (Wolak-Tuzimek, 2018, p. 1946; Gorynia, 2010, pp. 92–96; Shevelova, 2008, p. 370).

Practical attempts at measuring competitive potential should list those variables that are important when competing in a sector or enterprise group since the factors that determine successful competition may vary widely across sectors, markets, and enterprise sizes.

Methods

Under pandemic conditions, enterprises have been forced to adapt to the new market situation, e.g., by changing their customer relations. Firms that have invested in a number of channels are selling via fixed outlets, mobile applications, and Internet stores. They encourage staying home and shopping online. In addition, they offer free deliveries without limits on orders and extend the right to return. As a result, businesses have taken increasing advantage of new channels of distribution as factors of competitiveness. This leads to Research Hypothesis H1: under the conditions of the COVID-19 pandemic, the methods of distribution have had statistically significant effects on the competitive potential of enterprises.

The hypothesis was verified on the basis of the results of a survey of 264 (January 2018) and 253 (March 2020) Polish enterprises by means of exploratory factor analysis. The samples for both of the studies were selected at random from the large enterprises in Poland; 1,600 enterprises were drawn out of this population so that each unit of the general set had identical chances of selection. Assuming α = 95% and β = 6%, the results of the 2018 and 2020 surveys were representative of the general population.

The empirical study employed an original survey questionnaire. Data were generated with the aid of computer-assisted telephone interviews.

The first part of the survey concerned the particulars of the sample, including the legal organizations, sectors, and regions of the enterprises.

Most of the companies that were surveyed were limited liability companies – both in 2018 and 2020: in 2018, these constituted 72.35% of all of the enterprises, while their share declined by 3.56% points in the 2020 study. The studied enterprises engaged predominantly in trade and services (in 2018 – 104 enterprises; in 2020 – 118) and in industrial and chemical production (78 and 74 businesses, respectively). Most of the firms were based in Mazowieckie (56 in 2018; 46 in 2020) and in Śląskie regions (36 firms in 2018; 34 in 2020). The fewest companies that were examined were limited partnerships, accounting for 2.27% in 2018 and merely 0.1% more in 2020. Enterprises that dealt with consumer goods and fuel extraction numbered 6 and 7, respectively, in both studies. The lowest shares of enterprises were surveyed in Opolskie (1.89% – 2018) and Lubuskie (2.37% – 2020) regions.

The other part of the survey contained six questions, with responses recorded on a ten-point ordinal scale: 1 denotes a low significance and 10 denotes a high significance. This article presents the results that concerned 16 observable variables that defined the competitive potential of the enterprises. In 2018, these were the following variables: V1 – financial liquidity, V2 – profitability, V3 – level of equity in enterprise, V4 – customer loyalty, V5– expansive network of distribution, V6 – correct management of IT infrastructure, V7 – quality of management staff, V8 – creativity of staff, V9 – condition of plant and machinery, V10 – research and development activities, V11 – technical standard of products, V12 – mastery of technology, V13 – creation of strong product brand, V14 – availability of materials, V15 – standard of servicing, and V16 – implementation of Corporate Social Responsibility. The observable V5 and V6 variables were replaced with method of distribution and integrated IT system, respectively, in the 2020 survey.

The research hypothesis was verified by means of exploratory factor analysis – a statistical method for detecting an optimum group of core factors by explaining any correlations among observable variables (Thurstone,

1947). This consisted in examining the mutual relationships among a high number of variables and detecting the latent conditions that accounted for their presence in order to identify all of the factors that could actually be present in the correlations in a given system of variables while preserving as much information that was contained in the original variables as possible.

The procedure of factor analysis continued to separate those factors with the maximum contributions to the explication of the variables. To this end, the input space was rotated using Varimax, which was developed by Kaiser (1958). A regression line in space is determined that maximizes the variance (variability) of a first factor while minimizing the variance around it. Such a factor has the highest eigenvalue (variance); that is, it explains most of the variability of a studied phenomenon. Subsequent factors were identified that determined most of the remaining variability that was not covered by the previous factor (Wolak-Tuzimek and Duda, 2021, p. 317). The method simplifies the factor interpretation by minimizing the number of variables that are needed to explicate a given factor. The number of factors was determined by means of two methods:

- Kaiser criterion (1960): according to this, factors with at least the same variance as any standardized primary variable can be retained. Since the variance of each standardized primary variable is 1, the Kaiser criterion stipulates that only those factors with eigenvalues that are above or close to 1 are important.
- Cattell scree test (1966): a graph of the number and eigenvalues of the factors. A "breaking point" is identified, and the angle of the curve refraction (the "scree") is determined there. This point defines the number of factors that are eligible for further analysis. A point needs to be captured where continuing to increase the number of factors will only slightly contribute to an explanation of the variance (where the graph begins to "flatten out").

Results

The number of factors for the continuing analysis were determined in accordance with the Kaiser criterion and Cattell scree test. Based on the data that were generated in 2018 and 2020, four factors with eigenvalues above 1 were determined.

The eigenvalues concerning the responses suggested four factors whose eigenvalues were within the ranges of <1.09; 4.93> and <1.09; 4.96> as part of the surveys that were administered in 2018 and 2020. In both studies, the eigenvalue of the first factor was the highest and explicated ca. 31% of the total variance.

A comparative analysis of the data in Table 11.1 indicated that the responses that were gained in both 2018 and 2020 were very similar. Both

Table 11.1 Matrix of Eigenvalues for Factors That Describe Competitive Potential of Enterprises

Factor	*2018*				*2020*			
	Characteristic eigenvalue	*Percentage of general variance (%)*	*Accumulated characteristic eigenvalue*	*Accumulated percentage (%)*	*Characteristic eigenvalue*	*Percentage of general variance (%)*	*Accumulated characteristic eigenvalue*	*Accumulated percentage (%)*
F1	4.93	30.78	4.93	30.78	4.96	31.02	4.96	31.02
F2	1.95	12.16	6.88	42.94	1.96	12.25	6.92	43.27
F3	1.51	9.47	8.39	52.41	1.52	9.51	8.44	52.78
F4	1.09	6.82	9.48	59.23	1.09	6.84	9.53	59.62

Source: Authors' own compilation.

Table 11.2 Matrix of Factor Loadings for Factors That Describe Competitive Potential of Enterprises

Factor loads (normalized varimax) Main components (loads greater than 0.7 are highlighted)								
Variable	*2018*				*2020*			
	F1	*F2*	*F3*	*F4*	*F1*	*F2*	*F3*	*F4*
1	0.08	**0.93**	0.10	0.10	0.07	**0.93**	0.07	0.12
2	0.07	0.91	0.10	0.13	0.06	**0.91**	0.07	0.15
3	0.08	0.39	−0.30	0.42	0.09	0.37	−0.31	0.44
4	0.16	0.30	0.69	0.09	0.17	0.32	0.68	0.06
5	0.06	0.33	0.36	0.21	0.11	0.27	0.18	**0.71**
6	−0.03	0.15	0.28	0.54	−0.02	0.17	0.31	0.61
7	0.12	−0.12	**0.77**	0.09	0.10	−0.13	**0.76**	0.12
8	0.26	0.05	**0.76**	0.24	0.14	0.05	**0.76**	0.25
9	**0.75**	0.14	0.15	0.04	**0.74**	0.14	0.15	0.05
10	0.68	0.03	0.25	0.08	0.69	0.03	0.26	0.05
11	**0.85**	0.03	−0.02	0.21	**0.86**	0.03	−0.02	0.21
12	**0.78**	0.04	0.07	0.24	**0.78**	0.05	0.08	0.23
13	0.53	0.09	0.37	0.39	0.52	0.10	0.37	0.40
14	0.17	0.13	0.16	0.58	0.17	0.12	0.16	0.58
15	0.37	−0.04	0.17	0.60	0.41	−0.04	0.17	0.56
16	0.22	0.10	0.02	0.78	**0.18**	0.09	0.05	0.12

Source: Authors' own compilation.

of the results were reliable. The factors explicated 59.23% of the total variance in 2018 and 0.39% points of the variance in 2020.

The matrix of the factor loads was subjected to varimax rotation in order to generate a simple factor structure. Table 11.2 contains a matrix of the factor loads that described the competitive potential of an enterprise, that is, the correlation between the observable variables and the determined factors. A minimum correlation that qualifies as being significant is assumed to equal 0.7; those values above 0.7 are shown in bold to draw attention to the variables that loaded the particular factors.

The 2018 data imply that the first factor (F.1) explained 4.93% of the total variance, which was represented by three variables (9, 11, and 12, that is, condition of plant and machinery, technical standard of products, and mastery of technology). The second factor (F.2) explicated 1.95% of the total variance and was represented by two variables (1 and 2, i.e., financial liquidity and profitability of enterprise). The third factor (F.3) explained 1.52% of the total variance and was represented by two variables (7 and 8, namely, quality of management staff and creativity of staff). The fourth factor (F.4) explicated 1.09% of the total variance and was represented by a single variable (16, that is, implementation of corporate social responsibility).

Four more factors were specified on the basis of the responses that were provided in 2020. The first three were represented by the same variables as in the previous survey. The first factor (F.1) explained 4.96% of the total variance and was represented by three variables (9, 11, and 12, that is, condition of plant and machinery, technical standard of products, and mastery of technology). The second factor (F.2) explicated 1.96% of the total variance and was represented by two variables (1 and 2, i.e., financial liquidity and profitability of enterprise). The third factor (F.3) explained 1.52% of the total variance and was represented by two variables (7 and 8, namely, quality of management staff and creativity of staff). The fourth factor (F.4) explicated 1.09% of the total variance and was represented by a single variable (5; method of distribution).

As suggested by the literature, the factor names were derived from a shared characteristic. Using the foregoing terminology, a model was prepared that represented the factors of enterprise competitive potential (as shown in Figure 11.1).

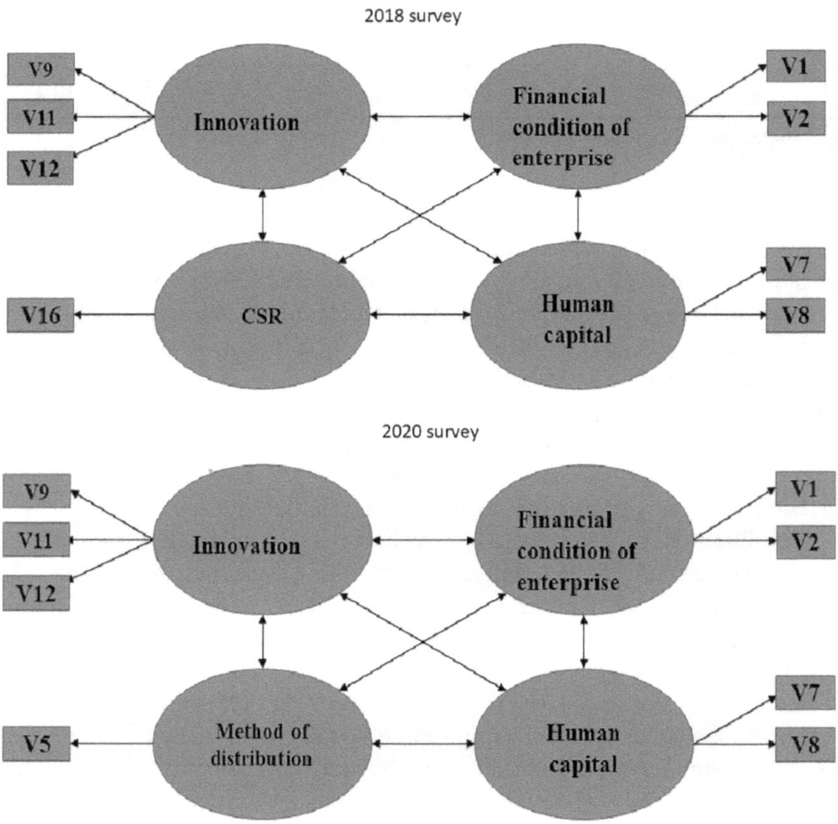

Figure 11.1 Factor-based model of enterprise competitive potential.

The individual observable variables in Figure 11.1 (the points on the scale) are represented by rectangles, and the factors are denoted as ovals. The cause-and-effect (regressive) relationships are shown as unidirectional arrows, and correlation dependencies are denoted as bidirectional arrows.

A comparison of the results that were produced by means of exploratory factor analysis in 2018 and 2020 indicated the following:

1 Both of the respondent groups shared three factors, i.e., innovation, financial standing, and human capital.
2 One more factor was determined by the data that were obtained in 2018 (CSR) and was loaded by a single variable, i.e., implementation of corporate social responsibility.
3 The 2020 data served to determine one more factor (method of distribution), which was loaded with a single variable of the same name.

The analysis demonstrated a difference in the structure of the factors of enterprise competitive potential before and during the initial phase of the economic crisis that was caused by the COVID-19 pandemic. In 2020, the respondents pointed to the method of distribution as a factor that influenced competitive potential, which corroborates the validity of the research hypothesis.

Discussion

Competitive potential (in particular, its significance and development) may constitute a major source of competitive advantage. As such, it has a considerable impact on the success of an enterprise. Analyzing competitive potential in contemporary enterprises seems interesting scientifically – especially during the time of the COVID-19 pandemic.

No results concerning the effects of COVID-19 on enterprise competitiveness were available in the literature; existing publications chiefly addressed the impact of the COVID-19 pandemic on international trade (International Trade Centre, 2020), enterprise strategy (Fabeil et al., 2020; Raflis et al., 2020), customer behavior (Hasanat et al., 2020), and the environment (Paradesi, 2020). No studies were available on the impact of distribution on enterprise competitiveness; thus, this paper fills a gap in the research. Its results clearly indicate that besides the traditional factors of competitive potential, businesses have taken advantage of distribution methods to gain a competitive edge during the time of the pandemic. This reaffirms an earlier observation that the issue of reaching customers was a key problem that was caused by COVID-19, while methods of distribution have allowed for a competitive advantage in the market.

A wide-ranging survey of 5,800 enterprises, employing up to 500 workers each, was carried out by researchers with the Harvard University Institutional Review Board during the period of March 27 through April

04, 2020 (Bartik et al., 2020). The board was concerned with the effects of COVID-19 on staffing, financial position, anticipated consequences of the crisis, and expectations of the government. The results were interpreted by means of a statistical analysis. During the initial phase of the crisis, 41.3% of the studied enterprises were temporarily shut down, and the numbers of full-time staff fell by 32% as compared to the January figures. More than a half of the enterprises faced financial difficulties; they held little cash during the beginning of the pandemic, which meant having to dramatically cut spending, take on more debt, or go bankrupt. All of the firms approved of the Coronavirus Aid, Relief, and Economic Security Act, which provided fast and direct economic aid to small businesses, workers, and their families and preserved jobs.

An analysis of the results that were generated prior to the pandemic points to the conformity of the results that are discussed in this paper with the global research.

In line with the factor-based model, four factors of competitive potential that could be regarded as statistically significant were determined, namely, innovation, financial standing, human capital, and CSR.

Capital is a necessary production factor in the contemporary economy as well as a fundamental structural part of an enterprise. Capital levels determine the existence of a business as well as its standing, survival, and development. If a firm is in good financial shape, it is able to implement new technological solutions or engage in research and development activities more often than other entities.

The results concerning the impact of innovation on enterprise competitiveness that are available in the literature show that innovation is treated as a basic condition of success and a source of competitive advantage (Mura et al., 2018; Cao et al., 2012; Rhee et al., 2010, p. 65).

A.N. Mustafin et al. (2019) believed that innovation was the basis of enterprise competitiveness as it can lead to increased productivity and the improved quality of products and services.

Studies by N. N. Abd Aziz and S. Samad (2016) reaffirmed the hypothetical effects of innovation on enterprise competitiveness. These studies were conducted on 220 enterprises in Malaysia, where the authors applied a survey questionnaire of 30 questions. The responses were recorded on a five-degree Likert-type scale. The results were subject to structural equation modeling using AMOS software. The results confirmed the fact that innovation makes a 73.5% contribution to changes in competitive advantage.

Workers are a very important factor that determines the innovative activities of an enterprise. These are people who create and introduce innovations; their attitudes toward innovation are key. Management, who should be open to ideas from staff members and provide adequate working conditions, plays an important role in forming the abilities and willingness to create innovation.

M. Dakhli and D. De Clercq (2004) believed that innovation (as activities that require knowledge) should be linked to human capital. M. Wright et al. (2007) pointed out that, according to the human capital theory, workers with greater human capital resources (measured with formal education or work experience) should be more productive since they are better able to solve emerging problems and adapt to changes in the market environment.

These hypothetical considerations were corroborated with the results that were reported by J. Xu and F. Liu (2020) concerning the effects of intellectual capital and its components on the performance of Korean manufacturing companies during the period of 2013–2018. They stated that intellectual capital is commonly understood as a major driver of improvements to enterprise competitiveness and value creation in a knowledge-based economy. The authors applied a modified and expanded Value Added Intellectual Coefficient (VAIC) model and concluded that intellectual capital was the key factor in goodwill creation.

In the opinion of N.N.A. Aziz (2019), management competencies are sources of competitive advantage for Malaysian food-processing enterprises. The results from a survey of 330 firms and structural equation modeling using AMOS demonstrated that the relationship between organizational capabilities and competitive advantage was statistically significant and positive (organizational capabilities accounted for 93% of the total variance of competitive advantage), while managerial skills fully mediated between organizational capabilities and competitive advantage.

The concept of corporate social responsibility is increasingly seen as a source of competitive advantage in the contemporary economy.

Carroll and Shabana (2010) analyzed the literature on CSR results and believed that CSR created goodwill by reducing risk and/or costs, improving an enterprise's reputation, enhancing its competitive advantage, and creating synergies with company stakeholders (Abernathy et al., 2017, p. 27). In addition, Porter and Kramer (2002, p. 66) argued that when firms "get the where and how right," philanthropic activities and competitive advantage reinforce each other and form a virtuous circle. They claimed that corporate philanthropy could serve to affect the competitive context of an enterprise, helping it to improve its competitiveness and satisfy the needs of some stakeholders.

The theory of CSR evolved from a philanthropic approach to a strategic business necessity that helps a firm achieve a competitive advantage in the market. The theoretical discussion was reaffirmed with the results from D. Gallardo-Vázquez and M. I. Sanchez-Hernandez (2014) of research into a sample of 67 Spanish enterprises. The authors employed structural equations based on least-square path modeling to prove the positive, direct, and significant impact of CSR on the competitive success of an enterprise.

Conclusion and recommendations

Under the conditions of the COVID-19 pandemic, enterprises have been forced to meet new challenges. Those sectors that are based on the movement of people and services and physical contact (that is, tourism, services, finances, and retail) have been especially exposed to the virus's challenges due to limited interactions and travel or problems with logistics and supply chains.

The destructive impact of the pandemic on businesses is evident, adversely affecting sales revenue, employment, and planned investments and innovations.

An analysis of the surveys of Polish enterprises in January 2018 and March 2020 indicated the following:

1 Based on the results of the 2018 survey, the factor-based model of competitive potential was upheld by research worldwide. Other authors (e.g., Mustafin et al., 2019; Xu and Liu, 2020; Aziz, 2019; Gallardo-Vázquez and Sanchez-Hernandez, 2014) reported the four factors that created the model (i.e., innovation, financial standing, human capital, and CSR) were perceived as sources of enterprise competitive advantage.
2 Based on the results of the 2020 data, the factor-based model of competitive potential was composed of the method of distribution factor, which was absent from the earlier model. The crisis that was associated with the global COVID-19 pandemic has altered the conditions of the sale and distribution of goods. Consumers have been more eager to resort to e-commerce and purchasing on the Internet. For this reason, enterprises found method of distribution to be an important factor of competitive potential that helps them gain a competitive advantage.

The research results and statistical analysis helped corroborate Hypothesis H1 that under the conditions of the COVID-19 pandemic, methods of distribution have had statistically significant effects on the competitive potential of enterprises. The studies suffered from certain limitations that can be subject to continuing research in order to include more dimensions of competitiveness, namely, the competitive standing of an enterprise in the market or instruments of competing. Furthermore, this research can extend to enterprises in the Visegrad Group countries and, thus, acquire an international character.

The trend in competition of switching from tangible to intangible resources can be noted during the time of the COVID-19 pandemic; therefore, managers should take advantage of the potential that is particularly inherent in intangible resources like human capital or methods of distribution so that they can play major parts in the creation of competitive advantage.

The results also suggested that managers should introduce changes to their methods of goods distribution. By switching to online channels of distribution, they could maintain the levels of their revenue and even attract new business partners. At the moment, a change in an enterprise's methods of distribution may lead to its competitive advantage in the market.

Literature

Abernathy, J., Stefaniak, C., Wilkins, A. and Olson J. (2017) Literature review and research opportunities on credibility of corporate social responsibility reporting, *American Journal of Business*, 32(1), 24–41.

Ahmedova, S. (2015) Factors for increasing the competitiveness of small and medium– sized enterprises (SMEs) in Bulgaria, *Procedia – Social and Behavioral Sciences*, 195, 1104–1112.

Aziz, N.N.A. (2019) Organisational capabilities and competitive advantage: the moderating influence of managerial competencies, *International Journal of Academic Research in Business and Social Sciences*, 9(2), 782–794.

Aziz, N.N.A. and Samad, S. (2016) Innovation and competitive advantage: moderating effects of firm age in foods manufacturing SMEs in Malaysia, *Procedia Economics and Finance*, 35, 256–266.

Barney, J.B. (1997) *Gaining and Sustaining Competitive Advantage*, Addison-Wesley Publishing Company, Inc., New York, NY.

Barney, J.B. (1991) Firm resources and sustained competitive advantage, *Journal of Management*, 17(1), 99–120.

Bartik, A.W., Bertrand, M., Cullen, Z., Glaeser, E.L., Luca, M. and Stanton C. (2020) The impact of COVID-19 on small business outcomes and expectations, *Proceedings of the National Academy of Sciences*, 117(30), 17656–17666.

Bednarz, J. (2013), *Konkurencyjność polskich przedsiębiorstw na rynkach europejskich na przykładzie wybranych branż*, Wydawnictwo Uniwersytetu Gdańskiego, Gdańsk.

Cao, Q., Baker, J., Wetherbe, J. and Gu, V. (2012) Organizational adoption of innovation: identifying factors that influence RFID adoption in the healthcare industry, *ECIS 2012 Proceedings*, Paper 94, Barcelona.

Carroll, A.B. and Shabana, K.M. (2010) The business case for corporate social responsibility: a review of concepts, research and practice, *International Journal of Management Reviews*, 12(1), 85–105.

Cattell, R. (1966) The scree test for the number of factors, *Multivariate Behavioral Research*, 1(2), 245–276.

Cherkesova, E.Y., Breusova, E.A., Savchishkina, E.P. and Demidova, N.E. (2016) Competitiveness of the human capital as strategic resource of innovational economy functioning, *Journal of Advanced Research in Law and Economics*, 7(21), 1662–1667.

Dakhli, M. and De Clercq, D. (2004) Human capital, social capital, and innovation: a multicountry study, *Entrepreneurship & Regional Development*, 16, 107–128.

Duda, J. and Wolak-Tuzimek, A. (2019) *Competitiveness Factors of Large Enterprises in Polish Economy*, In Duda, J. and Skalna, I. (eds.), *Functioning and Development of Enterprises – Contemporary Challenges*, Wydawnictwo AGH, Kraków, 127–145.

Fabeil, N.F., Pazim, K.H. and Langgat J. (2020) The impact of Covid-19 pandemic crisis on micro-enterprises: entrepreneurs' perspective on business continuity and recovery strategy, *Journal of Economics and Business*, 3(2), 837–844.

Flak, O. and Głód, G. (2014) Koncepcja i przykład metody badania konkurencyjności przedsiębiorstw, *Studia Ekonomiczne. Zeszyty Naukowe Uniwersytetu Ekonomicznego w Katowicach*, 187, 87–100.

Gallardo-Vázquez, D. and Sanchez-Hernandez, M.I. (2014) Measuring corporate social responsibility for competitive success at a regional level, *Journal of Cleaner Production*, 72, 14–22.

Gorynia, M. (2010) *Konkurencyjność w ujęciu mikroekonomicznym*, In Gorynia, M. and Łażniewska, E. (eds.) *Kompendium wiedzy o konkurencyjności*, Wydawnictwo Naukowe PWN, Warszawa, 48–99.

Hasanat, M.W., Hoque, A., Shikha, F.A., Anwar, M., Hamid, A.B.A. and Tat, H.H. (2020) The impact of coronavirus (Covid-19) on E-Business in Malaysia, *Asian Journal of Multidisciplinary Studies*, 3(1), 85–90.

International Trade Centre (2020) *SME Competitiveness Outlook 2020: COVID-19: The Great Lockdown and its Impact on Small Business*. ITC, Geneva.

Kaiser, H.F. (1958) The varimax criterion for analytic rotation in factor analysis, *Psychometrika*, 23, 187–200.

Kaiser, H.F. (1960) The application of electronic computers to factor analysis, *Educational and Psychological Measurement*, 20(1), 141–151.

Kusa, R. (2007) *Metodyka badania wybranych aspektów konkurencyjności małych i średnich przedsiębiorstw*, In Pyka, J. (ed.), *Nowoczesność przemysłu i usług. Procesy restrukturyzacji i konkurencyjności w przemyśle i usługach*, Katowice: TNOiK, 467–475.

Liu, J. and Huang, J. (2009) Research on enterprise international competitive advantage sustainability, *International Journal of Business and Management*, 40(2), 89–92.

Łobejko, S. and Pierścionek Z. (2011), *Zarządzanie strategiczne w praktyce polskich przedsiębiorstw*, Warszawa: Wydawnictwo SGH.

Maráková, V., Wolak-Tuzimek, A., Tučková, Z. (2021) Corporate social responsibility as a source of competitive advantage in large enterprises, *Journal of Competitiveness*, 13(1), 113–128.

Mitchelmore, S. and Rowley, J. (2010) Entrepreneurial competencies: a literature review and development agenda, *International Journal of Entrepreneurial Behavior and Research*, 16, 92–111.

Mura, L., Marchevska, M. and Dubravska, M. (2018) Slovak retail business across panel regression model, *Marketing and Management of Innovations*, 4, 203–211.

Mustafin, A.N., Kotenkova, S.N., Shlyakhtin, A.E., Kotulič, R., Kravčáková Vozárová I. and Benková, E. (2019) The governance of innovation in industrial enterprises, *Polish Journal of Management Studies*, 20(1), 318–331.

Nikitina, T., Lapina, I., Ozolinš, M., Irbe, M.M., Priem, M., Smits, M. and Nemilentsev, M. (2020), Competences for strengthening entrepreneurial capabilities in Europe, *Journal of Open Innovation: Technology, Market, and Complexity*, 6(3), 62–81.

Pansuwong, W. (2020) Business model and business model innovation: scholarly incongruence and implications to entrepreneurial firms, *International Journal of Trade and Global Markets*, 13(1), 31–41.

Paradesi, A. (2020) Impact of COVID 19 on environment' in ARTFEST & GRAPHIXREP 2020 On World Environment Day June 5 2020.

Petison, P. and Johri, L.M. (2006) Driving harmony: philosophy of Toyota Motor Thailand, *Strategic Direction*, 22(11), 3–5.

Porter, M.E. and Kramer, M.R. (2002) The competitive advantage of corporate philanthropy, *Harvard Business Review*, 80, 56–69.

Raflis, A., Ishak, S. and Jusoh, M. (2020) The impact of Covid-19 movement control order on SMEs' businesses and survival strategies, *GEOGRAFIA Malaysian Journal of Society and Space*, 16(2), 139–150.

Rhee, J., Park, T. and Lee, D.H. (2010) Drivers of innovativeness and performance for innovative SMEs in South Korea: mediation of learning orientation, *Technovation*, 30, 65–75.

Ryu, S. and Won, J. (2018) The relationship between competitive advantage and the value relevance of accounting information, *International Journal of Trade and Global Markets*, 1(1–2), 118–126.

Shevchenko, V.V., Kokuytseva, T.V. and Ovchinnikova, O.P. (2019) Competitiveness of the enterprises of the eurasian economic union: assessment methodology, *Revista ESPACIOS*, 40(37), 15–23.

Shevelova, S. (2008) Teoretyczne i metodologiczne aspekty pomiaru zdolności konkurencyjnej w agrobiznesi, *Stowarzyszenie Ekonomistów Rolnictwa i Agrobiznesu, Roczniki Naukowe*, 10(1), 367–372.

Sieradzka, K. and Luft, R. (2015) Theoretical aspects of enterprise competitiveness, *Central European Review of Economics & Finance*, 10(4), 133–141.

Sieradzka, K., (2013) Innovativeness of enterprises in Poland, *Acta Univarsitatis Agriculturae et Silviculturae Mendelianae Brunensis*, LXI(7), 2729–2735.

Sneader, K. and Singhal, S. (2020). Beyond coronavirus: the path to the next normal, Article McKinsey & Company. [online] https://www.mckinsey.com/industries. (Accessed 15 August 2020).

Sobolewski, H. and Narojczyk, S. (2018) Potencjał konkurencyjny przedsiębiorstw przetwórstwa przemysłowego, In Jaki, A., Kowalik, M. and Rojek, T. (eds.), *Zarządzanie restrukturyzacją. Rozwój i efektywność w obliczu zmian*, Kraków: Uniwersytet Ekonomiczny, 37–45.

Stankiewicz, J.M. (2005) *Konkurencyjność przedsiębiorstwa. Budowanie konkurencyjności przedsiębiorstwa w warunkach globalizacji*, Toruń: TNOiK.

Šproch, F., Nevima, J., (2021) Increasing competitiveness through innovation in an industrial enterprise – A case study of the company massag, *Advances in Science and Technology Research Journal*, 15(1), 110–125.

Thurstone, L.L. (1931) Multiple factor analysis, *Psychological Review*, 38, 406–427.

Wen-Cheng, W., Chien-Hung, L. and Ying-Chien C. (2011) Types of competitive advantage and analysis, *International Journal of Business and Management*, 6(5), 100–104.

Wolak-Tuzimek, A. (2018) Measures of Competitive Potential of Enterprises, In Löster, T. and Pavelka, T. (eds.), *The 12th International Days of Statistics and Economics*, University of Economics, Prague, Czech Republic, 1942–1951.

Wolak-Tuzimek, A. and Duda, A. (2021) The Concept of Corporate Social Responsibility as a Source of an Enterprise's Competitive Advantage, In Bukowski, S.I., Hyż, A., and Lament, M. (eds.), *Competitiveness and Economic Development in Europe: Prospects and Challenges*, New York: Routledge, 312–320.

Wolak-Tuzimek, A. and Luft, R. (2021) Effect of Integrated IT Systems on Enterprise Competitiveness at Time of "Industry 4.0", In Duda, J., and Gąsior, A. (eds.), *Industry 4.0. A Glocal Perspective*, New York: Routledge, 78–94.

Wright, M., Hmieleski, K.M., Siegel, D.S. and Ensley M.D. (2007) The role of human capital in technological entrepreneurship, *Entrepreneurship Theory and Practice*, 31, 791–806.

Xu, J. and Liu, F. (2020) The impact of intellectual capital on firm performance: a modified and extended VAIC model, *Journal of Competitiveness*, 12(1), 161–176.

12 Role of inter-organizational cooperation during times of crisis

Joanna Duda, Rafał Kusa, Marcin Suder, Zofia Gródek-Szostak and Kristina Grumadaitė

Introduction

Individuals, organizations, societies, and economies experience different crises. The current crisis was caused by the coronavirus pandemic (COVID-19). It started in China in December 2019 and seriously affected countries around the world. It has an impact on employees, enterprises, and economies (Kinnunen et al., 2021). The economic short-term consequences of the current pandemic crisis include the temporal suspension of business activities in many industries, which has resulted in a dramatic decrease in income; this has led to the bankruptcy of many businesses (Lu et al., 2021). The performance of companies has been affected by the interruption of logistic channels (resulting in a lack of resources) along with the increase in costs that was caused by the new organization of work or new resources that have been employed in response to the contagion risk. The long-term consequences of this crisis are difficult to assess at the moment. Consequently, the current pandemic crisis still affects individuals, organizations, societies, and economies in the economic and societal sphere across the world. Such conditions challenge entrepreneurs and managers; they must implement extraordinary solutions to secure their businesses (Pantano et al., 2020).

Despite some similarities, this crisis differs from previous crises. The differences include the source of the crisis (pandemic), scale (global), scope (all aspects and levels of life), threat subject (health and life), preventive measures (lockdown), and business consequences (in a short time: suspended production and services). Thus, our experience from previous crises and post-crisis proceedings may be only partly useful and insufficient regarding the current crisis that was caused by the COVID-19 pandemic.

At the organizational level, managers implement different actions in coping with a crisis (Klyver & Nielsen, 2021; Duda & Kusa, 2022; Suder

DOI: 10.4324/9781003368687-12

et al., 2022). In response to a shortage of resources (which is one of the peculiarities of the current crisis), managers initiate cooperation with other entities as one possible solution (Ebersberger & Kuckertz, 2021; García-Madurga, Grilló-Méndez, & Morte-Nadal, 2021; Kusa, Duda, & Suder, 2022). The inter-organizational cooperation in gaining resources (also during the time of a crisis) has been well-described in the literature. Thus, one question arises: what is the role of inter-organizational cooperation in terms of the current pandemic crisis?

The aim of this study is to initially identify the role and scope of inter-organizational relationships during the time of the current COVID-19 pandemic crisis. Through our research, we intend to contribute to the existing body of knowledge about inter-organizational cooperation during times of crisis with adjustments to the current pandemic crisis and its specifics. Additionally, we intend to support entrepreneurs and managers who may consider including cooperation with other entities in their response portfolio to this crisis.

In order to grasp the very essence of the role of inter-organizational cooperation during times of crisis, we employed a case study as a research method. Due to the expected differences in the impact of the crisis on particular enterprises, our sample is diverse; it includes companies that are both small and big, provide both services and production, and engage in commerce both locally and internationally.

The remaining content of this chapter is as follows: First, the crisis conditions and consequences are presented, along with cooperation behaviors in the crisis context; also, a research hypothesis is proposed. Second, the methodology and sample are described. Third, the results are presented and discussed regarding the existing literature. Finally, the study's limitations are indicated, as well as its contributions.

Theoretical background

Crises are a part of organizational reality. Crises can be sourced both in internal and external factors. Enterprises strive to prevent crises; when a crisis occurs, enterprises try to manage (crisis management is an important managerial ability). Crises, especially those that are sourced from external factors, affect many enterprises at the same time. They can be sudden, unexpected, extraordinary, and unpredictable – like those that are sourced from disasters or emergencies (Al-Dahash, Thayaparan, & Kulatunga, 2016). Crises may demand immediate action, the suspension of ordinary procedures, and decision-making based on uncertain information (Scholl & Carnes, 2017). Managers need to cope with high uncertainty, which is the case during the current pandemic crisis as well (Baker et al., 2020).

Crises may result in decreasing organizational performance, including profitability (Fusco & Migliaccio, 2019). However, different types of organizations may be differently affected by a crisis. For example, small and medium-sized enterprises can be more exposed to the consequences of a crisis than big companies (Bartik et al., 2020).

Wenzel, Stanske, and Lieberman (2020) identified four types of responses to crises: retrenchment, perseverance, innovation, and exit. Retrenchment refers to reductions (e.g., in costs, assets, and products) (Pearce & Robbins, 1993), while perseverance relates to mitigating adverse impacts in order to sustain a firm's business activities in response to a crisis (Wenzel, 2015). If a crisis lasts longer and firms need to look for alternative sources of revenue, innovation can enable them to sustain their survival (Wenzel, Stanske, & Lieberman, 2020).

Crises can require coordinated actions (Noori & Miralles, 2014; Scholl & Carnes, 2017). For example, resource mobilization needs to be coordinated due to insufficient resource accessibility (Bergström, Uhr, & Frykmer, 2016); this includes a wide range of capabilities that are possessed by different actors (Ekman & Uhr, 2015). However, these actors are diverse; they are both private and public organizations that work on local, regional, and national levels representing different organizational cultures, structures, methods, ambitions, and communication technologies. This is a challenge for managing collaborations during crises (Granåsen et al., 2019). Moreover, the speed of creating networks of organizations with valuable resources can be crucial when responding to crises (Curtis, 2018). On a community or national level, inter-organizational collaboration can affect one's capacity to prepare for and bounce back from disruptive crisis events; however, different types of crises may require different modes of collaboration (Nohrstedt et al., 2018).

Thus, when facing uncertainty, leadership, magnitude, costs, and urgency (which all are specific for crises), organizations need to network (Kapucu & Garayev, 2013; Harris & Doerfel, 2017) and manage a crisis collaboratively (Nohrstedt et al., 2018). Cooperation can include competitors as well (Crick & Crick, 2020).

The observations from previous crises indicate that multiparty collaboration and cross-organizational coordination in the field of crisis management determine the timely response to crises. However, the intensity of such changes during a crisis demands varying solutions in terms of forming networks and interacting within them as cooperating organizations need to be adaptive in responding to the crisis (Noori & Miralles, 2014).

Based on the above-presented studies, we propose the following hypothesis: A pandemic crisis leads to strengthening inter-organizational cooperation.

Methodology

In this study, we aim to initially explore the research problem, namely, what is the role of inter-organizational cooperation in terms of the current pandemic crisis? Thus, we employed a case study as a research method.

A case study is one of the qualitative methodologies, which is the best way to approach a case (cf. Yin, 2009; Piekkari et al., 2009). This method is an in-depth study of a phenomenon and includes threads, assumptions, or motives for action. A case study is most often utilized with research individuals or small groups of people as well as organizations (e.g., to describe their success or economic failure). However, a case study method can be successfully used in any field of science (not only social). A case study is typically used for one of two reasons: first, to present an unusual or original phenomenon, case, or situation, and second, to thoroughly understand an analyzed phenomenon (Yin, 2009). In the first situation, we describe an exceptional case that differs from the others. The analyzed cases are usually classified as being extreme or outliers. The analysis and description of such phenomena are aimed at broadening the knowledge that is related to a given field of science. This approach is a kind of complement to group studies in which unusual behaviors (those that occur extremely rarely) are not analyzed and are often even removed from a collection (as the so-called outliers). A case study can be a kind of analysis of exceptions to the rule – the application of which makes the theoretical knowledge of a given field of science richer and better understood. In the second situation (i.e., through understanding an analyzed phenomenon), the aim of the research is not to analyze outliers (at least that is not the reason for the study) but to get to know the process very well. In the case study method, the quality of the cognition of the overall character is emphasized; an in-depth analysis allows us to analyze mistakes that were made, behaviors that should be followed, or execution processes that should be copied (Yin, 2009).

According to the aim of our study, we selected five enterprises. These enterprises represented both small and big companies that provided services and production and engaged in local and international markets.

Company A is part of an international company with its headquarters in the United Kingdom. Company A has operated for 25 years and focuses on communication and printing services. They serve the publishers of magazines and catalogs as well as the producers and distributors of goods. Besides, it offers a wide range of point-of-sale marketing solutions for local and global retail chains. It runs three printing houses, which enable the production of materials of various sizes, volumes, and complexities. The Polish branch employs 1,400 workers. The interview was conducted with the HR Supervisor of Company A Europe branch.

Company B has operated in online marketing for ten years. In particular, it deals with search engine marketing, including Google AdWords (sponsored links, remarketing, advertising network, YouTube ads, and GMC), word-of-mouth marketing (i.e., writing positive opinions and comments and, thus, building the positive image of a company), publishing sponsored articles on selected portals, search engine optimization (i.e., website positioning and helping in reaching the top natural results in a search engine), supporting clients with service, and fundraising under

Google AdGrants. The company is settled in Krakow and employs seven specialists. The interview was conducted with the owner of the enterprise.

Company C is a leading online training provider in Poland. It has been recognized by "Computerworld" as one of the market leaders. According to "Trusted Training Radar® for AgilePM®" (ranking provided by "Course Conductor"), Company C has been a leader in AgilePM® as well as Project Management courses since last year. The interview was conducted with the owner of the company.

Company D is a leading global manufacturer of car body seals, fluid flow systems, and active and passive vibration-monitoring systems. Its headquarters is located in Novi, MI, USA. Company D currently employs more than 30,000 employees in 90 factories that are situated in 20 countries. In their factory in Poland, 2,400 employees are employed. The interview was conducted with the HR manager in Poland.

Company E is a leading international company in optics and optoelectronics industries. The company offers solutions for the semiconductor industry, automotive and mechanical engineering, biomedical research, and medical technology as well as eyeglass lenses and lenses for cameras, binoculars, and planetariums. It has branches in more than 30 countries and has representatives in more than 100 countries. Their production is located in Europe, North and South America, and Asia. The Polish branch employs 116 specialists. The interview was conducted with the mid-level manager of the branch in Poland.

The characteristics of the interviewed companies are presented in Table 12.1.

We interviewed the companies in our sample in July 2020 (i.e., four months after the beginning of the pandemic and lockdown in Poland and again more than two months after the end of the lockdown). The structured interviews were conducted with each company separately. The interviews comprised questions that were related to inter-organizational cooperation (with clients, suppliers, and competitors – before and after the beginning of the crisis), the consequences of the crisis, the actions that

Table 12.1 Basic Characteristics of Surveyed Enterprises

Company	*Industry*	*Scope of activity*	*Foundation year*	*Number of employees in Poland*
A	Production/printing	International	1994	1,400
B	Service/online marketing	Local	2008	7
C	Service/online training	National	2007	52
D	Production	Global	1960	2,400
E	Production	Global	1846	116

were implemented in response to the crisis, and the general perception of this crisis and any expectations that were related to the post-crisis future (the next months). The lengths of the interviews varied in time within a range of 50–120 minutes.

Results

Our respondents described several ways through which the current pandemic crisis impacted inter-organizational cooperation as well as how inter-organizational cooperation was utilized by the enterprises during the current pandemic crisis.

As stated before, the pandemic crisis has had a significant impact on delivery chains; thus, it has affected the relationships between suppliers and buyers:

> In general, the crisis has a positive impact on inter-firm relationships. People were willing to help each other. This was especially visible in supplier-client relationships; these relationships became closer. For example, we suspended all rules related to the terms of orders and payments despite the fact that it was highly costly for us because of the high scale of the reduction of orders (actually, all orders for advertisements were canceled on March 11) and delays in payments. However, we were conscious of the extent of the problems faced by our clients; their situations were much worse than ours (for example, our clients who served in beauty salons or tourism who had to close their businesses temporarily). Now, I can say it was worth doing so; after two months, most of our clients came back to our business; now, they order more services than usual. Consequently, we are profitable despite several weeks of losses. And additionally, we have reached new clients.
>
> (Company B)

> The relationships that were built before the crisis were crucial during the first stage of the pandemic crisis when we served only our previous clients; there were no new clients. We were engaged in developing our relationships even before the crisis; however, the crisis strengthened these relationships. Our clients were very friendly and gracious toward us, as we were toward them. Actually, I would say that we have survived the first stage of the crisis thanks to our partnerships.
>
> (Company E)

The statements of our respondents reveal the importance of strong relationships in order to survive a crisis. In addition, these statements correlate to the suggestion of Ritter and Pedersen (2020) that decisions that are made during a crisis may become foundations of strength after the crisis; for example, these decisions may lead to increased customer loyalty:

> In our business, we depend on our suppliers – also during the crisis. Our suppliers reacted in different ways; however, many of them became flexible and indulgent. During the crisis, delays in delivery or payments were acceptable without consequences being written in an agreement. In general, the crisis resulted in strengthening our relationships with suppliers as well as customers. I believe it will be our asset in the future.
>
> (Company C)

> All businesses were affected by the crisis; thus, all understood the difficulties on the side of their business partners. Consequently, our partners proposed to suspend penalty payments that were agreed upon before in the case of delivery delays. We all had to change ourselves. Additionally, the crisis resulted in the development of cooperation with suppliers.
>
> (Company D)

One should emphasize that trust plays a significant role within business partnerships (as was stated by our respondents). For example, the manager from Company E highlighted "*the trust of clients*."

The results of the study confirmed our hypothesis that the current pandemic crisis has led to a strengthening of inter-organizational cooperation. However, the results exposed specific issues that need to be explored; these include attitudes toward delays in delivery and payments (despite their short-term consequences), flexibility in terms of agreements, the role of long-term partnerships, and the role of trust during a crisis. These issues are recommended as the subjects of future studies.

The study results are in line with the reactions that were reported by Ritter and Pedersen (2020) that some firms were helping their network partners (for instance, by offering better payment conditions); however, others constrained their partners by tightening conditions. The above observations indicate the examination of the role of business networks during crisis and post-crisis times as an avenue of future studies.

Moreover, entrepreneurs and managers look for solutions even together with their competitors. Our respondents reported the following:

> We cooperate with our competitors from Poland and other European countries. During the time of the COVID-19 crisis, this cooperation is like an 'insurance policy' for the case of long-term lockdowns in one or all countries; in such a case, we are prepared to share access to clients. This cooperation is accompanied by ongoing competition.
>
> (Company A)

> We cooperate with our competitors. One of them (which has suspended its activities) released its clients to us. In general, companies started to help each other rather than fighting after the crisis began.
>
> (Company B)

> We have 'exchanged' our employees with other companies on our market; however, not with our direct competitors.
>
> (Company D)

The presented behaviors indicate the role of coopetition during times of crisis. This finding is in line with the propositions of Crick and Crick (2020), who suggested engagement in complementary coopetition activities with trustworthy partners. Thus, we share the proposition to explore coopetition in terms of the current crisis.

Additionally, our study unveils the role of business networks and asks for a further examination of the role of business networks during crisis and post-crisis times. One of our respondents belongs to the local business network Krak-Business and the local branch of Business Network International (BNI). He reported the following:

> My company belongs to two business networks: SME's Association "Krak-Business" (local network) and the local branch of BNI. Additionally, we belong to one of the non-formal cooperation groups; such groups were founded shortly after the pandemic crisis began in order to support each other. Since the beginning of the pandemic crisis, Krak-Business has provided us with information about available donations and supporting projects and initiatives. BNI has increased the functionality of its online platform. It had been implemented before the crisis began; previously, it was used for online meetings and courses, and the crisis exacted its development. Now, we meet managers and entrepreneurs from abroad online; this offers us a new cooperation opportunity and, consequently, the opportunity to increase our sales and income. Moreover, it supports our internationalization; it has let us go beyond our current markets, and we have started to think about our expansion in the future.
>
> (Company B)

Thus, business networks offer access to information, markets, and business partners; this can be crucial for survival during times of crisis, but it can also be supportive for future expansion and development. Our observation is in line with previous studies. For example, Kraatz (1998) wrote about the impact of strong network links on better cooperation, communication, information exchange, access to knowledge and, consequently, reductions of total costs. Gavirneni (2002) emphasized the impact of network links on stable and sustainable economic activity. Barringer and Ireland (2016) analyzed the utilization of business networking to connect more with other enterprises in order to enhance efficiency operations, while Goes and Park (1997) highlighted the impact of networking on innovation. Additionally, business networking can strengthen entrepreneurial orientation and help capture emerging business opportunities (Li & Zhou, 2010; Barringer & Ireland, 2016). Taking the fact that opportunities appear alongside threats into account, entrepreneurial orientation is of a significant importance during times of crisis.

All of our respondents shared the observation that the crisis has been a source of opportunities. For example, the current pandemic crisis sparked new needs in the market.

> In general, the crisis will have a negative impact on firm performance; until now, we have had losses. However, new opportunities appeared, and we have used them. For example, there was a need for printed promotional newsletters with a bacteria-proof surface of the pages; one of our clients (a supermarket network) ordered it. Such newsletters gave them an advantage (their clients were afraid to touch traditional paper newsletters), and for us, it was a new source of income.
>
> (Company A)

> The crisis has resulted in new market needs; thus, we need to be flexible. Our managers are ready to react quickly and catch new opportunities.
>
> (Company D)

Some needs that were served before the crisis have increased, which caused an increase in market demand:

> Ca. 2 weeks after the beginning of the lockdown, we started to get new orders; increasingly, firms have recognized the need to move to the Internet, and they needed our support to proceed. This change was a great opportunity for us. In particular, we have observed a huge increase in online sales and marketing of our new business clients. Additionally, some of our clients are motivated by banks, which have offered better conditions for firms that are highly positioned on the Internet.
>
> (Company B)

The last statement signals an important managerial implication that is related to the accessibility of financial resources, which tend to decrease during crises (Brown & Rocha, 2020).

However, the current pandemic crisis has resulted in the bankruptcy of numerous companies. For those companies that are strong, the bankruptcy of others is an occasion for acquisition and is perceived as an opportunity:

> The bankruptcy of some firm in my market is an opportunity for me.
>
> (Company B)

> We hope to get stronger after the crisis. Our market is highly fragmented. The bankruptcy of weak enterprises will enable market consolidation; this will be an opportunity for bigger companies, as we are.
>
> (Company A)

This observation is in line with Wan and Yiu (2009), who indicated that opportunities for corporate acquisitions were opened up by crises:

> The crisis will eliminate some weak and unfair companies from the market. Consequently, the market will be more trustworthy. Such a change would be good for us.
>
> (Company C)

The above-mentioned observation indicates the role of the entrepreneurial approach (wherein opportunity pursue is essential) during times of crisis. The entrepreneurial approach helps companies to survive as well as strengthen them when facing a crisis. Such an entrepreneurial posture of managers and entrepreneurs is a good prognosis for post-crisis restoration and development. Lessons from previous crises (e.g., Hurricane Katrina and the tornadoes in Tuscaloosa, Alabama) have shown that entrepreneurs contribute to recovery just after a crisis (e.g., by supplying necessary resources to disaster victims) (Grube & Storr, 2018) as well as to long-term restructuring and adaptation during the aftermath of the crisis (Kuckertz et al., 2020). Thus, we recommend to further explore entrepreneurial behaviors during times of crisis as a direction of future studies.

We have found that the crisis is perceived by our respondents as a stimulus and trigger and sometimes as an accelerator of the development of their firms. The interviewed managers provided different examples of activities that were somehow provoked by the current pandemic crisis:

> A crisis mobilizes us to act. A crisis accelerates actions. This crisis has accelerated everything with extraordinary power. This crisis has shown solutions that were new for many enterprises; for example, online meetings. Due to the crisis, we have had to introduce changes and build new processes and new procedures.
>
> (Company B)

> During the crisis, our organization has improved itself; in response to the crisis, we initiated actions that allowed us to keep the quality and low costs. This cost-reduction was implemented quickly (despite the fact that we had not done it before), and we will benefit from it starting now.
>
> (Company A)

> A crisis makes decisions about implementing new solutions faster. During this crisis, we internally popularized new channels of communication. We had them before, but we only used them occasionally; they used to play a supporting role. We improved them, and they became our main way of communication. A crisis is inspiring; it is an opportunity. It creates new needs, also inside an organization. We experienced it in the HRM department, wherein we had rebuilt relationships with our employees.
>
> (Company D)

> A crisis accelerates (turbo-accelerates) actions. Throughout the last years, we considered the inclusion of online training into our offer several times; however, there was never time for this, neither any motivation. During the crisis, we did it within four days! We have built the entire system of customer service. We have rebuilt our advertisement channel. Within five days, we moved our firm to online mode; this required us to train our trainers as well as our customers. However, this saved us – this restrained a decrease in orders. This gave hope to our employees for jobs; finally, this strengthened team spirit and helped us survive the crisis.
>
> (Company C)

> A crisis makes one look for new solutions and accelerates actions. We increased the scale of online repairs. This was waiting in the queue for implementation; before the crisis, we used online reparations only occasionally. During this crisis, we commonly started to offer an online diagnosis of equipment to our clients. Thus, in our case, the crisis resulted in spreading the online services. A crisis shows new ways and new solutions, which we were not looking for before the crisis; however, they will remain with us. New solutions as well as new rules of cooperation and communication with customers will stay with us. During the crisis, we had less work, and we used this time to train our staff; we developed online training and tools to share knowledge and experience. In general, we were meeting together (online) more often than before the crisis. Due to the crisis, we limited business travels and moved to online meetings. It is good for the environment. And it resulted in a decrease in our costs.
>
> (Company E)

Thus, all of the interviewed managers shared the opinion about the accelerating impact of this crisis on organizational development. The observed role of a crisis in firm development corresponds with previous studies, including the Greiner Growth Model (Greiner, 1998), wherein growth is interrupted periodically by crises. This observation was confirmed in recent studies (e.g., Rosenbloom, 2000; Westergård-Nielsen & Neamtu,

2012). Consequently, we propose to investigate the role of the pandemic crisis in accelerating the development of a firm.

The pandemic crisis has had an impact on cooperation matters inside organizations. Our respondents indicated the specifics of this crisis in terms of relationships between employers and employees as well. Specifically, the crisis has led to strengthening the ties between both sides and increasing employee involvement. One of the factors behind such changes is the situation in the labor market. The current pandemic crisis affects the employees' ties with the company:

> Employees recognized the changes in the labor market, wherein the unemployment rate increased significantly in a very short time. Consequently, employees became more flexible and engaged as compared to the situation before the beginning of the crisis.
>
> (Company E)

> Employees strived to understand the situation of the company. They recognized that their work-place was not secure and that they could lose the jobs day by day.
>
> (Company B)

> In regions wherein the unemployment rate is traditionally high, employees were thankful for sustaining their jobs.
>
> (Company D)

> Employees have identified themselves with the company stronger than before the crisis. They care about the company, which is their workplace.
>
> (Company A)

Managers reported positive changes in the relationships between employees within teams:

> Last year was very good for our company in terms of income. However, the relationships between employees were tense, which was caused by the amount of work and pressure for results. The occurrence of the crisis has switched employees to integration. All were conscious that they needed to cooperate in order to survive; other tasks lost their importance. Actually, I was surprised by the posture of my staff; I had to reduce the salaries, and the employees were thankful I did so instead of reducing the staff. Additionally, they proposed a reduction in salaries for the next month if necessary. Moreover, my managers proposed reducing their salaries to cut costs and avoid firing their subordinates. It was amazing!
>
> (Company C)

The crisis was a challenge for employers to manage work processes under uncertain circumstances:

> We have to support our employees and co-workers. And we have to keep them informed.
>
> (Company C)

> All were afraid of the contagion. Thus, we moved many jobs to online mode, especially in the case of employees who had relatives in the high-risk group; however, it was not easy, because we provide maintenance services. In some cases, we moved an employee to another job. This was also the case of our training staff. They provided training mainly 'in place.' During the pandemic, most of our clients canceled training sessions, and we wanted to reduce the risk of the contamination of our staff during training 'in place.' We prepared online training; but still, we had to move some of our trainers to other tasks.
>
> (Company E)

This leads us to propose a deeper exploration of the impact of the situation in the labor market on employers' decisions during times of crisis.

The current pandemic crisis has affected the relationships between workers' unions and employers:

> Of course, the workers' union was concerned with the new conditions that were caused by the pandemic. However, they were very open and constructive, which eased the negotiations despite the difficult situation.
>
> (Company D)

Additionally, human resource management can be a subject of inter-organizational cooperation. One of our respondents described the following situation:

> One of my colleagues, who is a manager in company that organizes events, called me one day and asked: 'Could you offer a temporary job for my sales representatives? They would work on commission just to earn some money until we reopen our business.' She wanted to avoid firing her staff despite the fact that her company's income approached to zero day by day.
>
> (Company B)

The above-cited situations show that internal cooperation (within teams, between employees and employers, and between workers' unions and employers) is an important issue and requires additional studies. In addition, we recommend a deeper exploration of the impact of the crisis on social and economic development on a macro level (society and economy). On a macro scale, the impact of the pandemic crisis is already visible in innovativeness and the labor market. Our respondents point to this directly:

> The current pandemic crisis has changed the labor market in Poland. Before the crisis began, there was a high demand for employees; as a consequence, everybody could find a job from day to day, and companies had problems finding workers. After the beginning of the crisis, big employers and temporary employment agencies released their labor resources, which has changed the situations of employees and employers.
>
> (Company A)

One of the interviewed managers stated the following:

> This pandemic crisis began during good times in the labor market. Before the beginning of the crisis, it was difficult to find employees; consequently, managers did not want to fire any of them. If such a crisis had begun during times of high unemployment, the reduction of jobs would have reached a massive scale.
>
> (Company B)

Finally, our study unveils the role of a company's strategy and the consequences of the crisis for the strategy. One of our respondents reported the following:

> We have survived thanks to our diversity strategy; we serve clients that represent different markets and industries. Some of the companies in my market have gone bankrupt due to focusing on only one industry (e.g., gastronomy).
>
> (Company B)

Another interviewed manager pointed out that the crisis had caused a change in his company:

> Due to the crisis, we postponed our development plans. Additionally, we changed our competition strategy; just after the beginning of the crisis, we redirected our energy toward cooperation and building relationships instead of competition. Actually, we lost the habit of competing.
>
> (Company C)

These observations suggest the next research proposition: The pandemic crisis has resulted in changes in a firm's strategy. Additionally, we propose to examine the strategies that support the survival of a firm during the time of a pandemic crisis.

However, one should emphasize that cooperation is the key toward survival and development, as one of our respondents stated:

> Inter-organizational cooperation became a part of our strategy. We expect benefits sourced from cooperation in the future; namely, we expect increases in our income and profit.
>
> (Company A)

Limitations

Although the case study method that was applied in this study provides more-realistic answers than quantitative research, it has some limitations. First, the case study method does not allow us to generalize conclusions; even a few cases constitute only a narrow part of the reality under study. Usually, the use of case studies is a starting point for applying quantitative methods in forthcoming research.

This study explores the situations and reactions of five enterprises, which were selected intentionally by convenience. Namely, we selected those enterprises that were expected to be affected by the COVID-19 crisis. All of the analyzed enterprises have faced the crisis that was sourced from a global pandemic; in parallel, however, they have faced country-specific conditions (such as times and rules of lockdowns and scopes and terms of public support). Thus, our observations can be irrelevant in other contexts.

In addition, the study focuses on the extraordinary conditions that were defined by the deep changes that were caused by the crisis and the high variability of business conditions after these changes occurred. Consequently, our respondents were often not able to identify the main factors, reasons, or relationships that were related to the situations of their enterprises, and they were not able to propose solutions for all of their challenges. Furthermore, the respondents were not able to assess the previously implemented solutions in terms of their effectiveness.

One should emphasize that, despite its current limitations, the study indicates the numerous factors and solutions and allows us to define areas for future research.

Conclusions and implications for future research

The results of this study show that the current pandemic crisis can lead to strengthening inter-organizational cooperation, both with suppliers and customers. The common understanding of the roots of the problems that have been faced by enterprises have led to changes within delivery chains between suppliers and customers. Moreover, the results of the study show that entrepreneurs and managers have cooperated with their competitors in order to survive during the crisis; this indicates the need to explore the role of coopetition during times of crisis.

In the area of supplier–customer relationships, the results have exposed specific issues that need to be explored further; these include attitudes toward delays in deliveries and payments (despite their short-time consequences), flexibility in terms of agreements, the role of long-term partnerships, and the role of trust during a crisis.

This cooperation can be significantly supported by business networks. Network membership is profitable, especially during times of crisis; the business networks that were mentioned in the interviews provided its members with access to current information and contact with new business partners. Networking has been especially important during the current pandemic crisis, which resulted in the isolation of most enterprises around the world. Additionally, our study shows the impact of the crisis on the relationships between employers and employees as well as internal cooperation (within teams, between employees and employers, and between workers' unions and employers); the latter can also determine the survival of a firm.

The study's findings confirm the important role of a company's strategy and the consequences of a crisis for the strategy. The presented cases can serve other entrepreneurs and managers as inspirations and examples of good practices for coping with the current crisis. Finally, the study's highlight is that a crisis can be a source of opportunities and that a crisis can play the role of a stimulus, trigger, and (occasionally) accelerator of organizational development. The presented cases exemplify how highly motivated entrepreneurs and managers have introduced new solutions in a short amount of time, which helped them survive the crisis and even develop their organizations. Thus, some of the implemented solutions were not temporary because they will also be applied after the pandemic crisis lifts.

Taking these observations into account, the study contributes to both theory and practice; the study's results indicate ways of future research development and solutions that can be implemented by managers who are coping with the crisis.

References

Al-Dahash, H., Thayaparan, M., Kulatunga, U. (2016). Understanding the terminologies: Disaster, crisis and emergency. *Management*, 2, 1191–1200.

Baker, S.R., Bloom, N., Davis, S.J., Terry, S.J. (2020). *Covid-Induced Economic Uncertainty (No. W26983)*. Cambridge, MA: National Bureau of Economic Research.

Barringer, B.R., Ireland, R.D. (2016). *Entrepreneurship: Successfully Launching New Ventures*, 5th ed. Upper Saddle River, NJ: Prentice Hall.

Bartik, A.W., Bertrand, M., Cullen, Z.B., Glaeser, E.L., Luca, M., Stanton, C.T. (2020). *How Are Small Businesses Adjusting to COVID-19? Early Evidence from a Survey (No. W26989)*. Cambridge, MA: National Bureau of Economic Research.

Bergström, J., Uhr, C., Frykmer, T. (2016). A complexity framework for studying disaster response management. *Journal of Contingencies and Crisis Management*, 24(3), 124–135. DOI: 10.1111/1468-5973.12113.

Brown, R., Rocha, A. (2020). Entrepreneurial uncertainty during the Covid-19 crisis: Mapping the temporal dynamics of entrepreneurial finance. *Journal of Business Venturing Insights*, 14, e00174. DOI: 10.1016/j.jbvi.2020.e00174.

Crick, J.M., Crick, D. (2020). Coopetition and COVID-19: Collaborative business-to-business marketing strategies in a pandemic crisis. *Industrial Marketing Management*, 88, 206–213. DOI: 10.1016/j.indmarman.2020.05.016.

Curtis, C.A. (2018). Organizational networks in times of crisis: Lessons from Katrina. *Journal of Contingencies and Crisis Management*, 26(2), 202–211. DOI: 10.1111/1468-5973.12138.

Duda, J., Kusa, R. (2023). Mitigating impact of crisis in the multi-industry perspective – Summary of the studies. In: J. Duda, R. Kusa (Eds.), *Entrepreneurship, Innovation, and Crisis: SME Responses to the COVID-19 Pandemic* (pp. 170–177). New York, NY: Routledge. DOI: 10.4324/9781003279891-8.

Ebersberger, B., Kuckertz, A. (2021). Hop to it! The impact of organization type on innovation response time to the COVID-19 crisis. *Journal of Business Research*, 124, 126–135. DOI: 10.1016/j.jbusres.2020.11.051.

Ekman, O., Uhr, C. (2015). Global model for direction and coordination in multi-actor crisis management. In: *Proceedings of the 20th International Command and Control Research and Technology Symposium (ICCRTS)*. Cambridge, MA: Academic Press.

Fusco, F., Migliaccio, G. (2019). Cooperatives and crisis: Economic dynamics in Italian context. *International Journal of Business and Globalisation (IJBG)*, 22(4), 638–654. DOI: 10.1504/IJBG.2019.100258.

García-Madurga, M.A., Grilló-Méndez, A.J., Morte-Nadal, T. (2021). The adaptation of companies to the COVID reality: A systematic review. *Retos Revista de Ciencias de la Administración y Economía*, 11(21), 55–70. DOI: 10.17163/ret.n21.2021.04.

Gavirneni, S. (2002). Information flows in capacitated supply chains with fixed ordering costs. *Management Science*, 48(5), 644–651.

Goes, J.B., Park, S.H. (1997). Interorganizational links and innovation: The case of hospital services. *Academy of Management Journal*, 40(3), 673–696.

Granåsen, M., Olsén, M., Oskarsson, P., Hallberg, N. (2019). Assessing interorganizational crisis management capability: A systematic literature review. *International Journal of Information Systems for Crisis Response and Management (IJISCRAM)*, 11(2), 38–56. DOI: 10.4018/IJISCRAM.2019070103.

Greiner, L.E. (1998). Evolution and revolution as organizations grow. *Harvard Business Review*, July–August.

Grube, L.E., Storr, V.H. (2018). Embedded entrepreneurs and post-disaster community recovery. *Entrepreneurship and Regional Development*, 30, 800–821.

Harris, J.L., Doerfel, M.L. (2017). Interorganizational resilience: Networked collaborations in communities after superstorm sandy. In: E.C. Jones, A.J. Faas (Eds.), *Social Network Analysis of Disaster Response, Recovery, and Adaptation* (pp. 75–91). Oxford: Butterworth-Heinemann. DOI: 10.1016/B978-0-12-805196-2.00006-6.

Kapucu, N., Garayev, V. (2013). Designing, managing, and sustaining functionally collaborative emergency management networks. *The American Review of Public Administration*, 43, 312–330.

Kinnunen, J., Georgescu, I., Hosseini, Z., Androniceanu, A.-M. (2021). Dynamic indexing and clustering of government strategies to mitigate Covid-19. *Entrepreneurial Business and Economics Review*, 9(2), 7–20. DOI: 10.15678/EBER.2021.090201.

Klyver, K., Nielsen, S.L. (2021). Which crisis strategies are (expectedly) effective among SMEs during COVID-19? *Journal of Business Venturing Insights*, 16, e00273. DOI: 10.1016/j.jbvi.2021.e00273.

Kraatz, M.S. (1998). Learning by association? Interorganizational networks and adaptation to environmental change. *Academy of Management Journal*, 41(6), 621–643.

Kuckertz, A., Brändle, L., Gaudig, A., Hinderer, S., Morales Reyes, C.A., Prochotta, A., Steinbrink, K.M., Berger, E.S.C. (2020). Startups in times of crisis – A rapid response to the COVID-19 pandemic. *Journal of Business Venturing Insights*, 13, e00169. DOI: 10.1016/j.jbvi.2020.e00169.

Kusa, R., Duda, J., Suder, M. (2022). How to sustain company growth in times of crisis: The mitigating role of entrepreneurial management. *Journal of Business Research*, 142, 377–389. DOI: 10.1016/j.jbusres.2021.12.081.

Li, J.J., Zhou, K.Z. (2010). How foreign firms achieve competitive advantage in the Chinese emerging economy: Managerial ties and market orientation. *Journal of Business Research*, 63(8), 856–862.

Lu, L., Peng, J., Wu, J., Lu, Y. (2021). Perceived impact of the Covid-19 crisis on SMEs in different industry sectors: Evidence from Sichuan, China. *International Journal of Disaster Risk Reduction*, 55, 102085. DOI: 10.1016/j.ijdrr.2021.102085.

Nohrstedt, D., Bynander, F., Parker, C., Hart, P. (2018). Managing crises collaboratively: Prospects and problems – A systematic literature review. *Perspectives on Public Management and Governance*, 1(4), 257–271. DOI: 10.1093/ppmgov/gvx018.

Noori, N.S., Miralles, F. (2014). The role of C2C in facilitating coordination in emergency response networks. *The 11th International ISCRAM Conference* (May 2014), University Park, PA.

Pantano, E., Pizzi, G., Scarpi, D., Dennis, C. (2020). Competing during a pandemic? Retailers' ups and downs during the COVID-19 outbreak. *Journal of Business Research*, 116, 209–213. DOI: 10.1016/j.jbusres.2020.05.036.

Pearce, J.A., Robbins, K. (1993). Toward improved theory and research on business turnaround. *Journal of Management*, 19(3), 613–636. DOI: 10.1177/014920639301900306.

Piekkari, R., Welch, C., Paavilainen, E. (2009). The case study as disciplinary convention: Evidence from international business journals. *Organizational Research Methods*, 12(3), 567–589. DOI: 10.1177/1094428108319905.

Ritter, T., Lund Pedersen, C. (2020). Analyzing the impact of the coronavirus crisis on business models. *Industrial Marketing Management*, 88, 214–224. DOI: 10.1016/j.indmarman.2020.05.014.

Rosenbloom, R.S. (2000). Leadership, capabilities, and technological change: The transformation of NCR in the electronic era. *Strategic Management Journal*, 21(10–11), 1083–1103.

Scholl, H.J., Carnes S. (2017). Managerial challenges in early disaster response: The case of the 2014 Oso/SR530 landslide disaster. In: Montarnal A., Hanachi M.L.C., Comes F.B.T. (Eds.), *Proceedings of the 14th International Conference on Information Systems for Crisis Response and Management* (pp. 961–972), Albi: ISCRAM.

Suder, M., Kusa, R., Duda, J., Dunska, M. (2022). How small printing firms alleviate impact of pandemic crisis? Identifying configurations of successful strategies with fuzzy-set qualitative comparative analysis. *Entrepreneurial Business and Economics Review*, 10(2), 61–80. DOI: 10.15678/EBER.2022.100204.

Wan, W.P., Yiu, D.W. (2009). From crisis to opportunity: Environmental jolt, corporate acquisitions, and firm performance. *Strategic Management Journal*, 30(7), 791–801. DOI: 10.1002/smj.744.

Wenzel, M. (2015). Path dependence and the stabilization of strategic premises: How the funeral industry buries itself. *Business Research*, 8(2), 265–299. DOI: 10.1007/s40685-015-0021-4.

Wenzel, M., Stanske, S., Lieberman, M. (2020). Strategic responses to crisis. *Strategic Management Journal*, 41, V7–V18. DOI: 10.1002/smj.3161.

Westergård-Nielsen, N., Neamtu, I. (2012). How are firms affected by the crisis and how do they react? *IZA Discussion Paper No.* 6671, DOI: 10.2139/ssrn.2096801.

Yin, R.K. (2009). *Case Study Research. Design and Methods.* Thousand Oaks, CA: Sage Publications.

13 Dynamic capabilities of small enterprises during global crisis caused by the COVID-19 pandemic

Renata Lisowska and Andriy Pekhnyk

Introduction

The current COVID-19 pandemic that spread worldwide has caused an economic crisis in almost all countries. The closure of or large reduction in the operations of certain sectors of the economy ordered in many countries, including Poland, has undoubtedly yielded beneficial effects from an epidemiological point of view, but it has certainly taken its toll on the global economy.

The difficulty in assessing the impact of SARS-CoV-2 on the economy lies, among others, in the fact that it has affected the demand and supply sides at the same time. Many industries are at risk, as are many sectors of the economy. Although the effects of the COVID-19 pandemic on the economy are difficult to accurately predict, there is no doubt that the situation of the owner of an average small business and the financial condition of such a business are deteriorating. A significant proportion of companies, including small companies, have already experienced the crisis that was caused by COVID-19, which is spiraling in most cases; i.e., the original sources of the crisis triggered a chain reaction of the subsequent causes and effects, resulting in a growing crisis. The deteriorating condition is a consequence of the domino effect (i.e., the weakening of one cell); e.g., the quality of production in the short term leads to the weakening of the next link – a decrease in sales (Lim et al., 2020; OECD, 2020; Clampit et al., 2021; Klein and Todesco, 2021). An entrepreneur should therefore observe the symptoms of the crisis in the form of signals that inform about phenomena that are unfavorable to his/her company; e.g., difficulties in financing day-to-day and innovative activities; adverse changes in sales volume, dynamics, and structure; the imbalance between the growth rate of the market and the rate of increase in sales of the company's products expressed by a decrease in a relative market share; and a decrease in the value of the company (Mitroff, 2005; Maior and Camisao, 2021).

An important issue in the event of a crisis that results from many unpredictable phenomena and processes (such as the COVID-19 pandemic) is the resilience of a company to a crisis, which is often equated with crisis management. This resilience is seen as the ability to anticipate

DOI: 10.4324/9781003368687-13

future changes and disruptions and mitigate their effects before they turn into a crisis situation. Crisis resilience is a company's long-term development potential and good economic standing that persist despite changes in its operating conditions (Eggers, 2020; Fairlie, 2020).

Referring to the current situation of small businesses that was caused by the COVID-19 pandemic, it can be concluded that their resilience to the crisis is low, as evidenced by numerous surveys that have conducted in this group of entities (Lim et al., 2020; OECD, 2020; Clampit et al., 2021). Companies rarely declare that their situation is stable during the era of coronavirus – they rather point to a crisis. The dynamics of the environment require companies to adjust to new rules of the game, e.g., by developing dynamic capabilities that will allow them to survive and build a competitive advantage. Dynamic capabilities should enable a company to quickly and efficiently react to changes in its environment (especially the market and competitive environment) and within the company itself (changes in the internal processes that are carried out in the company as well as those changes that are related to the results of these processes) (Pisano, 2017). The dynamic capabilities of a company should enable it to achieve the expected level of efficiency – assessed in terms of both market value (from the perspective of value and benefit to the customer) and economic value (from the perspective of value and benefit to the company). By developing dynamic capabilities, companies can more effectively achieve their goals of creating value for the customer, value for the company, and value for individual stakeholders.

Due to the reasons presented above, the study was aimed at assessing the impact of the COVID-19 pandemic crisis on the dynamic capabilities of small businesses. To achieve this goal, the following research hypothesis was adopted: *There is a relationship between the crisis that was caused by the COVID-19 pandemic and the dynamic capabilities of small businesses.*

Concept of dynamic capabilities: literature review

The dynamic capabilities of enterprises have already been quite widely described in the literature (e.g., Teece and Pisano, 1994; Teece et al., 1997; Lampel and Shamsie, 2003; Winter, 2003; Teece, 2018) and have been the subject of many scientific studies (e.g., Zahra et al., 2006; Helfat et al., 2007). However, it is recognized that this issue is important due to the high cognitive potential for explaining the behaviors of small businesses in a turbulent environment; undoubtedly, the COVID-19 pandemic constitutes a component of this environment nowadays.

There is a lively ongoing debate in the scientific community as to whether dynamic capabilities can be a source of sustainable competitive advantage according to the concept of Teece et al. (1997) or a source of temporary competitive advantage according to the concept of Eisenhardt and Martin

(2000). In this context, the type of market in which a company operates may influence the perception of its dynamic capabilities. In the case of a moderately dynamic market, dynamic capabilities are a set of processes that can be identified and analyzed, e.g., product development through innovative changes, and creating alliances. In such a market, dynamic capabilities are somewhat similar to routines and can result in good practices that other companies will emulate. On the other hand, dynamic capabilities are based on uncertain processes that require experimentation in a rapidly changing market; therefore, their results are unpredictable (Teece 2018). According to the resource-based approach, the term *dynamic* refers to a company's ability to renew resources and competencies in response to changes in the environment, and the term *abilities* emphasizes the role of strategic management in the adaptation, integration, and reconfiguration of *know-how*, resources, and competencies so that a company can deal with a turbulent environment (Pisano, 2017). According to Pavlou and El Sawa (2011), dynamic capabilities are embedded in organizational processes and routines that allow an enterprise to adapt to changes in the environment through the reconfiguration of its resources. According to Helfat et al. (2007), dynamic capabilities are a company's capabilities to purposefully create and expand its resource base, adapting to changing environmental conditions. In the presented definitions, attention has been focused on a company's access to resources in the context of improving its strategic potential; this means that dynamic capabilities constitute the basis for the company's flexibility, allowing it to adapt to changing environmental conditions. Thus, the resource-based approach to dynamic capabilities has significant practical limitations as it ignores the issue of the time horizon (Teece, 2007); therefore, these capabilities cannot be considered a source of sustainable competitive advantage:

- competition can use these capabilities faster;
- configuration of a resource base that is dependent on dynamic capabilities may be effective for one company but not for another because of the organizational context; the processes of acquiring and configuring a resource base may be more or less random in various companies (Leoncini and Montresor, 2008; Pisano, 2017).

The dynamic capabilities of small enterprises concern better product design, the development of existing and generating new markets, and the reconfiguration and integration of company resources in order to gain and maintain a competitive advantage. The strength of these capabilities is manifested in the speed of identifying business opportunities, adjusting a company to the environmental conditions, and the flexibility of its strategy. However, owners/managers with dynamic capabilities are able to generate new values for customers in the absence of an opportunity (Teece, 2018). The dynamic approach emphasizes the balance between customer needs and opportunities, focusing on opportunities to derive benefits from new knowledge (Teece, 2014) that results from experience-based organizational learning (Zollo and Winter, 2002).

On the one hand, organizational learning is the search for new knowledge – exploration (taking risks, experimenting, discovering, and searching aimed at adapting to a turbulent environment); on the other hand, it is the use of new knowledge – exploitation (improvement and implementation) (Clampit et al., 2021). In order for an enterprise to be successful, it should find a balance between exploitation and exploration. This is not an easy task as there is a contradiction between these processes; i.e., companies are forced to exchange long-term efficiency that is gained through exploration for short-term exploitation (Arend, 2014). Nevertheless, an enterprise should explore dynamic capabilities through learning new ways of operating while using its already possessed capabilities in order to achieve high efficiency in a strategic perspective (Kump et al., 2019). The learning process in the case of small enterprises is mainly based on experience, starting with experimentation in the framework of which ideas emerge that are subsequently modified by new experiences (Kolb, 1984).

Dynamic capabilities are also seen as options that allow one to follow opportunities that arise in the market. The greater the dynamics of the environment, the greater the possibility of the emergence of market opportunities. The emergence of new market opportunities is the result of changing customer needs, expectations, and preferences. Unexploited opportunities usually do not come along again; therefore, it is important that entrepreneurs should have the ability to identify and exploit them. An active approach to an opportunity means creating such ventures that can become opportunities, while a passive approach means turning ventures that already exist into opportunities (Teece, 2011).

The uncertainty of the environment reveals opportunities, while its dynamics positively influences the creation of new ventures. Processes of analyzing the environment and the enterprise are aimed at collecting information about opportunities and threats, while the task of owners/managers is to transform this information into opportunities (Martinelli, 2018; Stoyanova, 2018). The dynamic nature of an enterprise that is obtained as a result of its dynamic capabilities may lead to an increase in its flexibility, which is related to identifying opportunities in the environment. Flexibility in the context of a strategic dimension is understood as a company's ability to respond and adapt to changes, and it is related to the reconfiguration of resources that lead to organizational changes.

Dynamic capabilities are perceived as a set of specific organizational capabilities that emerge from the development trajectory of enterprises, creating company market value through the reconfiguration of resources (Teece, 2011). The specificity of these capabilities depends on the nature of the environment in which an enterprise operates as well as its processes of exploration and exploitation of resources. Therefore, it is important that company managers who strive to achieve the desired levels of operational efficiency should introduce changes in a systemic manner, designing, implementing, and improving the process of shaping and developing dynamic capabilities. This process should not be treated as a one-off passive action but as a process that anticipates change continuously because the lack of the continuity of this process will force the enterprise to introduce abrupt changes that may lead to the inefficiency of the management system in the event of the emergence of a strategic gap; this may result in a reduction in operational efficiency (Arend, 2014).

Dynamic capabilities are influenced by market dynamics; i.e., the greater the market dynamics, the greater a company's propensity for using dynamic capabilities to shape its strategy (Wang and Ahmed, 2007). Therefore, the development of dynamic capabilities is dictated by a company's development strategy as it has an impact on the company's market and financial results in the long term as well as on improving its competitive position (Kump et al., 2019).

The concept of dynamic capabilities refers to strategic management and includes various sets of dimensions that constitute interdependent components. According to Wang and Ahmed (2007), dynamic capabilities are a construct that is composed of three elements:

- Adaptability –a company's ability to adapt to changes in the environment through resource flexibility.
- Absorptive capacity –a company's ability to recognize and acquire new knowledge from the environment and integrate it with its existing knowledge in order to exploit it.
- Innovative capacity –a company's ability to seek new solutions in order to develop new products/services as well as new manufacturing or service provision processes in order to achieve a sustainable competitive advantage.

According to Tecce et al. (2007), the dimensions of the construct of dynamic capabilities include the ability to integrate, build, and reconfigure external and internal resources. According to Barreto (2010), dynamic capabilities include making strategic sense, timely decision-making, and implementing changes. Cyfert and Krzekiewicz (2019) considered the following elements as components of dynamic capabilities:

- Learning related to the acquisition of knowledge, knowledge transfer, allocation, and preservation within the enterprise.
- Search for opportunities - analyzing phenomena in the environment, creating new ideas.
- Coordination seen as building employee loyalty and commitment, implementing innovations and new technologies.

- Configuration and reconfiguration related to acquiring, creating, and integrating resources, creating innovations, implementing new technologies, acquiring skills, and disposing of unnecessary resources.
- Adaptation of the organization related to the reconfiguration of the business model, improvement of the company, implementation of good practices in the field of management, ensuring the flexibility of the organizational structure, and organizational identity management.

The presented literature review shows that researchers recognize the significant role of dynamic capabilities in the adaptation of enterprises to the conditions of the changing environment. Therefore, the development of these capabilities by enterprises (including small ones) during the age of the COVID-19 pandemic is essential for reducing the effects of the crisis by adapting economic agents to current market needs. For the efficiency of the enterprise, it is essential that managers view dynamic capabilities as a component of enterprise management. Thus, the process of developing dynamic capabilities should not be treated as a single action that represents the enterprise's response to the crisis but as a proactive action that allows it to seize opportunities.

Importance of crisis caused by the COVID-19 pandemic for development of dynamic capabilities of small enterprises: research results

Research methodology and characteristics of research sample

Research into the process of developing the dynamic capabilities of small businesses amid the COVID-19 pandemic crisis began with literature studies that were conducted with the use of the critical analysis method. Due to the multiplicity of approaches toward defining dynamic capabilities and identifying the components of this construct, the concept of Cyfert and Krzakiewicz was adopted for the further analysis, which was mentioned in the first part of the following publication. Afterward, the research methods and tools were selected. The research was aimed at assessing the impact of the COVID-19 global crisis on the dynamic capabilities of small businesses.

The research, which was based on a structured and standardized survey questionnaire, was conducted with the use of the computer-assisted telephone interviewing (CATI) and computer assisted web interview (CAWI) techniques between May and June 2020 among owners of micro- and small enterprises that operated in Poland. A pilot study on a sample of 15 small enterprises was carried out to test the research questionnaire and amend it as needed. The reliability of the research tool was then assessed using the Cronbach alpha test, the Kaiser–Meyer–Olkin coefficient (KMO), and the Bartlett sphericity test. The measurement of dynamic capabilities was carried out using a measuring tool based on a five-point Likert scale that consisted of five statements that corresponded to the following dimensions: organizational adaptation, configuration and reconfiguration, coordination, opportunity search, and organizational learning.

In the next step, the accuracy of the construct and the reliability of the scale were assessed using the reliability coefficient of Cronbach alpha.[1] The coefficient for the scale was 0.905, which indicates the high reliability of the research tool. Importantly, the level of dynamic capabilities was calculated as the arithmetic mean of the respondents' answers as related to the issues that were included in this one-dimensional construct.

The next step in assessing the theoretical validity was to conduct the KMO[2] exploratory factor analysis and the Bartlett sphericity test.[3] The conducted factor analysis (KMO = 0.868; Bartlett sphericity test: chi-square approximation = 1,450.571; degrees of freedom – 10, $p = 0.000$) with the use of the varimax rotation method with Kaiser normalization indicated that all five dimensions were loaded into one dimension of dynamic capabilities, explaining almost 74% of the variance among the questions. The loading strength of the individual questions into one identified dimension of dynamic capabilities was high, ranging from 0.794 to 0.906; this indicated that the respondents' answers constituted one dimension. Therefore, dynamic capabilities are a one-dimensional construct.

The research that was carried out assumed the acquisition of a representative sample so that it was possible to generalize the results that were obtained to the entire general population from which it was taken. The sample size was determined on the basis of a formula that was based on the estimation of the stratum weight and simple random sampling that were proposed by Steczkowski (1995):

$$n = 0.25 \times u\alpha 2 \times N/[0.25 \times u\alpha 2 + N \times d2],$$

where
n is the minimum sample size;
N is the size of the analyzed population;
d is the maximum allowable error of estimate;

$u\alpha$ is the value of a random variable u with standardized normal distribution for which confidence interval $(-u\alpha/2 < U < u\alpha/2) = 1 - \alpha$.

The following were adopted for the calculations:
$d = 0.05$; $\alpha = 0.05$; $1 - \alpha = 0.95$; $u\alpha = 1.96$; $N = 4268606$.[4]

On this basis, a minimum sample size of 384 business entities was calculated. The entities met the condition of belonging to a group of domestic micro- and small enterprises (employing up to 49 people) that operated in various industries.

The study used stratified random sampling, with the strata formed on the basis of two criteria: the size of the company (the number of employees: micro-enterprises that employed 0–9 people, and small enterprises that employed 10–49 people) and the region (voivodeship) in which the company was based. The sample distribution was developed on the basis of data that were contained on the websites of the Central Statistical Office (as of December 31, 2019) concerning the proportional distribution of the number of micro- and small enterprises in each voivodeship (taking the number of employees into account).

The sampling frame was the database of the Register of National Economy, which is considered to be a complete sampling frame of companies that operate in Poland. The sample size was set at 1,200 companies (400 in the basic sample and 800 in the reserve sample) and was proportionally divided into different strata. The substituted sample was used due to the respondents' refusal to participate in the study and outdated records in the database. In addition, the sample was controlled from the point of view of the enterprises' locations in voivodeships, which allowed us to eliminate excessive concentrations in one group. Finally, 438 completed questionnaires were obtained, of which 429 remained after verification due to data inconsistencies.

Due to the large disparities in the number of micro- and small enterprises in Poland, an over-representation of small enterprises was assumed (see Table 13.1) – otherwise, analyses by company size would not have been possible with the assumed sample size.

Due to the disproportional sampling, the analyses used post-stratification weighting to adapt the structure of the sample to the population structure from the point of view of employment size. These ex-post weights also included an uneven response rate within the sample. Thanks to the post-stratification weights that were applied, generalizations for the micro- and small business populations were carried out with the risk of a Type I error of not more than 5%.

Table 13.1 Population and Sample Structure of Enterprises by Employment Size

Description	*Number of companies*		*Percentage of enterprises*	
	Poland (2019)	*Sample (2020)*	*Poland (2019)*	*Sample (2020)*
Micro (up to nine employees)	4,341,325	282	96.7	65.7
Small (10–49 employees)	136,675	147	3.3	34.3
Total	4,509,916	429	100.0	100.0

Source: Own elaboration based on Local Data Bank (www.stat.gov.pl).

The surveyed sample consisted of 429 business entities that operated in Poland and included 282 micro-enterprises (i.e., 65.7%, which employed fewer than ten employees) and 147 small enterprises (i.e., 34.3%, which employed from 10 to 49 employees).

Taking the ages of the surveyed enterprises into account, it should be noted that enterprises that had operated in the market for six to ten years were the most numerous - accounting for slightly more than 42.0%, followed by enterprises that had operated for 11–20 years (33.2%) and for two to five years (16.8%). The least numerous groups of enterprises (4%) were the so-called start-ups with histories of less than one year in the market as well as companies that had operated for more than 20 years.

In terms of the type of dominant activity, service and commercial enterprises dominated (accounting for 39.6 and 33.1%, respectively). Taking the range of a company's market operations that dominated in terms of turnover into account, almost 80% of the surveyed entities operated in domestic and regional markets (38.9 and 40.1%, respectively), and only 10.5% participated in the international market.

Effects of crisis caused by the COVID-19 pandemic in surveyed companies

During the first stage of the study, the entrepreneurs assessed the current condition of their companies on a 1–5 scale, where 1 meant very poor condition, 2 meant poor condition, 3 meant neither good nor bad condition, 4 meant good condition, and 5 meant very good condition. The average rating was 2.1 points - negative ratings (1 and 2 points) were indicated by nearly 70% of the respondents, while positive ratings (4 and 5 points) were indicated by only 9.8% of them. An analysis of the data that was collected by type of dominant activity and age of the company confirmed that manufacturing enterprises and enterprises that had operated for six to ten years were in the best condition (average ratings of 2.4 and 2.3, respectively). Service enterprises and enterprises with little market experience were in the worst condition (average ratings of 1.7 and 1.9, respectively). The respondents then assessed whether the COVID-19 pandemic caused a crisis in their company; the results confirmed that, for most companies, this was the case - nearly 91% of the responses.

The respondents identified decreases in both domestic and foreign demand as well as the late payments from customers and contractors that caused payment gridlocks (69.3 and 61.8%, respectively) as the main causes of the crisis. The representatives of the surveyed companies pointed to supply chain disruptions and the more difficult cooperation with other companies (32.5 and 30.6%, respectively) as less significant reasons for the crisis situation.

As a further step in the analysis of the research results, an attempt was made to answer the question of whether there were any dependencies between the causes of the crisis in the company that were caused by the COVID-19 pandemic and the metric data of the enterprise (i.e., the size, age, type of dominant activity, and dominant range of activity in terms of turnover). A chi-squared test of independence was used to assess the statistical significance of these dependencies. The condition for applying the chi-squared independence test was met since all of the theoretical counts were greater than 5. The results of this test showed that the analyzed dependencies were not statistically significant.

Identifying the measures that were undertaken by companies related to the negative impact of the COVID-19 pandemic on their business activities was another research area. Most of the surveyed companies pointed to two measures that were used to overcome the crisis, i.e., reducing the volume of orders and reducing the workforce (72.8 and 69.2% of the responses, respectively), while the least often indicated were changes in the business profile and the suspension of business activities (21.7 and 23.5%, respectively). In the "other" category, the respondents pointed out the following: the use of government assistance, the sale of vouchers for later use, and late payments to customers.

In the next step of the analysis, an attempt was made to answer the question of whether there were any dependencies between the measures that were undertaken by the surveyed companies to overcome the crisis that was caused by the COVID-19 pandemic and the metric data of the enterprise (i.e., the size, age, type of dominant activity, and dominant range of activity in terms of turnover). A chi-squared test of independence was used to assess the statistical significance of these dependencies. The condition for applying the chi-squared independence test was met since all of the theoretical counts were greater than 5. The results of the test showed statistically significant dependencies only in the case of one grouping variable - type of dominant activity.

The results of the analysis (i.e., the chi-squared statistics, the number of degrees of freedom [*df*], test probability [*p*], and the measure of association [Cramer's *V*]) are included in Table 13.2. The probability in the chi-squared test was less than $\alpha = 0.05$ for the five measures that were undertaken by the surveyed companies to overcome the crisis that was caused by the COVID-19 pandemic (i.e., change in the profile of their business [e.g., starting new production], production reduction, workforce reduction, working remotely, and increasing online sales) for which the dependencies were statistically significant and linked to the dominant activity. The strength of this dependency was the highest for remote work, as evidenced by a Cramer's *V* value of 0.243.

The conducted analysis of the responses according to the dominant type of activity highlighted the diversity of the measures that were undertaken by the surveyed companies to overcome the crisis that was caused by the COVID-19 pandemic. Every fifth manufacturing enterprise and every tenth service enterprises decided to change the profiles of their activities.

Table 13.2 Significance and Strength of Dependency between Measures Undertaken by Companies to Overcome Crisis Caused by COVID-19 Pandemic and Dominant Type of Activity

Dominant activity (a)	*Chi-squared statistic*	*df*	*p*	*Cramer's V*
Suspension of business activities	0.648	2	0.723	
Reduction in volume of orders	0.661	2	0.718	
Change in business profile (e.g., starting new production)	11.169	2	0.004*	0.161
Production reduction	20.548	2	0.000*	0.219
Workforce reduction	12.952	2	0.009*	0.123
Remuneration reduction	3.925	2	0.141	
Remote work	25.423	2	0.000*	0.243
Increase in online sales	8.907	2	0.012*	0.144

Source: own elaboration.
*Statistically significant dependency.

Every second manufacturing firm decided to reduce production. Among the commercial enterprises, every second company decided to increase online sales – but not on such a scale that the sales would compensate for the losses that were incurred by these companies (e.g., due to closures of shopping centers). In turn, the most common response to the crisis that was caused by the COVID-19 pandemic in the case of service enterprises was the reduction of the workforce and remote work – especially in area of business service provision.

Crisis caused by the COVID-19 pandemic and dynamic capabilities of surveyed companies

Another research area was the assessment of the components of the dynamic capabilities construct by the studied enterprises as compared to their direct competitors. The respondents assessed these capabilities on the basis of a theoretical construct that consisted of five variables on a 1–5 scale, where 1 meant much worse than those of their direct competitors, 2 meant worse than those of their direct competitors, 3 meant comparable to those of their direct competitors, 4 meant better than those of their direct competitors, and 5 meant much better than those of their direct competitors.

The highest scores were obtained in the area of organizational learning capabilities (61.8% of the responses (see Table 13.3) – 34.3% of the responses indicated better capabilities than those of the competition and 27.5% of the responses indicated much better capabilities than those of the competition) and organizational adaptation (61.5% of the responses –

Table 13.3 Assessment of Components of Dynamic Capabilities Construct as Compared to Direct Competitors

Characteristics of dynamic capabilities	*Assessment**				
	1	*2*	*3*	*4*	*5*
Opportunity search	4.0%	11.2%	29.6%	29.6%	25.6%
Configuration and reconfiguration	8.4%	23.5%	24.0%	25.6%	18.5%
Organizational adaptation	2.6%	12.1%	23.8%	33.3%	28.2%
Coordination	4.9%	19.8%	31.5%	31.7%	12.1%
Organizational learning	4.9%	11.9%	21.4%	34.3%	27.5%

Source: Own elaboration.

*Respondents assessed dynamic capabilities on a 1–5 scale, where 1 denoted dynamic capabilities much worse than those of their direct competitors, 2 denoted dynamic capabilities worse than those of their direct competitors, 3 denoted dynamic capabilities comparable to those of their direct competitors, 4 denoted dynamic capabilities better than those of their direct competitors, and 5 denoted dynamic capabilities much better than those of their direct competitors.

33.3% of the responses indicated better capabilities than those of the competition and 28.2% of the responses indicated much better capabilities than those of the competition). On the other hand, the entities assessed their capabilities of configuration and reconfiguration at the lowest level - 31.9% of the responses (as being worse and much worse than those of the competition).

The research also attempted to determine whether there was a link between the COVID-19 pandemic crisis in the company and the components of the dynamic capabilities construct.

The respondents assessed the impact of the COVID-19 pandemic on the components of the dynamic capabilities construct on a 1–5 scale, where 1 indicated a very weak impact, 2 indicated a weak impact, 3 indicated neither a weak nor a strong impact, 4 indicated a strong impact, and 5 indicated a very strong impact. According to the respondents, the crisis had the strongest impact on the company's adaptability (4.3) as related to the reconfiguration of the business model, improving the company, implementing good management practices, ensuring flexibility in the organizational structure, managing the identity of the organization, and the ability to configure and reconfigure (4.21) related to the acquisition, creation, and integration of resources, creating innovations, implementing new technologies, acquiring skills, and disposing of unnecessary resources. In an attempt to examine this situation, attention should be drawn to the fact that the measures that were undertaken within the framework of these capabilities formed the basis for the survival and development of a company in a turbulent environment (such as the one that was caused by the COVID-19 pandemic crisis). By contrast, the weakest impact of the crisis could be seen on the ability to coordinate (3.67) as related to the implementation of innovations and new technologies, the creation of a vision integrating stakeholders, building employee loyalty and commitment, and the ability to learn (3.79) aimed at knowledge acquisition, transfer, allocation, and preservation within the company. This may indicate the company's passivity in responding to changes in the environment and passivity in the knowledge-management process.

Conclusions

The conducted research concerning the process of developing the dynamic capabilities of small businesses during the time of the crisis that was caused by the COVID-19 pandemic allowed for the following observations to be made:

1 According to the assessments that were made by the respondents, the conditions of the surveyed companies were poor (70% of responses). It turns out that manufacturing enterprises and enterprises that had operated for six to ten years were in the best condition, while service enterprises and enterprises with little market experience were in the worst situation. The reason for this was undoubtedly the fact that nearly 91% of the surveyed companies were in a crisis situation due to the COVID-19 pandemic.
2 The respondents identified decreases in both domestic and international demands as well as the late payments from customers and contractors that caused payment gridlocks (69.3 and 61.8%, respectively) as the main causes of this crisis. The representatives of the surveyed companies indicated supply chain disruptions and more difficult cooperation with other companies (32.5 and 30.6%, respectively) as less significant reasons.
3 Most often, the respondents pointed to two measures that were undertaken to overcome the crisis (i.e., reducing the volume of orders and reducing the workforce), while the least frequently indicated were changes in the profile of their activities and the suspension of business activities. One in five manufacturing enterprises and every tenth service enterprise decided to change their business profiles, while every second manufacturing enterprise decided to reduce production. Among the commercial enterprises, one in two decided to increase online sales. In turn, the most common response to the crisis that was caused by the COVID-19 pandemic in the case of service enterprises was the reduction of the workforce and remote work – especially in the case of business services provision.
4 The assessment of the components of the dynamic capabilities construct by the surveyed companies as compared to their direct competitors indicated that the highest ratings were achieved by the ability to

learn and adaptability. On the other hand, the studied entities assessed their ability to configure and reconfigure to be at the lowest level, which may indicate their small capacity to make innovative changes as well as to acquire and integrate resources.

5 Based on the analysis of the research results, it can be concluded that there is a relationship between the crisis that was caused by the COVID-19 pandemic and the dynamic capabilities of small businesses (which confirms the research hypothesis).
6 According to the respondents, the COVID-19 pandemic crisis has had the strongest impact on their adaptability and ability to configure and reconfigure. By contrast, it has had the weakest impact on their ability to coordinate and to learn aimed at knowledge acquisition, transfer, allocation, and preservation within the company. This may indicate that a given company is reacting passively to changes in a turbulent environment.

The results of the conducted research have an application value for the managers of small enterprises. The conducted research allows us to formulate a conclusion that the dynamic abilities of these entities make it possible to gain and maintain a competitive advantage in a changing environment. Developing these abilities allows for shaping and modifying the enterprise's skills and resources to build a market advantage and competitive position.

The study that is presented in this paper has some research limitations, such as the fact that it discusses Polish conditions that are characterized by a lower level of experience in the analysis of the dynamic capabilities of small businesses during the COVID-19 pandemic than other world economies. The research is static as it concerns only one period; therefore, future research should focus on a deeper understanding of the possibilities of using dynamic capabilities to deal with a crisis by small enterprises that operate in countries with different stages of development of these entities. It would also be interesting to study different periods, which would allow us to compare changes in the use of dynamic capabilities by small businesses as related to overcoming the crisis that was caused by the COVID-19 pandemic. Empirical verification of these issues can become a source of new knowledge for entrepreneurs, which will increase the efficiency of managing small businesses.

Notes

1 Cronbach's alpha coefficient ranged from 0 to 1, and the recommended value was within a range of 0.6–0.94. Values that are below the reference value may indicate, for example, the weak reciprocity of the relationships among the coefficients or an insufficient number of questions, while in the case of a too high coefficient, the problem may be too many similar variables.
2 It is recommended that KMO should have a value that is not lower than 0.5.

3 Bartlett's test for sphericity tests the null hypothesis (H_0): the correlation matrix is an identity matrix, against H_1: ~H_0 (thus, $p < \alpha$ is expected).
4 As of the end of 2019, Local Data Bank, www.stat.gov.pl.

References

Arend, R. (2014) Entrepreneurship and dynamic capabilities: How firm age and size affect the capability enhancement–SME performance relationship. *Small Business Economics* 42(1), 33–57.

Barreto, I. (2010) Dynamic capabilities: A review of past research and an agenda for the future. *Journal of Management* 36(1), 256–280.

Clampit, J.A., Lorenz, M.P., Gamble, J.E., and Lee, J. (2021) Performance stability among small and medium-sized enterprises during COVID-19: A test of the efficacy of dynamic capabilities. *International Small Business Journal: Researching Entrepreneurship* 40 (5), 1–17.

Cyfert, S., and Krzakiewicz, K. (2019) *Dynamiczne zdolności polskich przedsiębiorstw.* PWN, Warszawa.

Eggers, F. (2020) Masters of disasters? Challenges and opportunities for SMEs in times of crisis. *Journal of Business Research* 116, 199–208.

Eisenhardt, K.M. and Martin, J.A. (2000) Dynamic capabilities: What are they? *Strategic Management Journal* 21, 1105–1121.

Fairlie, R. (2020) *The Impact of COVID-19 on Small Business Owners: Continued Losses and the Partial Rebound in May 2020.* Working paper 27462. National Bureau of Economic Research, Cambridge, MA.

Helfat, C.E., Finkelstein, S., Mitchell, M., Peteraf, M., Singh, H., Teece, D., and Winter, S. (2007). *Dynamic Capabilities: Understanding Strategic Change in Organizations.* Blackwell Publishing, Malden, MA and Oxford.

Klein, V. B., and Todesco, J.L. (2021) COVID-19 crisis and SMEs responses: The role of digital transformation. *Knowledge and Process Management* 28 (2), 117–133.

Kolb, D.A. (1984) *Experiential Learning: Experience as the Source of Learning and Development.* Prentice-Hall, Hoboken, NJ.

Kump, B., Engelmann, A., Kessler, A., and Schweiger, C. (2019) Toward a dynamic capabilities scale: Measuring organizational sensing, seizing, and transforming capacities. *Industrial and Corporate Change* 28(5), 1149–1172.

Lampel, J., and Shamsie, J. (2003). Capabilities in motion: New organizational forms and the reshaping of the Hollywood movie industry. *Journal of Management Studies* 40(8), 2189–2210.

Leoncini, R., and Montresor, S. (2008) *Dynamic Capabilities between Firm Organisation and Local Systems of Production.* Routledge, London.

Lim, D., Morse, E., and Yu, N. (2020) The impact of the global crisis on the growth of SMEs: A resource system perspective. *International Small Business Journal* 38(6), 492–503.

Maior, P., and Camisao, I. (2021) *The Pandemic Crisis and the European Union COVID-19 and Crisis Management.* Routledge, London.

Martinelli, E., Tagliazucchi, G., and Marchi, G. (2018) The resilient retail entrepreneur: Dynamic capabilities for facing natural disasters. *International Journal of Entrepreneurial Behavior & Research* 24(7), 1222–1243.

Mitroff, I.I. (2005) *Why Some Companies Emerge Stronger and Better from a Crisis: 7 Essential Lessons for Surviving Disaster.* Amacom, New York.

OECD, (2020) *Coronavirus (COVID-19): SME Policy Responses.* https://read.oecd-ilibrary.org/view/?ref=119_119680-di6h3qgi4x&title=Covid-19_SME_Policy_Responses

Pavlou, P.A., and El Sawy, O.A. (2011) Understanding the elusive black box of dynamic capabilities. *Decision Sciences* 42(1), 239–273.

Pisano, G.P. (2017) Toward a prescriptive theory of dynamic capabilities: Connecting strategic choice, learning, and competition. *Industrial and Corporate Change* 26(5), 747–762.

Steczkowski, J. (1995) *Metoda reprezentatywna w badaniach zjawisk ekonomiczno-społecznych, PWN,* Warszawa, Kraków.

Stoyanova, V. (2018) *An Analysis of David J. Teece's Dynamic Capabilites and Strategic Management Organizing for Innovation and Growth.* Routledge, London.

Teece, D., (2011) Dynamic capabilities: A guide for managers. *Ivey Business Journal* 75(2), 29–32.

Teece, D.J. (2007) Explicating dynamic capabilities: The nature and micro foundations of (sustainable) enterprise performance. *Strategic Management Journal* 28 (13), 1319–1350.

Teece, D.J., Pisano, G., and Shuen, A. (1997) Dynamic capabilities and strategic management. *Strategic Management Journal* 18(7), 509–533.

Teece, D.J., and Pisano, G. (1994) The dynamic capabilities of firms: An introduction. *Industrial and Corporate Change* 3(3), 537–556.

Teece, D.J. (2014). The foundations of enterprise performance: Dynamic and ordinary capabilities in an (economic) theory of firms. *Academy of Management Perspectives* 28(4), 328–352.

Teece, D.J. (2018) Business models and dynamic capabilities. *Long Range Planning* 51, 40–49.

Wang, C.L., and Ahmed, P.K. (2007). Dynamic capabilities: a review and research agenda. *The International Journal of Management Reviews,* 9(1), 31–51.

Winter, S.G. (2003) Understanding dynamic capabilities. *Strategic Management Journal* 24, 991–995.

Zahra, S.A., Sapienza, H.J., and Davidson, P. (2006) Entrepreneurship and dynamic capabilities: A review, model and research agenda. *Journal of Management Studies* 43(4), 917–955.

Zollo, M., and Winter, S.G. (2002) Deliberate learning and the evolution of dynamic capabilities. *Organization Science* 13(3), 339–351.

14 Impact of COVID-19 on risk management in projects

Hanna Soroka-Potrzebna

Introduction

Nowadays, integrating risk into project activities is an increasing problem, as the external environment has become more and more competitive, complex, and unpredictable. The reality that surrounds us, which is dynamically changing, creates huge opportunities for development but increases the risk of making decisions at the same time. As compared to other areas of business activity, projects are associated with a higher level of risk due to their uniqueness. In addition, the implementation of most projects entails high investment outlays, with a lack of full knowledge about future periods of project implementation.

Significant help for project teams is the implementation of risk management in projects. The relationship between risk management and the success or failure of a project has been analyzed in the literature over the last years (Hatamleh, 2020; Carvalho and Rabechini, 2015; Hwang et al., 2014; Hwang, Zhao, and Toh, 2014; De Bakker et al., 2010; Banaitiene and Banaitis, 2012). The theory is focused on techniques, methods, and formalities that are related to the implementation of a project, while project teams are focused more on soft skills (Hatamleh, 2020; Söderlund and Maylor, 2012; Eskandari et al., 2007; Rabelo, 2006).

The situation changed after the outbreak of the COVID-19 pandemic in December 2019, which had a huge impact on all of the entities that operated throughout the world (including project teams). It is still impossible to estimate the impact of theCOVID-19 pandemic on the activities of entities (Khanna et al., 2020, p. 703), but it is possible to develop recommendations and guidelines that will help project teams properly prepare for similar emergencies in the future.

The purpose of the chapter is to show how COVID-19 influenced risk management in projects and to formulate recommendations for similar crisis situations. A literature analysis, the CAWI method, and statistical analysis were used to prepare the chapter. The results have shown that actions by project teams are needed to expand both the risks and methods of their analysis as well as to implement updated risk management plans that take the risk register and more flexible operation into account.

DOI: 10.4324/9781003368687-14

Project risk

Risk is an inseparable element of each decision that is made while conducting business activities, which accompanies every entrepreneur. Risk management plays an important role in the areas of the business activities of enterprises, especially during their projects. Many researchers and practitioners have claimed that introducing risk management has had the effect of increasing the chances of a project's success (Schwindt and Zimmermann, 2015; Yeo and Ren, 2009; Olechowski et al., 2016; Hillson, 2006; Holzmann and Spiegler, 2011; Cagliano et al., 2015). The importance of project management can also be seen in the literature, where it has been receiving more and more attention in recent decades (Hillson, 2006; Yaraghi and Langhe, 2011; Verbano and Venturini, 2011). Practical analyses show, however, that risk management has not been fully implemented in projects or can be improved when being utilized (Olechowski et al., 2016; Dyer, 2016; Mu et al., 2014; Yaraghi and Langhe, 2011).

There are many definitions of risk in the literature. Risk is a combination of internal and external factors that affect the implementation of an adopted project's objectives and significantly affect the profitability of both the project and the entire organization. This is also a chance to realize the event that will affect the achievement of the intended goal or the experience of failure. Risk is very broadly defined in terms of uncertainty and its consequences, and the risk effect is defined as the deviation from the expected (Luko, 2013, p. 293). D. Hillson (2016, p. 6) even stated that risk is uncertainty that matters.

Project risk is defined as "the likelihood that a project will fail to achieve its objectives" (Mars and Weir, 2019, p. 225). The ISO 31000: 2009 risk-management standards define these factors in the context of the following (ISO, 2009):

- impact on project – as deviation from expected result;
- various aspects (financial, health, safety, environmental protection) implemented at various levels (strategic, tactical, operational) of entire organization, project, product, or process;
- uncertainty – as state of partial lack of information about event, its consequences, or probability of its occurrence.

Due to the type of criterion, the most general risk classification divides risk into the following:

- typical – occurring during implementation of each project regardless of field it concerns;
- specific – closely related to specificity of field to which it relates; occurs in case of specific project implemented (e.g., on individual orders, based on special non-standard methodology, or using special tools).

According to the criterion of the information level, the following are distinguished (Mankad, 2012, p. 291):

- known risk – occurs on basis of design analysis, potential sources of risk, and simulations that are carried out; it is possible to identify it and determine events that may occur with certain accuracy specific;
- predictable risk – occurs when, based on knowledge of project team members, potential sources of risk can be determined and level of risk for project due to risk;
- unpredictable risk – occurs when undesirable events or their effects cannot be predicted.

The classification of project risk by cause distinguishes the following risks (Posokhov and Zhadan, 2016, p. 286):

1 Brought about by external causes – determined by external forces and not under the control of the entity that manages the project. This risk is related to forces of nature, the economic conditions of the market, and the decisions that are made in the political or legal spheres.
2 Brought about by internal causes – can be controlled by the entity that manages the project and includes the method of project planning that is used. This risk is associated with the human factor.

According to the standards of the Project Management Institute project, risk is defined as "an uncertain event or condition that, if it occurs, has a positive or negative effect on one or more project objectives such as scope, schedule, cost, or quality" (PMI, 2013, p. 301).

Project risk-management process

Project risk management "is a systematic process that aims to identify and manage risk in order to act on its appearance (eliminating, minimizing, or controlling it) by implementing systems and procedures to identify, analyze, evaluate, and address the risks that are inherent to any project" (Marcelino-Sádaba et al., 2014). This is identifying any threats to a project and determining the actions to eliminate the detected threats or minimize their impact on the project (Zaskórski et al., 2013, p. 31). It is also fundamental to achieving project goals, not only by minimizing bad results but also by acting as a guide to maximizing positive results (Górecki, 2018).

The risk-management process is sequential; this means that it should be implemented on a continuous basis. As part of the process, six stages (Figure 14.1) can be distinguished as follows (Pritchard, 2015, pp. 37–38):

1 plan risk management – establishing project risk infrastructure and risk-management plan;

Figure 14.1 Project risk-management process.

2 identify risks – consisting of identifying potential events, including both individual risks and sources of overall project risk;
3 qualify risks – process of prioritizing risk factors, carried out by assessment, and reference of probability of risk factors to their effects;
4 quantify risks – process of analyzing impact of identified risk factors on overall objectives of project;
5 plan risk responses – involving development of acceptable solutions and activities that aim to maximize opportunities and minimize risks of project;
6 monitor and control risk – process of implementing risk-response plans, monitoring identified risk, and identifying new risk.

Following the stages of the risk-management process improves the transparency of the analysis as well as makes the members of a project team aware of the possibility of interference in the management process (Rodrigues-da-Silva and Crispim, 2014, p. 943; Thamhain, 2013, p. 23). However, it is important to consider the risk to not only be full of threats but also of opportunities (Rehacek, 2017, p. 13).

Concept of risk and risk management by project teams

During the period of October to December 2019, a survey was conducted among 1,325 project management practitioners in Poland. The survey included 24 questions, including six metric questions; these were asked of entities by using the CAWI (computer-assisted web interview) method. One hundred and 52 answers were obtained, which were analyzed by using the statistical method and MS Excel 2016 software.

The research sample included public institutions and local government units (43.2%), medium-sized enterprises (17.6%), and micro- and small enterprises (25.7%). The entities represented various industries, including education and upbringing (27.6%), industry (18.4%), health care (10.5%), construction (7.9%), physical culture, tourism, and the rest (7.9%). The entities were dominated by small project teams that consisted of a maximum of three-person (39.5%) and four-person teams (15.8%).

The projects that were implemented by the surveyed entities overwhelmingly lasted less than two years (82% of the respondents), while those projects that lasted up to a year were almost half of them (41% of the respondents). The budgets of the analyzed projects were quite diverse in terms of their sizes: Budgets below 500,000 PLN accounted for 22% of the analyzed projects, between 500,000 and one million PLN – 20% of the projects, one to two million PLN– 17% of the projects, and two to five million PLN – 26% of the projects; the rest were projects with budgets that were above five million PLN. The funds for implementing the projects mostly came from EU subsidies (88%), while the rest came from loans, grants, or a company's own funds.

The first question asked of the respondents concerned the concept of risk and, thus, the way project team members perceived risk. As many as 67% of the surveyed project team members admitted that they understood risk as a threat, while 33% described it as both an opportunity and a threat. Positive information is that all of the respondents saw risk as a threat, but awareness of the other part of risk was still largely lacking. The results that were obtained with this question (that the majority of the project teams perceived risk as a threat) were consistent with the research that has been presented in the literature (e.g., Hartono et al., 2014).

The second question that was asked of the project teams was whether they identified and analyzed risk before starting a project's implementation. Unfortunately, only 87% had identified and analyzed risk despite the fact that 100% of the respondents saw risk as the possibility of loss. The entities that responded positively to the question analyzed the risk of maintaining a time frame (30%), financial risk (27%), the risk that is related to planned technical and technological solutions (19%), and legal risk (12%). There was no force majeure among the answers, which has had a huge impact on the implementation of all ongoing projects in recent months.

The obtained results are in line with the results of studies that were conducted in other countries; according to these, the most frequently analyzed risks by project teams included cost risk, schedule risk, performance risk, legal risk, government risk, strategical risk, operational risk, and market risk (e.g., Van et al., 2015; ICCPM, 2011; PM Project management.com, 2021).

The surveyed entities were also asked about the methods of risk identification and analysis that they used in their projects. The most frequently mentioned methods were brainstorming (44%) and documentation review (42%), while SWOT analysis (30%) and checklists (21%) were mentioned slightly less frequently. The least frequent answers included specialized software (2%), the morphological method (2%), lotus flower (2%), and the snowball technique (1%). Individuals also pointed to the observations of macroeconomic and legislative changes, market reviews and analysis, and ongoing monitoring. Similar methods were indicated by respondents in studies that were conducted in other countries, where the largest share was brainstorming and checklists (Raz and Michael, 2001; Akintoy and MacLeod, 1997; Lyons and Skitmore, 2004).

The choice of the indicated methods was mainly motivated by their effectiveness (38%), ease of implementation (36%), and low cost (17%). When asked about the existence of identified risk during the implementation of a project, as many as 62% of the respondents answered that risk had occurred. Only 17% of the respondents admitted that there was risk that they did not identify before starting the project. Among the unidentified types of risk that appeared were the human factor, price increases, bad weather conditions, and political decisions.

Finally, 76% of the surveyed entities admitted that a project was successful, 3% indicated that it was still in progress, and 21% ended with deviations as to the dates, budgets, or scopes of the project work. Nearly all of the respondents (93%) admitted that risk identification and analysis was an important point before starting project implementation and, thus, for a project's success.

Risk management in projects during COVID-19 epidemic

In December 2019, a phenomenon of collective pneumonia appeared in Wuhan, Hubei Province, China (Huang et al., 2020). The National Health Commission sent experts to Wuhan to investigate. A coronavirus (COVID-19 – Corona VIrus Disease 19) was detected in the Laboratory of Virology, Chinese Center for Disease Control and Prevention on January 7, 2020 (Wang et al., 2020). The number of patients with the virus had skyrocketed, and it eventually spread throughout China and the rest of the world. The global COVID-19 pandemic confronted project managers with a new unknown that inevitably changed the dynamics of risk management. This adversely affected the activities of enterprises, including those that were implementing projects. According to data that was collected by Euler Hermes, the global default rate will reach a record level of +35% in 2021 as a result of the pandemic. Thus, half of the analyzed countries will record new records since the 2009 financial crisis: the United States (+57% by 2021 as compared to 2019), Brazil (+45%), China (+40%), and major European countries such as the UK (+43%), Spain (+41%), Italy (+27%), Belgium (+26%), and France (+25%) (Lemerle, 2020). The insolvency of enterprises also means a lack of funds for implemented or planned projects.

The proper implementation of a project requires the implementation of all assumptions of the application documentation, which include the periods of the implementations of individual tasks as well as their material scopes, among others. The effects that are associated with the occurrence of epidemic risk have an influence on all areas that are related to an implemented project. Such areas include the following in particular:

- Prepared project schedule (i.e., all of the activities that are undertaken during the implementation of a project). The effects in this area are manifested by delays in the implementation dates of individual activities. This applies, among others, to the deliveries of ordered equipment or machines, which can last from several to even dozens of months. In the context of an epidemic when there are limitations in the production staff of many companies or even their cessations of production, orders may prove to be impossible to fulfill. Delays in deliveries, limiting the work of offices, or closing some enterprises cause the extensions of entire projects. This becomes particularly burdensome when the implementation of a project depends on starting subsequent projects or obtaining funds from the EU.
- Project budget (i.e., the financial dimension of an entire project). The effects in this area are linked to timetables. Any delays in a project's implementation are reflected in increased expenses, which is synonymous with increases in the costs of implementing the entire project. This may also cause problems with the payment of remuneration – especially for entities that were forced to limit or suspend their activities. With very limited revenues, maintaining a full staff becomes a huge cost for a company.
- Enterprise resources (i.e., people, materials, technical means). Disruptions in a project's implementation change these resources and cause changes in their use, which may result in its lack of completion or its incompatibility with a plan.
- The quality of the work that is performed by suppliers and the final value of the product; the latter being particularly important for customers.

All of the above effects are consequences of the risk of an epidemic. However, the most important thing is that similar risks may reappear in the near or distant future. The possibility of another wave of illness or a new virus has been repeated many times by experts. Hence, the possibility of the emergence of further difficulties in the implementation of a project is recognized by everyone. Risk awareness, however, does not mean taking on the appropriate risk-management measures. Project teams should identify and analyze risks and then plan their risk responses. For this purpose, it is necessary to verify the catalog of risks that are presented in the "Concept of risk and risk management by project teams" subsection. Undoubtedly, epidemic risk should be added to the catalog of risks that are analyzed by project teams as being one of the most important risks. In addition, it is also necessary to expand the methods that are used for risk analysis. The brainstorming and checklists that have been mentioned so far seem insufficient. Experience-based methods such as risk-log analysis or experience analysis should be disseminated among project teams.

One positive example is the research that was conducted among students in Poland. During the period of April to June 2020, the students implemented a risk-management process in the projects that they created as part of their activities. A total of 49 project teams were created in their full-time and part-time studies. By using a properly selected method, each team identified risks that may occur during the implementation of a project. One hundred percent of the surveyed teams mentioned the risk of the case of force majeure in the form of a pandemic among the listed risks. Proper risk identification and analysis allowed all of the teams to choose those risks that most threatened the success of their projects and then plan their responses and create plans for monitoring their progress.

The importance of risk management was also confirmed by International Project Management Association certification assessors, who deal with assessing project managers' competencies in project risk management, among others. During interviews that were conducted with five CERT IPMA assessors at the end of 2019, everyone agreed that risk management was an important point in a project and that choosing the right methods of analyzing and respond to risk helped to avoid negative events or supported positive events during the project.

Conclusion

Project risk management is extremely important for the success of a project. The research results that have been discussed in this chapter have confirmed that this is one of the most important elements of project management, which was acknowledged by both project implementers and specialists in project management. However, it is necessary to develop recommendations and guidelines for project teams that would help in the effective planning of actions in the event of subsequent crisis situations. Some researchers point to six critical lessons that are worth implementing (Darwish et al., 2021):

1. identify activities;
2. work and be confident in planning;
3. look at present and future developments;
4. research lessons from actions already taken;

5 be imaginative – expect something worse;
6 understand limitations.

Useful in this respect is a risk log in which a project team records all of the risks that have occurred in its implemented projects. Unfortunately, the document has not been recommended by all methodologies; however, it should become an obligatory document. It is important for project teams to focus on solutions in order to understand a problem and be able to easily plan actions to reduce its effects. A log should be kept so that everyone understands a potentially dangerous situation. It is essential to ensure that any actions that are taken lead to a greater control of the risk. In risk management, direct actions can lead to better outcomes and timely results (Richter and Wilson, 2020).

There is also a need to update a project's risk-management plan to take account of any government regulations regarding COVID-19. Implemented projects carry minimal risks that are related to any recurrence of the epidemic at the closure stages. However, for projects that are in the planning stages, the need to consider revising plans to include current COVID-19 legislation as well as any future implications of the legislation is vital. On the other hand, projects that are already at the implementation stage should be updated to take the required regulations into account.

The authors emphasize that there is a positive relationship between project schedule overruns and project cost overruns (Larsen et al., 2016; Plummer-Braeckman et al., 2019). The more a project is delayed, the more money will be spent on it (Larsen et al., 2016; Plummer-Braeckman et al., 2019). Hence, it is necessary to reserve additional funds to cover such costs (if any). Therefore, project managers, project sponsors, and consultants will need to re-plan, rethink, re-learn, and adapt to any changing factors that are associated with the COVID-19 pandemic in order to achieve their projects' goals.

Taking the above recommendations into account will certainly contribute to the more effective preparation of project teams for the possible emergence of crisis situations that are similar to those at the end of 2019 and beginning of 2020. Perhaps future threats will no longer be associated with the COVID-19 virus itself, but a force majeure risk will certainly remain in force. This research is an introduction to the further analysis of risk management in projects that will be continued while taking the future evolution of the epidemic into account.

References

Akintoye, A.S. and MacLeod, M.J. (1997) Risk analysis and management in construction. *International Journal of Project Management*, 15(1), 31–38.

Banaitiene, N. and Banaitis, A. (2012) *Risk management in construction projects* [in:] Banaitiene, N. (ed.) *Risk Management – Current Issues and Challenges.* IntechOpen, Croatia, 429–448.

Cagliano, A.C., Grimaldi, S., and Rafele, C. (2015) Choosing project risk management techniques. A theoretical framework. *Journal of Risk Research,* 18(2), 232–248.

Carvalho, M.M. and Rabechini, J.R. (2015) Impact of risk management on project performance: The importance of soft skills. *International Journal of Production Research*, 53(2), 321–340.

Darwish, S., Gomes, A.M. and Ahmed, U. (2021) Risk management strategies and impact on sustainability: The disruptive effect of Covid-19. *Academy of Strategic Management Journal*, 2(20), 1–19.

De Bakker, K., Boonstra, A. and Wortmann, H. (2010) Does risk management contribute to IT project success? A meta-analysis of empirical evidence. *International Journal of Project Management*, 28(5), 493–503.

Dyer, R. (2016) Cultural sense-making integration into risk mitigation strategies towards megaproject success. *International Journal of Project Management*, 35(7), 1338–1349.

Eskandari, H., Sala-Diakanda, S., Furterer, S., Rabelo, L., Crumpton-Young, L. and Williams, K. (2007) Enhancing the undergraduate industrial engineering curriculum. *Education and Training*, 49(1), 45–55.

Górecki, J. (2018) *Big data as a project risk management Tool*[in:] Oduoza, Ch.F. (ed.), *Risk Management Treatise for Engineering Practitioners.* IntechOpen, London, 25–32.

Hartono, B., Sulistyo, S.R., Praftiwi, P.P. and Hasmoro, D. (2014) Project risk: Theoretical concepts and stakeholders' perspective. *International Journal of Project Management*, 32, 400–411.

Hatamleh, M.T. (2020) *Exploring the project risk management: Highlighting the soft side of project management* [in:] Moynihan G. (ed.) *Concepts, Applications and Emerging Opportunities in Industrial Engineering.* IntechOpen, Croatia, 117–134.

Hillson, D. (2006) *The Risk Management Universe: A Guided Tour.* BSI Standards, London.

Hillson, D. (2016) *Managing Risk in Projects.* Routledge, London.

Holzmann, V. and Spiegler, I. (2011) Developing risk breakdown structure for information technology organizations. *International Journal of Project Management,* 29(5), 537–546.

Huang, C., Wang, Y., Li, X., Ren, L., Zhao, J., Hu, Y., ... and Cao, B. (2020) Clinical features of patients infected with 2019 novel coronavirus in Wuhan, China. *The Lancet*, 395(10223), 497–506.

Hwang, B.G., Zhao, X. and Toh, L.P. (2014) Risk management in small construction projects in Singapore: Status, barriers, and impact. *International Journal of Project Management,* 32(1), 116–124.

ISO, ISO31000 (2009) *31000: 2009 Risk Management–Principles and Guidelines.* International Organization for Standardization. Geneva, Switzerland.

Khanna, R.C., Cicinelli, M.V., Gilbert, S., Honavar, S.G. and Murthy, G.V. (2020) COVID-19 pandemic: Lessons learned and future directions. *Indian Journal of Ophthalmology*, 68(5), 703.

Larsen, J.K., Shen, G.Q., Lindhard, S.M. and Brunoe, T.D. (2016) Factors affecting schedule delay, cost overrun, and quality level in public construction projects. *Journal of Management in Engineering*, 32(1), 1–29.

Lemerle, M. (2020) *Calm Before the Storm: Covid-19 and the Business Insolvency Time Bomb.* Allianz and Euler Hermes, Munich.

Luko, S.N. (2013) Risk management terminology. *Quality Engineering*, 25(3), 292–297.
Lyons, T. and Skitmore, M. (2004) Project risk management in the Queensland engineering construction industry: A survey. *International Journal of Project Management*, 22(1), 51–61.
Marcelino-Sádaba, S., Pérez-Ezcurdia, A., Lazcano, A.M.E. and Villanueva, P. (2014). Project risk management methodology for small firms. *International Journal of Project Management*, 32(2), 327–340.
Mars, G. and Weir, D.T.H. (2019), *Risk Management: Volume II: Management and Control*. Routledge, London.
Mankad, D. (2012) Risks management in software engineering. *International Journal of Advances Computer Research*, 2(4), 290–293.
Mu, S., Cheng, H., Chohr, M. and Peng, W. (2014) Assessing risk management capability of contractors in subway projects in mainland China. *International Journal of Project Management,* 32(3), 452–460.
Olechowski, A., Oehmen, J., Seering, W. and Ben-Daya, M. (2016) The professionalization of risk management: What role Can the ISO 31000 risk management principles play? *International Journal of Project Management,* 34(8), 1568–1578.
Plummer-Braeckman, J., Disselhoff, T. and Kirchherr, J. (2019) Cost and schedule overruns in large hydropower dams: An assessment of projects completed since 2000. *International Journal of Water Resources Development*, 1–16.
PMI (2013) *A Guide to the Project Management Body of Knowledge*. PMBOK®, Newtown Square, PA.
Posokhov, I.M. and Zhadan, U.V. (2016) The improvement of approaches to the classification of risks of industrial enterprises. *Маркетинг і менеджмент інновацій*, 4, 285–300.
Pritchard, C.L. (2015) *Risk management. Concepts and Guidance*. Taylor & Francis Group. New York, NY.
Rabelo, L. (2006) Emerging topics for industrial engineering curriculum. *American Society for Engineering Education*, Chicago, IL.
Raz, T. and Michael, E. (2001) Use and benefits of tools for project risk management. *International Journal of Project Management*, 19, 9–17.
Rehacek, P. (2017) Risk management standards for project management. *International Journal of Advances and Applied Sciences*, 4(6), 1–13.
Richter, A. and Wilson, T.C. (2020) Covid-19: Implications for insurer risk management and the insurability of pandemic risk. *The Geneva Risk and insurance review*, 45(2), 171–199.
Rodrigues-da-Silva, L.H. and Crispim, J.A. (2014) The project risk management process, a preliminary study. *Procedia Technology*, 16, 943–949.
Schwindt, C. and Zimmermann, J. (2015) *Handbook on Project Management and Scheduling, Vol. 2*. Springer, Cham.
Söderlund, J. and Maylor, H. (2012) Project management scholarship: Relevance, impact, and five integrative challenges for business and management schools. *International Journal of Project Management*, 30(6), 686–696.
Thamhain, H. (2013) Managing risks in complex projects. *Project Management Journal*, 44, 20–35.
Van Os, A., Van Berkel, F., De Gilder, D., Van Dyck, C. and Groenewegen, P. (2015) Project risk as identity threat: Explaining the development and

consequences of risk discourse in an infrastructure project. *International Journal of project management*, 33(4), 877–888.

Verbano, C. and Venturini, K. (2011) Development paths of risk management: Approaches, methods and fields of application. *Journal of Risk Research,* 14(5), 519–550.

Wang, C., Cheng, Z., Yue, X.G. and McAleer, M. (2020) Risk management of COVID-19 by universities in China. *Journal of Risk and Financial Management,* 13, 36.

Yaraghi, N. and Langhe, R.G. (2011) Critical success factors for risk management systems. *Journal of Risk Research,* 14(5), 551–581.

Yeo, K.T. and Ren, Y. (2009) Risk management capability maturity model for complex product systems (CoPS) projects. *Systems Engineering*, 12(4), 275–294.

Zaskórski, P., Woźniak, J., Szwarc, K. and Tomaszewski, Ł. (2013) *Zarządzanie projektami w ujęciu systemowym*. Wojskowa Akademia Techniczna, Warszawa.

Online sources

International Centre for Complex Project Management (ICCPM) (2011). The task force report "global perspectives and the strategic agenda to 2025" is available at https://iccpm.com/content/taskforce-report

PM Project Management.com (2021). "Types of risk in project management" is available at https://project-management.com/types-of-risk-in-project-management/

15 Hedging strategy as protection of insured capital during pandemic period

Magdalena Homa

Introduction

At the time of writing this chapter, the pandemic continues, and nobody knows its real scale. We are all concerned about the possible economic effects of the crisis that was caused by COVID-19, including its impact on the financial markets. It is therefore reasonable to expect a great deal of interest in the very near future concerning the role of the pandemic in finance. This is especially true in the context of financial products, which require a certain amount of activity on the part of investors in terms of analyzing the economic situation to better guarantee their future profits. This is a particularly important issue during times of instability in financial markets that are caused by random events, such as the COVID-19 pandemic. An example of such a product is unit-linked insurance plan (ULIP), where making the right decision on optimal coverage and adopting a specific fund investment strategy guarantees an adequate payout to the insured. In addition, given that insurance should protect the capital of insured persons, the relevant question becomes: do the fund's hedging strategies perform this function during times of crisis?

Making the right decision when it comes to optimal coverage and adopting a specific fund investment strategy guarantees the insured an appropriate payout. Defined as the policy value, the payout value is not usually guaranteed by the insurer and depends on the market price of the securities in which the funds are deposited and is, thus, a random variable. Because ULIP is transparent and open, it gives the insured the possibility to decide about the portfolio content in its duration. It should be mentioned that this insurance offers many ways of investing. However, there is a financial risk in each case that determines the policy value. This problem has been addressed in the literature with the acknowledgement of the legal, formal, actuarial, or financial aspects – especially from the point of view of the insurer. Yet, the specifics of ULIP in Poland that result from the fact that it is a type of insurance in which the investment risk and any negative consequences of their decisions are borne by the insured constitutes the premise to analyze this type of insurance from the point of view of the insured. Thus, the actuarial value of a referential ULIP portfolio was examined depending on the application of risk-prevention strategies,

DOI: 10.4324/9781003368687-15

thus providing information that would enable the insured to gain control over the effectiveness and the fund risk being the consequence of using hedge-type strategies. This constitutes the basis for making optimal decisions in terms of the ways of investing and protecting funds within the range of possibilities of hedge applications during periods of increased risk while guaranteeing the optimization of future payout amounts.

ULIP insurance with capital fund as hybrid insurance

A ULIP policy with a capital fund belongs to the so-called universal life insurance group; however, it significantly differs from classic life insurance. This combines the element of insurance with the element of saving in an extraordinarily flexible way, thus creating many possibilities in terms of managing capital. The idea of ULIP is associated with its savings and investment nature. The most significant feature of a capital fund-based life insurance (referred to as unit-linked) is linking it to the separate fund or funds in which the premiums are being invested. In contrast to classic life insurance (where the insurance cost [expressed in the paid premium] is constant throughout the entire duration of the policy and is not the result of the amount of risk in a given year but from the average risk of the whole insurance period), the cost of ULIP is dependent on the age of the insured and varies depending on payments, interest rates, unit prices, administrative costs, burdens related to death, etc. In this type of insurance, the insured invests part or all of the paid premiums in funds that are offered by the insurer (which differ in terms of risk level). This means that the premium is invested in the financial market. Nevertheless, the insured bears the investment risk while also bearing the responsibility for any possible negative consequences of his or her decisions since insurance companies do not know the consequences of such activities in advance. Therefore, many aspects have been considered in the literature regarding the fair valuation of ULIP insurance (Karim & Dhaene, 2019; Melnikov, 2011; Dahl & Møller, 2006; Bacinello, 2003).

Importantly, such contracts allow for the collection of savings in an individually created investment portfolio that consists of various investment funds that are run by external investment fund insurance companies that are independent of the insurer. What is equally important is the fact that, because these types of policies are open and transparent, it is possible to adjust a portfolio on an ongoing basis depending on changing situations on the market. This is a crucial element in the situation of an unstable market economy. Then, contracts of this type enable the insured to collect savings in his or her individually created investment portfolio that consists of investment funds; these can be divided into two groups:

- classic;
- specialist hedging strategies.

The essence of classic funds is reducing the investment risk by diversifying the investment portfolio. In the case of specialized funds like hedge funds, however, the basic principle is the additional fund protection and the reduction of investment risk by applying protection strategies, which managers are able to do due to the flexible investment policy. In this case, the payout value of life insurance is influenced by both the positive and negative effects of this activity. Especially during periods of market instability (including pandemic periods), the financial risk is particularly significant and determines the size of the insurance payment. Offering ULIP-type insurance extended actuarial risk should be taken into account as well as covering the financial market and its related risks in the case of insurance institutions (which are, after all, institutions of public trust) when. Filtering in the case of hybrid insurance should, therefore, not only be based on the mortality process but also take extended actuarial risk into account (including the following):

- activation of additional insurance options;
- interest rate developments;
- price developments of selected assets.

All of these financial processes are particularly sensitive to market failures that are caused, inter alia, by random events (such as the COVID-19 pandemic); therefore, ULIP portfolio managers should include safeguards to protect the capital of the insured in their investment strategies. In addition to the problems that are widely discussed in the literature concerning the correct valuation of products, the correct analysis of the risk of investment strategies (classical and hedging) is equally important. However, this problem is discussed much less in the literature (Homa, 2018; Melnikov, 2018; Wang et al., 2017; Melnikov & Romanyuk, 2006).

Actuarial value of ULIP portfolio and payout function

In ULIP insurance (as in traditional insurance), the insurance company undertakes to pay a benefit depending on the type of contract at the moment of the expiration of the insurance policy (n) or in the case of the death of the policyholder (T) according to the contract. Unlike in the case of traditional insurance, however, the payment of the benefit depends on the value of the portfolio – both in the case of death during the insurance period and at its maturity (i.e., the survival of the insured through the end of the insurance period). Thus, not only the moment of payment is random in ULIP insurance – the amount of the benefit that is paid is also random. Payout is therefore the appropriate function of the accumulated investment (meaning the value of the insurance portfolio) (Moller, 2007):

$$B_t = b\left(FV_t\right), \tag{15.1}$$

where: FV_t – value of insurance (referential) portfolio at moment t.

The value of the reference portfolio determines the amount of the payout, as the insurer pays the insured the higher of the guaranteed amount (G_Π) and the market value of the portfolio (FV_t) in ULIP insurance at the time of the occurrence of the event that is covered by the contract. Therefore, the insurance payment at time t is an appropriate function of the accumulated investment depending on the price of the fund units and is equal to the following (Bacinello, 2003, 2008):

$$\left(FV_t\right) = \max\left\{G_\Pi, FV_t\right\} = G_\Pi + \left(FV_t - G_\Pi\right)^+. \tag{15.2}$$

Considering the changing money value, the insurance payment (which is the function of the market value of the portfolio) is expressed by the following formula:

$$b\left(FV_t\right) = \frac{\upsilon(T)}{\upsilon(t)} G_\Pi + \frac{\upsilon(T)}{\upsilon(t)} \left(FV_t - G_\Pi\right)^+. \tag{15.3}$$

The above formula shows that ULIP insurance is a product of a hybrid nature whose structure is based on classic insurance or the endowment model with investments in selected capital funds. Taking this fact into consideration, a unit-linked type of contract may be interpreted as traditional insurance with insurance sum G_Π with premium $\pi(t)$ and a potential surplus dependent on the asset price (S_t). So, the value of the insurance portfolio is random depending on the unit prices of the selected fund that result from the strategy that is adopted by the insured. This is obtained by investing part of the insurance premium that is paid at moment t_i, $i = 0, 1, 2, \ldots, n-1$, until the expiration of policy $t_n = T$. The premium part that is invested at the t_i moment is defined as $\pi\left(t_i\right)$ and is called an investment premium. Therefore, the insured builds the value of the referential portfolio by investing in the chosen assets with a price that is defined as process S_t. Assuming that the insured invests a part of the insurance premium of $\pi\left(t_i\right)$ in the selected assets with a price defined as the S_{t_i} process at time t, he/she purchases $\pi\left(t_i\right)\left(S_{t_i}\right)^{-1}$ units of assets. Thus, the market value of the portfolio at time T is equal to the following (Homa, 2017):

$$FV_T = \sum_{i=0}^{\tilde{n}(t)-1} \frac{S_T}{S_{t_i}} \cdot \pi\left(t_i\right), \tag{15.4}$$

$$\tilde{n}(t) = \min\left\{i \middle| t_i \rangle t\right\}.$$

where

This means that the discounted (relative to S) portfolio value is equal to the discounted value of all of the investments. Then, the ULIP payout can be defined as follows:

$$b(FV_t)=\frac{\upsilon(T)}{\upsilon(t)}G_\Pi+\frac{\upsilon(T)}{\upsilon(t)}\left(S_T\sum_{i=0}^{\tilde{n}_T-1}\pi(t_i)\cdot S_{t_i}{}^{-1}-G_\Pi\right)^+. \tag{15.5}$$

The second component of the sum is the function of the payout of the European call option with expiration date T and a strike price that is equal to the guaranteed sum (Ballotta & Habermann, 2006). The execution of the option means that the option holder receives an amount that is equal to the difference between the value of the underlying instrument and the price of its execution. Therefore, the insured can expect a surplus to the guaranteed sum of the insurance only in the case when a call option is included in the price ("in the money"), which means that the value of the insurance portfolio exceeds the guaranteed value. Therefore, it is very important that the appropriate valuation of the option will not only allow one to achieve an advantage over the competition but also effectively manage their financial risk – especially during difficult periods of financial market collapses that result from a COVID-19-type pandemic, for example. While conducting a UFK portfolio valuation, it is necessary to examine its actuarial value by taking the extended risk into account. This encompasses not only the market price and financial risk but also the risk that is associated with the subject of the insurance as well. The consideration of extended risk means that the actuarial value of the referential portfolio is the following expected conditional value (Homa, 2018):

$$E\left[B_t^{ULIP}\right]=E\left(b(FV_T)\right)|\mathcal{L}_t\wedge\mathcal{F}_t\wedge\mathcal{H}_t\right), \tag{15.6}$$

where $\mathcal{L}_t$ – knowledge of contract options; $\mathcal{H}_t$ – interpreted as knowledge of price and value of monetary unit; $\mathcal{F}_t$ – knowledge of mortality process.

Interpreted as the risk of the contract option, filtration L_t determines the types of cash flows that result from the insurance policy that is entered into. Filtration $\mathcal{H}_t=\sigma\{(B_t,S_t),0\le t\le T\}$ means that information is received solely from the observation of the pricing process and the process of the monetary unit value. However, H_t is the knowledge that is gained until moment t about the mortality process, and information about it is determined by the future life expectancy of the insured; therefore, the following has been assumed: $\mathcal{F}_t=\{\mathrm{I}(T\le t),0\le t\le T\}$. Assuming the independence of both of these risks, the valuation of the payout at the end of the insurance period is made as follows:

$$\begin{aligned}EB_t^{ULIP}&=E\left(b(FV_T)\mid\mathcal{H}_t\right)\cdot E\left(\mathrm{I}_{\{T>t\}}|\{T>t\}\right)\\&+\int_t^{T\vee n}E\left(b(FV_T)\mid\mathcal{H}_t\right)\cdot E\left(d\mathrm{I}\{\tau\le T\}\mid\{T>t\}\right)\end{aligned}$$

$$= \left(\frac{\upsilon(T)}{\upsilon(t)} G_\Pi + \frac{\upsilon(T)}{\upsilon(t)} \left(S_T \sum_{i=0}^{\tilde{n}_T - 1} \pi(t_i) \cdot S_{t_i}^{-1} - G_\Pi \right)^+ \mid \mathcal{H}_t \right)$$

$$\cdot E\left(\mathrm{I}_{\{T>t\}} \mid \{T > t\} \right)$$

$$+ \int_t^{T \vee n} E \left(\frac{\upsilon(T)}{\upsilon(t)} G_\Pi + \frac{\upsilon(T)}{\upsilon(t)} \left(S_T \sum_{i=0}^{\tilde{n}_T - 1} \pi(t_i) \cdot S_{t_i}^{-1} - G_\Pi \right)^+ \mid \mathcal{H}_t \right)$$

$$\cdot E\left(d\mathrm{I}\{\tau \le T\} \mid \{T > t\} \right);$$

hence:

$$EB_t^{ULIP} = {}_{T-t}p_{x+t} E \left(\frac{\upsilon(T)}{\upsilon(t)} \left(G_\pi + \left(S_T \sum_{i=0}^{\tilde{n}_T - 1} \pi(t_i) S_{t_i}^{-1} - G_\pi \right)^+ \right) \mid \mathcal{H}_t^{S \wedge B} \right) +$$

$$+ \int_t^{T \vee n} {}_{\tau-t}p_{x+t} \mu(x+\tau) E \left(\frac{\upsilon(T)}{\upsilon(t)} \left(G_\pi + \left(S_T \sum_{i=0}^{\tilde{n}_T - 1} \pi(t_i) S_{t_i}^{-1} - G_\pi \right)^+ \right) \mid \mathcal{H}_t^{S \wedge B} \right) d\tau =$$

$$= \frac{\upsilon(T)}{\upsilon(t)} {}_{T-t}p_{x+t} E\left(G_\pi \mid \mathcal{H}_t^{S \wedge B} \right) + \int_t^{T \vee n} \frac{\upsilon(T)}{\upsilon(t)} {}_{\tau-t}p_{x+t} \mu(x+\tau) E\left(G_\pi \mid \mathcal{H}_t^{S \wedge B} \right) d\tau$$

$$+ {}_{T-t}p_{x+t} \frac{\upsilon(T)}{\upsilon(t)} E \left(\left(S_T \sum_{i=0}^{\tilde{n}_T - 1} \pi(t_i) S_{t_i}^{-1} - G_\pi \right)^+ \mid \mathcal{H}_t^{S \wedge B} \right) +$$

$$+ \int_t^{T \vee n} \frac{\upsilon(T)}{\upsilon(t)} {}_{\tau-t}p_{x+t} \mu(x+\tau) E \left(\left(S_T \sum_{i=0}^{\tilde{n}_T - 1} \pi(t_i) S_{t_i}^{-1} - G_\pi \right)^+ \mid \mathcal{H}_t^{S \wedge B} \right) d\tau.$$

Using the definition of the arbitrage pricing of European-type instrument $h(S_t)$ at moment t, assuming the following denotation (Jajuga & Jajuga, 2006):

$$E\left[\frac{\upsilon(T)}{\upsilon(t)} \cdot (X_T - G_\pi)^+ \mid \mathcal{H}_t \right] = C_t(X_T, G_\Pi),$$

it yields the following:

$$EB_t^{ULIP} = \frac{\upsilon(T)}{\upsilon(t)} {}_{T-t}p_{x+t} E\left(G_\pi \middle| \mathcal{H}_t^{S\wedge B}\right) + \int_t^{T\vee n} \frac{\upsilon(T)}{\upsilon(t)} \cdot {}_{\tau-t}p_{x+t} \cdot \mu(x+\tau) \cdot E\left(G_\pi \middle| \mathcal{H}_t^{S\wedge B}\right) d\tau + {}_{T-t}p_{x+t} C_t\left(X_T, G_\Pi\right) + \int_t^{T\vee n} \frac{\upsilon(T)}{\upsilon(t)} \cdot {}_{\tau-t}p_{x+t} \cdot \mu(x+\tau) C_t\left(X_T, G_\Pi\right) d\tau. \tag{15.7}$$

When a death benefit is to be paid out to the insured during the $\left[t_{j-1}, t_j\right)$ period, a probability of death that is equal to ${}_{t_{j-1}-t}p_{x+t} \cdot {}_{t_j-t_{j-1}}q_{x+t_{j-1}}$ is considered accordingly. Even more complete information can be obtained by analyzing not only the value of the ULIP portfolio but also the probability with which it may occur.

Financial and mortality market model

In the case of valuating the ULIP contracts and establishing the portfolio value, what becomes salient is the issue of the accurate valuation of the financial instrument according to the last presented Formula (15.7); this is option $C_t\left(X_T, G_\Pi\right)$. Depending on the insurance variation, this is accordingly the European or American call option (Glasserman, 2010). The European option can be executed only at the expiration moment of *T*; however, the American option can be executed at any time. In the classic approach (which is the Black-Scholes model), the price of the European option is defined by the analytic function, whereas the valuation of the American option is not as simple and requires the application of simulation methods in order to establish its price. This is the reason why the work is concentrated around simulation methods and uses the Monte Carlo (MC) method to establish their prices. In this method, the distribution of the underlying instrument on the expiry date of the option is determined by a certain stochastic process. Through knowing this process and applying the Monte Carlo method, the distribution of the final values of the primary instrument for which the option is issued is obtained by using multiple simulations.

In order to carry out the cash flow valuation and define the payout, therefore, one must first carry out a pricing simulation with the assumption of the financial market model. In this chapter, the Black-Scholes (Black-Merton-Scholes) model with horizon T has been adopted as the financial market model. It has been assumed that an ideal market is being dealt with where there are units of the fund that are chosen by the insured with the price being estimated by the following formula (Milevsky &Salisbury, 2006):

$$dS_t = \mu_S(t)S_t dt + \sigma_S(t)S_t dW_t, \tag{15.8}$$

where: W_t – Wiener process (geometrical Brownian motion); S_t – presumed price of derivative contract; S_0 – actual price of derivative contract; μ_S – process average; σ_S – standard deviation of process.

The only solution of the above differential equation follows a process that has a lognormal distribution:

$$S_t = S_0 \exp\left(\sigma_S W_t + \left(\mu_S - \frac{1}{2}\sigma_S{}^2\right)\cdot t\right).$$

Next, a simulation of the prices process must be implemented in order to carry out the valuation of the unit-linked flow as well as to calculate the amount of the payment (with attention being paid to the presumed financial market model).

This chapter uses the pricing model that is called the standard Brownian motion process. Hence, the price of stock fund unit S_t is described by this (including an appropriate drift ratio that may be defined by using the Euler method). Applying this mathematical apparatus, we obtain a formula that simulates the future value of the base instrument (Perna & Sibillo, 2008):

$$S_{t_k}^i = S_{t_{k-1}}^i \exp\left[\left(r - \frac{\sigma^2}{2}\right)(t_k - t_{k-1}) + \sigma\sqrt{t_k - t_{k-1}}\varepsilon_k^i,\right]$$

where ε_k^i are the independent values that are generated by the normal distribution, r is the risk-free interest rate, and σ describes the price volatility of the instrument.

The share price process is simulated in the finite number of time points (t_k). We also assume that the payout function is only dependent on the share prices in those points. For a single trajectory of the share prices, the discounted price of any option is as follows:

$$C_0 = \frac{\upsilon(T)}{\upsilon(t_0)}\left(S_0, S_{t_1}, \dots, S_{t_1}\right), \tag{15.9}$$

while this amounts to the following for the N trajectory:

$$C_0 = \frac{\upsilon(T)}{\upsilon(t_0)}\left[\frac{1}{N}\sum_{i=1}^{N} f\left(S_0^i, S_{t_1}^i, \dots, S_{t_n}^i\right)\right]. \tag{15.10}$$

Therefore, the option price can be determined by simulating the discounted value of the payout portfolio, followed by the average after all of the implementations.

To determine the actuarial value of the payoff, we need to determine the survivability and mortality functions. In this chapter, the Gompertz-Makeham model was used in order to create an accurate description of the mortality rate. The model describes the actual intensity of deaths by considering factors that are dependent on age. Gompertz claimed that mortality was the result of two types of causes; the first was illness (which affects both young and old people equally), while the second was the decline of a human's ability to oppose death. However, Makehan noticed that certain factors also affected this force regardless of age. These factors are aggregated and appear in the model in a constant form. The obtained model is called the Gompertz-Makeham law, and the distribution function takes the following form (Dahl, 2004):

$$F(x) = \begin{cases} 0 & x \leq 0 \\ 1 - \exp\left(-Ax - \frac{B}{C}\left(e^{Cx} - 1\right)\right) & x > 0 \end{cases},$$

and mortality rate can be described by the following formula:

$$\mu(x+t) = A + Bc^{x+t}.$$

In order to create an accurate description of the mortality rate in the population of men aged 30 to 80, we next used the data from the life tables from 2018 to approximate the function and obtained the maximum likelihood estimation of the parameters of the Gompertz-Makeham function of mortality are equal (Ostasiewicz, 2011):

$$A = 0.0004; B = 0.0000034674; c = 10^{0.06}$$

On this basis, the appropriate probabilities were determined by solving the Chapman-Kolmogorov differential equations using a standard approach that was based on national mortality rates.

Simulation of reference portfolio value payout for exemplary ULIP insurance as related to investment strategy during pandemic time

As an example, a ULIP policy (in particular, an n-year term endowment contract for a 30-year-old man) was examined. It was assumed that the insured paid premiums were in an amount of $\tilde{\pi}(t_k)$ at time $t_k \in T$, where $T = \{0 = t_0 < \ldots < t_n = T\}$; from each one, the investment part is equal to $\pi(t_k)$, which constitutes the adequate % of the total gross premium (assumed 100%) under the contract. According to the contract, the insurer will pay the beneficiary the insurance sum that results from the referential portfolio value if the insured dies at the $t_i \in \Theta / \{t_0\}$ moment. The actuarial value of the referential portfolio is the expected conditional value equal (7). An analogical payment would also be paid in the situation of the insured being alive at the moment of the contract's termination.

Moreover, it was assumed that the insured can implement various investment strategies, thus differentiating the profits that resulted from the volatility of the portfolio's value. The analysis encompasses insurance capital funds of those investment strategies that include both classic and specialized portfolios within their range and further divide them (due to the use of protection strategies) into groups of classic (*C*) and hedge (*H*) investment funds. Therefore, the classic and specialized funds whose managers used protection strategies in the insurance portfolios were taken into account from the following groups:

- SHARES:
  - universal;
  - global;
  - growth.
- MIXED:
  - stable;
  - balanced;
  - active allocation;
  - dynamic.

Being developed on the basis of the aforementioned funds, the insurance portfolios that are listed above differ in terms of the investment strategy, and hence, the financial risk and period analysis (including the standard and pandemic periods) make it possible to assess the impact of the investment strategy and the pandemic an the financial risk and the capital level. In other words, this analysis will verify the following hypothesis:

A hedging strategy has allowed for protecting the capital of the insured during the COVID-19 pandemic

For this purpose, a simple risk assessment of the funds in the individual groups was conducted in the first stage, taking basic measures such as the standard deviation and Sharpe Ratio (S_p) into consideration. On this basis, one fund was selected from each group with the highest rank.[1] Then, the distribution of the final values of the primary model for which the option was issued was attained by using the described price-development model and applying the Monte Carlo method. The starting point for the valuation was the generating the possible prices of the underlying instrument (insurance capital funds) on the expiry date of the option, followed by determining its payout function. In the next step, a calculation of the basic characteristics of the portfolio value was conducted depending on the investment strategy while taking the mortality process model into account. This way, the basic quantity that was used by the insurers to value the life insurance (meaning the actuarial value) was examined. Because the expected value does not provide full information on the distribution of the payout, it is also necessary to analyze the investment risk and other parameters of the portfolios. This actuarial value, risk, skewness, and kurtosis for the ULIP insurance portfolio with the adopted scenario and an iteration number that is equal to 10,000 in two periods (pre-pandemic and pandemic [COVID-19]) is presented in Table 15.1.

Based on the above data regarding the MC-simulated actuarial value of the ULIP portfolio at time n, it can be assumed that the investment strategy that is adopted by the insured as well as the issue of whether protection strategies are being applied by the managers does not in any significant way determine the portfolio value in the **pre-pandemic period**, with the insurance period being the only salient factor here. However, the payout results for the **pandemic period** indicate that both the duration of the insurance as well as its investment strategy determine the policy actuarial value. Only for such funds has the pandemic period not changed the value of the payout, which means that only these funds protect the capital of policyholders during periods of financial instability. More importantly, the expected value in each of the presented cases exceeds the traditional insurance sum, which means that the insured can expect a surplus as compared to traditional life insurance regardless of the chosen investment strategy. However, the above results apply to the best funds in each group. For the weakest funds (whose managers did not have the skills to correctly apply hedging strategies), different results were obtained. Moreover results indicate that the investment strategy that was adopted by the insured significantly determined the insurance portfolio risk too (regardless of the established insurance period). At the same time, these results confirm that the increase in investment strategy risk causes an increase in all of the measures that attest for the differentiation, asymmetry, and flattening of the distribution. The application of protection strategies not only affects the reduction of investment risk but also reduces the skewness and kurtosis, which is particularly important during periods of financial market instability. Investing during a pandemic period increases a fund's risk, thus increasing the asymmetry and kurtosis of the distribution. In all cases, kurtosis takes a positive value, which means that the distribution is leptokurtic (more slender than normal); along with the increase in risk, this value also rises. These properties are proven by the boxplots of the payout that are presented in the figures below (Figures 15.1 and 15.2).

Based on the above plots, it can be concluded that the insurance period significantly determines the differentiation of the distribution, while the adopted investment strategy keeps the value of the investment portfolio at

Table 15.1 Referential Portfolio Actuarial Value, Risk, Skewness (A_S), and Kurtosis (K) With Investment Strategies and Periods

Group		Pre-pandemic					Pandemic			
		Strategy protection	*Actuarial value*	*Risk*	A_S	K	*Actuarial value*	*Risk*	A_S	K
SHARES	Universal	Classic	2216.16	24.41	4.05	30.06	2198.09	24.598	4.66	50.51
		Hedge	2222.81	13.43	2.1	6.95	2229.76	27.152	6.93	8.73
	Global	Classic	2216.99	10.39	1.51	4.32	2213.14	18.074	2.94	17.08
		Hedge	2216.51	8.74	1.23	2.75	2216.45	10.21	1.48	4.06
	Growth	Classic	2219.31	66.66	2.99	8.82	2208.41	33.289	6.37	8.86
		Hedge	2245.47	10.66	1.51	4.03	2248.17	17.787	2.75	4.03
MIXED	Stable	Classic	2218.84	14.97	2.32	10.84	2215.71	15.019	2.35	10.9
		Hedge	2220.03	3.33	0.46	0.38	2220.48	4.9778	0.7	0.88
	Balanced	Classic	2218.58	7.88	1.13	2.42	2216.85	7.9068	1.13	2.47
		Hedge	2218.63	3.63	0.48	0.39	2219.35	7.3834	1.03	1.93
	Active allocation	Classic	2218.01	7.93	1.11	2.2	2217.93	9.5512	1.59	4.48
		Hedge	2220.34	5.82	0.8	1.1	2223.73	11.308	1.35	3.34
	Dynamic	Classic	2217.9	12.29	1.86	6.87	2216.25	12.834	1.9	4.01
		Hedge	2219.56	3.5	0.48	0.41	2220.89	10.276	1.47	6.81

Source: *Own elaboration.*

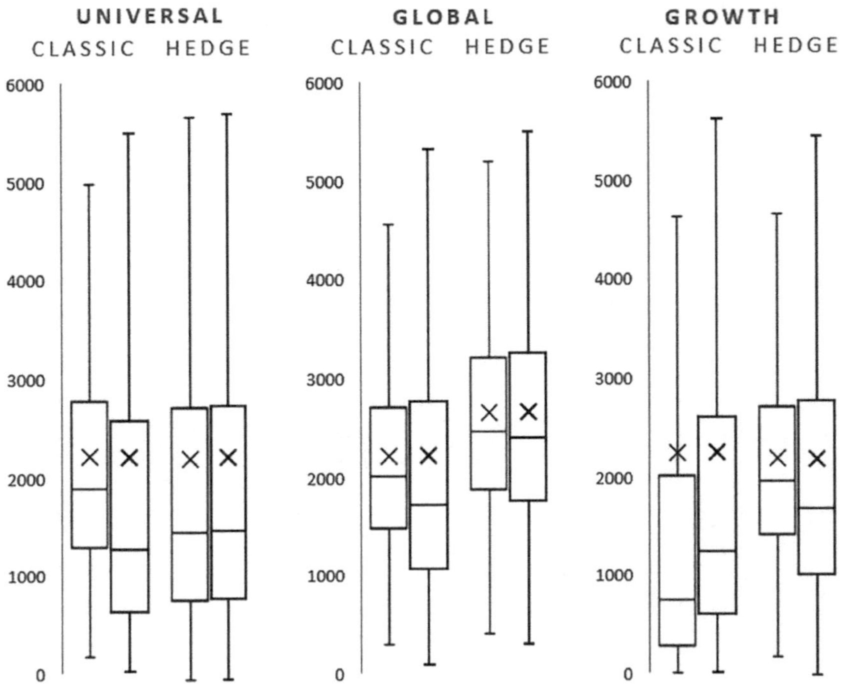

Figure 15.1 Boxplots of classic and hedge portfolios with different strategies during pre-pandemic (gray) and pandemic (black) periods – group SHARES.

Source: *Own elaboration.*

the expected level in terms of fund specialization. This reduces the investment risk as well as the asymmetry and kurtosis of the distribution of the insurance portfolio value, making it more similar to a normal distribution. This means that the use of hedging strategies is a guarantee of protecting the capital of the insured. Moreover, the above results indicate that the insured can control of the portfolio value and the ULIP payout amount by selecting the adequate risk-aversion strategy, therefore establishing the premium parts that build the investment portfolio value depending on his or her expectations. Therefore, this means that the insured can differentiate the profits that result from the variable portfolio value by implementing various investment strategies.

The presented results indicate that, in the case of ULIP life insurance, the content of the referential portfolio becomes far more important than the insurance period itself. As a result, this type of insurance is not to be thought of only in the long-term perspective; above all, it is necessary to adjust the strategy to the current market situation, remembering that hedge portfolios are undoubtedly the most beneficial ones during a pandemic period.

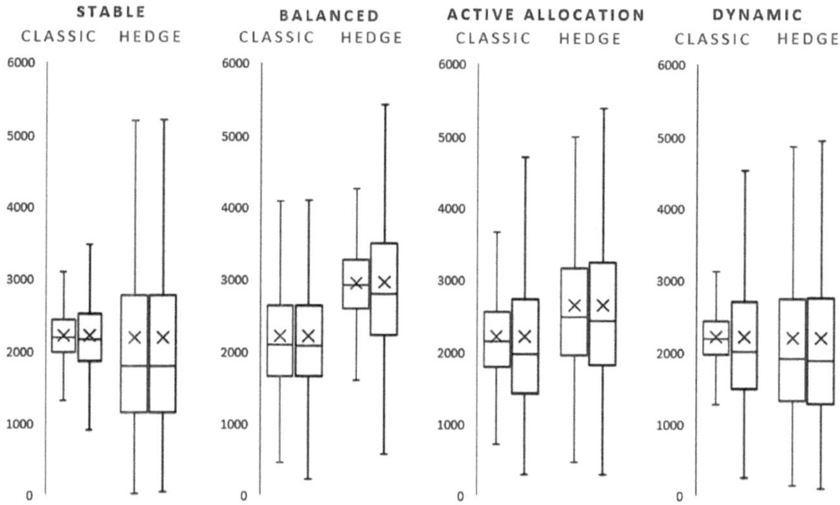

Figure 15.2 Boxplots of classic and hedge portfolios with different strategies during pre-pandemic (gray) and pandemic (black) periods – group MIXED.

Source: *Own elaboration.*

Conclusions

The aim of this chapter was to verify the following hypothesis: a hedging strategy has allowed for protecting the capital of the insured during the COVID-19 pandemic. The conducted analysis reveals that, in the case of ULIP (as opposed to classic insurance), the insurance period is of utmost importance – not the referential portfolio content (especially during periods of financial market instability). As a result, this type of insurance is not to be thought of only in the long-term perspective; above all, it is necessary to adjust the strategy to the market reality. This work demonstrates the following:

1 During the pre-pandemic period, using hedge strategies did not change the characteristics of a portfolio's value distribution in any significant way.
2 A hedging strategy has allowed for protecting the capital of the insured during the COVID-19 pandemic.

Additionally, the conducted analysis of portfolio value distribution with the acknowledgement of protection strategies proved that the awareness of the insured is an important element ofULIP, for it is the insured who has the ability to maximize a portfolio's value while minimizing its risk when matching the appropriate strategy with the insurance period. Moreover, it is important that the universality of the methods makes the conducted analysis and all of the obtained results usable by insurers who offer ULIP insurance in other countries.

Note

1 Because of editorial limits, these results are not included but can be provided on request.

References

Bacinello, A.R. (2003) *Equity-linked policies with embedded guarantee options, summer school in stochastic finance for insurance.* Springer, Berlin.

Bacinello, A.R., Perna, C., Sibillo, M. (2008) A full Monte Carlo approach to the valuation of the surrender option embedded in life insurance contracts, *Mathematical and Statistical Methods for Insurance and Finance,* Perna C., Sibillo M. (eds.), Springer, Berlin, 19–26. Ballotta, L., Habermann, S. (2006) The fair valuation problem of guaranteed annuity options: the stochastic mortality environment case, *Insurance Mathematics and Economics*, 38, 195–214.

Dahl, M. (2004) Stochastic mortality in life insurance: market reserves and mortality-linked insurance contracts, *Insurance: Mathematics and Economics*, 35, 113–136.

Dahl, M., Møller, T. (2006) Valuation and hedging of life insurance liabilities with systematic mortality risk, *Insurance: Mathematics and Economics*, 39, 193–217.

Glasserman, P. (2010) *Monte Carlo methods in financial engineering, Stochastic Modelling and Applied Probability.* Springer-Verlag, New York.

Homa, M. (2017) Unit-linked life insurances as a form of protection for the future, *Economic and Environmental Studies*, 17(1), 35–49.

Homa, M. (2018) Risk capital in unit-linked insurance policies, *Research Papers of Wroclaw University of Economics*, 519, 99–108.

Jajuga, K., Jajuga, T. (2006) *Inwestycje: instrumenty finansowe, aktywa niefinansowe, ryzyko finansowe, inżynieria finansowa, PWN,* Warszawa.

Karim, B., Dhaene, J. (2019) Fair valuation of insurance liabilities via mean-variance hedging in a multi-period setting, *Scandinavian Actuarial Journal*, 2, 163–187.

Melnikov, A. (2011) *Risk analysis in finance and insurance.* CRC Press, Taylor & Francis Group, Boca Raton, FL.

Melnikov, A., Nosrati, A. (2018) *Equity-linked life insurance partial hedging methods.* CRC Press, Taylor & Francis Group, Boca Raton, FL.

Melnikov, A., Romanyuk, Y. (2006) Efficient hedging and pricing of equity-linked life insurance contracts on several risky asset, *Bank of Canada Working Paper,* 43.

Milevsky, M., Salisbury, T.S. (2006) Financial valuation of guaranteed minimum withdrawal benefits. *Insurance: Mathematics and Economic*, 38, 18–35.

Moller, T., Steffensen, M. (2007) *Market valuation methods in life and pension insurance.* Cambridge University Press, Cambridge.

Ostasiewicz, S. (2011) Modelowanie trwania życia w populacjach niejednorodnych (Approximation of survival function for heterogeneity population), *Research Papers of Wroclaw University of Economics*, 230, 99–122.

Perna, C., Sibillo, M. eds (2008) *Mathematical and statistical methods for insurance and finance*. Springer-Verlag Italia, Milano.

Wang, C., Yang, S., Huang, J. (2017) Analytic option pricing and risk measures under a regime-switching generalized hyperbolic model with an application to equity-linked insurance, *Quantitative Finance*, 10, 1567–1581.

16 COVID-19 pandemic crisis – impact on business and society: summary

Joanna Duda and Aleksandra Gąsior

Introduction

The COVID-19 crisis is the third crisis in the last 100 years. The causes of the crisis were varied; this is one reason for the wealth of literature on the impacts of crises that have occurred in the past (Faulkner, 2001; Ritchie, 2004; Prayag, 2018; Ritchie and Jiang, 2019). Published research results show that some organizations are more resilient and effective than others in managing crisis situations and adapting to new market situations during post-crisis periods (Scott et al., 2008), while others are less resilient.

The COVID-19 pandemic has affected business in every industry and sector worldwide (Song et al., 2022). Scientists, practitioners, and policymakers remain committed to understanding the effects of lockdowns, social distancing measures, and other trade restrictions; the impacts of government incentives and support measures and the ways in which companies have adapted their operations. The dynamic nature of the virus and the changing political and economic landscape made it necessary to change the behavior of companies that operated in various areas of the economy.

This publication "***COVID-19 pandemic crisis – impact on business and society***" provides an overview of the various actions, decisions, and actions that were taken during the pandemic. This was a completely unpredictable event with a huge impact on economies worldwide. References to it can be found in light of the Black Swan theory (Taleb, 2014). This shows that the consequences of the pandemic and the circumstances in which they arose were difficult to predict, taking into account their scopes (worldwide) and the sizes of dysfunctional events in all sectors of global economies. This approach allows for an analysis of the past but also allows us to estimate and predict the effects of the situation on the future global economic future, as related to both individual consumers and enterprises.

This publication focuses on three key areas that were related to the unpredictability of the events that were triggered by the COVID-19 crisis; these were as follows:

– flexibility of companies and organizations in face of pandemic;

DOI: 10.4324/9781003368687-16

- impact on competitiveness of business entities;
- state support for business and society.

Flexibility of companies and organizations

The research results suggest that flexibility in running a business plays a large role for business entities; thus, companies can adapt to changes that are caused by unpredictable events (Hadjielias et al., 2022). The reactions of companies usually boiled down to taking two types of actions to overcome the COVID-19 crisis (i.e., reducing their volumes of orders, and reducing their workforces), while the least frequently indicated was a change in the profile of the business and the suspension of economic activity. It should be emphasized here that the crisis was easier for those companies in which the digitization process was highly advanced. In this context, the effects of the pandemic were twofold: both negative and positive. The negative ones were the consequence for entities and societies, while the positive ones were the actions of companies and organizations. The big business examples that have been referred to regarding their activities (which were developed efficiently during the pandemic) were Google and Facebook. The operating strategies of these organizations were built in such a way as to be resistant to such events.

A key element of these efforts was the "adaptive innovation" that was implemented by companies as an escape from simple destruction during the COVID-19 pandemic. Excluding these innovations from economic processes would mean that changes in productivity would only result from an incorrect selection of strategies. Under these conditions, the most optimistic version of what was happening after the COVID-19 pandemic from a productivity standpoint would be a return to the previous growth path. In this context, adaptive innovations seem to be a necessary condition not only to reverse the tendencies that are typical for simple destruction but also to break the productivity stagnation that has been observed in many countries for years. It should be emphasized that such adaptive innovations resulted mainly from the implementation of available technical and organizational solutions that were developed before the COVID-19 pandemic.

An important factor that contributed to the flexibility of companies' activities was the updates of project risk-management plans. Among other things, this was due to the need to comply with government regulations regarding COVID-19. For projects that are at the design or planning stages, one should take revised plans into account that now consider the current COVID-19 legislation as well as any future implications of these developments. On the other hand, projects that are already under implementation should update their risk-management plans while considering the required regulations. Considering the above recommendations will certainly contribute to the more effective preparation of project teams for the possible emergence of crisis situations that were similar to those at the end of 2019 and beginning of 2020. Perhaps future threats will no longer be related to the COVID-19 virus itself, but the risk of force majeure will certainly remain.

Businesses also had to adopt specific capital-protection strategies – especially if they operated in the financial markets. The adopted hedging strategies allowed for the protection of the insured capital during the COVID-19 pandemic. The analysis showed that, in the case of life insurance, the insurance period is of great importance – not the content of the reference portfolio (especially during times of financial market instability). The research showed that, during the period before the pandemic, the use of hedging strategies did not significantly change the characteristics of portfolio value distributions, while a hedging strategy allowed for the protection of insured capital during the COVID-19 pandemic.

Enterprises also had to be flexible regarding their methods of raising capital. During the pandemic, organizing the share issue process was technically more difficult due to restrictions and the wild fluctuations in stock prices. On the other hand, the competition among those companies that sought financing on the capital market was less intense. An important characteristic of the pandemic period was the appearance of a large number of new investors on the stock exchange. Hoping to compensate for losses that resulted from the pandemic, these investors planned to increase their capital relatively quickly by investing in small stock exchanges. The success of such small markets was, therefore, closely related to biotechnology and gambling companies, which saw growth during the pandemic. These two sectors have been the driving force behind alternative financial markets.

In the face of a pandemic, the main advantages of an innovative organization or enterprise are its high flexibility and market expansion, efficient exchange of resources, quick response to external opportunities, and partner support in difficult situations. This allows a business to not only survive the crisis but also develop by achieving more and more ambitious goals, overcoming the autonomous thinking of enterprises, or even fearing cooperation as a result of one's distrust.

Competitiveness of enterprises

Modifying competition factors seems to have been a response to the changes in the market that were caused by the pandemic and crisis (Momaya, 2020; Oorschot van et al., 2022). During the pandemic, it was found that the competition factors that had been applied thus far did not bring the expected results. Therefore, entrepreneurs were forced to use new competitive factors. These included the method of distribution, the level of equity in the enterprise, and integrated IT systems. Moreover, complete isolation prevented physical contact in the supply chain between suppliers and customers. Access to stationary facilities was difficult or impossible. The solution, therefore, was that suppliers, customers, and consumers resorted to e-commerce. For this reason, businesses should start offering their products online for home or business delivery. This will allow them to implement the mechanisms of business globalization and integrate connections between market partners, cooperating organizations (banks, social insurance, broadly understood administration), and social networking sites to a greater extent. The research confirms the important role of a company's strategy and the consequences of a crisis for the strategy.

This is in line with research that was conducted during previous crises by authors such as Pearce and Michael (2006) and Alonso-Almeida et al. (2015), who wrote about reactive strategies that aimed to: defend a company's market position through initiatives such as cost reductions (e.g., layoffs), cancellations of investment projects and liquidations of parts of the businesses, or proactive strategies that focused on innovation and marketing actions, finding new customers and increasing values for existing customers, and investing in new technologies (Miles et al., 1978; Alonso-Almeida et al., 2015).

Another way to maintain or increase the competitiveness of entities was to tighten inter-organizational cooperation – both with suppliers and customers. It was also important that entrepreneurs and managers cooperated with their competitors in order to survive the crisis. Collaboration can be significantly fostered by various business networks where network membership is important, especially during times of crisis. Entrepreneurs received significant support, such as assistance in obtaining government funds for financial aid that was directed to entrepreneurs or the mutual assistance of members of associations in acquiring lost resources through interrupted supply chains. The development of competitiveness occurs through business networks that provide their members with access to up-to-date information and contacts. Such networking is a common understanding of the sources of the problems that are faced by enterprises. Cooperation among employers and employees as well as internal cooperation (in teams, among employees and employers, and between labor unions and employers) are also elements of cooperation that may determine a company's survival.

An important factor of competitiveness during the period of a pandemic is also the dynamic ability of an entity (changing attitudes and capturing opportunities) that allows it to obtain and maintain a competitive advantage in a changing environment. The crisis changed the needs of consumers; this is why it is so important that companies analyze the market in response to these changes. They are ready to introduce changes in their functioning, offered products, and services in order to meet the new needs of customers and participants in the supply chain. Developing these skills allows firms to shape and modify their skills and resources in response to building a market advantage and competitive position.

The results of the research and statistical analysis show that, under the conditions of the COVID-19 pandemic, distribution methods had a statistically significant impact on the competitive potential of enterprises. This trend was seen during the COVID-19 pandemic: It was a shift from tangible to intangible assets. Therefore, the potential of intangible resources such as human capital or distribution methods should be used so that they can play an important role in creating a competitive advantage. By switching to online distribution channels, for example, companies can maintain their levels of revenues and even attract new business partners. Changing distribution methods can therefore lead to acquiring new customers, reducing costs, and gaining a competitive advantage on the market.

Another factor in building a competitive advantage was shaping a company's entrepreneurial knowledge and attitudes based on digital competencies. Knowledge, entrepreneurial, and employee competencies that are rooted in digital skills determine success in the era of Industry 4.0. The COVID-19 pandemic has significantly accelerated the digitization processes of many enterprises.

The lockdown, which caused social separation and the disappearance of shops and companies for a longer period, forced consumers to change their purchasing behaviors. A new model of consumer behavior has emerged, which is conditioned by various factors – the main determinant being the issue of caring for one's own health and following the rules that are set by national authorities. These changes are reflected in both the structural approach to consumerism and the growing importance of e-commerce, which has an impact on building competitive advantages for enterprises that notice such behavior. This trend is expected to continue in the near future.

State support

The speed of the governments' response to the spread of the SARS-CoV-2 virus was conditioned by objective factors (the numbers of infected, and the numbers of deaths) and subjective factors (the assessment of the epidemic risk's scale by decision-makers) (Lee, 2022). Governments have taken extraordinary measures to try to contain the epidemic; these have included general isolation and the halt of large-scale economic activity. Countries announced aid and recovery packages to support enterprises and workers (as well as their economies as a whole). Actions in the field of fiscal and monetary policy were applied. These systems appeared to be effective, but they did not always mitigate the negative effects of the coronavirus crisis.

State policy should, first of all, lead to support for adaptive innovations. Failure to do so may lead to the consolidation of an ineffective technologically obsolete economic structure and, as a result, deprive the economy of the long-term benefits that result from resource-reallocation processes. The pandemic also emphasized that the future belongs to Industry 4.0. The progressive automation of industrial practices and traditional production will form the basis of economic development and learning to operate in this virtual environment as a prerequisite for businesses, workers, and consumers.

It can also be stated that crisis management in the context of central management is more effective than in the case of the decentralization of power in this area. An example may be countries where the healthcare system was centrally managed showed lower incidents and deaths (Poland, the Netherlands, Denmark) than those countries where there was a division of responsibilities (e.g., by regions). In activities that may reduce the size of a pandemic and minimize its consequences, healthcare facilities should therefore cooperate with other organizations such as government administrations, local or regional administrations, universities and research units, or experts. Therefore, it is important to prepare emergency plans that should become the basic undertaking that enables the proper functioning of medical facilities and the continuity of health services.

The three above-mentioned areas of relationships between business activities and the effects of the crisis that was caused by COVID-19 (the flexibility of entities, changes in competitiveness, and the role of the state) are not the only ones. However, their impact can be noticed in every economy and for every entity. Whether it is a business or an individual consumer, it is important to be prepared for future unpredictable events. As today's reality shows – Russia's aggression toward Ukraine and its global impact on the economies of all countries – make it worth knowing and understanding the mechanisms that operate in such situations as well as their consequences.

References

Alonso-Almeida, M., Bremser, K., Llach, J. (2015), Proactive and reactive strategies deployed by restaurants in times of crisis: effects on capabilities, organization and competitive advantage. *International Journal of Contemporary Hospitality Management.* 27 (7), pp. 1641–1661, https://doi.org/10.1108/IJCHM-03-2014-0117

Faulkner, B. (2001), Towards a framework for tourism disaster management. Tourism Managerial. 22 (2), pp. 135–147.

Hadjielias, E., Christofi, M., Tarba, S. (2022), Contextualizing small business resilience during the COVID-19 pandemic: evidence from small business owner-managers. *Small Business Economics.* 59, pp. 1351–1380, https://doi.org/10.1007/s11187-021-00588-0.

Lee, S.Y. (2022), The political economy of early COVID-19 interventions in U.S. states: comment. *Journal of Economic Dynamics and Control.* 140, p. 104304, https://doi.org/10.1016/j.jedc.2022.104304.

Miles, R.E., Snow, C.C., Meyer, A.D., Coleman, Jr., H.J. (1978), Organizational strategy, structure, and process. *Academy of Management Review.* 3 (3), pp. 546–562.

Momaya, K.S. (2020), Return from COVID-19: thinking differently about export competitiveness and sustainability. *International Journal of Global Business and Competitiveness.* 15, pp. 1–9, https://doi.org/10.1007/s42943-020-00012-6.

Oorschot van, K.E., Van Wassenhove, L.N., Jahre, M. (2022), Collaboration–competition dilemma in flattening the COVID-19 curve. *Production and Operations Management*. 1–17. https://doi.org/10.1111/poms.13709.

Pearce, J.A., Michael, S.C. (2006), Strategies to prevent economic recessions from causing business failure. *Business Horizons*. 49 (3), pp. 201–209.

Prayag, G. (2018), Symbiotic relationship or not? Understanding resilience and crisis management in tourism. Tourism Management Perspectives. 25, pp. 133–135.

Ritchie, B.W. (2004), Chaos, crises and disasters: a strategic approach to crisis management in the tourism industry. *Tourism Management*. 25 (6), pp. 669–683.

Ritchie, B.W., Jiang Y. (2019), A review of research on tourism risk, crisis and disaster management: launching the annals of tourism research curated collection on tourism risk, crisis and disaster management. *Annals of Tourism Research*. 79, p. 102812.

Scott, N., Laws, E., Prideaux, B. (2008), Tourism crises and marketing recovery strategies. *Journal of Travel & Tourism Marketing*. 23 (2–4), pp. 1–13.

Song, J., Xia, S., Vrontis, D., Sukumar, A., Liao, B., Li, Q., Tian, K., Yao, N. (2022), The source of SMEs' competitive performance in Covid-19: matching big data analytics capability to business models. *Information Systems Frontiers*. 24, pp. 1167–1187, https://doi.org/10.1007/s10796-022-10287-0.

Taleb, N. (2014), *Black Swan*. Penguin Books, Dublin.

Index

Kolibri 360 GmbH
Ferdinand-Jühlke-Straße 7
99095 Erfurt, Deutschland
produktsicherheit@kolibri360.de